THE LIFE AND JOURNEY
OF GOD'S CHOSEN VESSEL

My Story

THE LIFE AND JOURNEY
OF GOD'S CHOSEN VESSEL

My Story

(Breaking the Chains of Generational Curses)

By
APOSTLE PROPHET
PATRICIA VEAL-SHANNON

Edited by:
Prophet Tammy Moore
Elizabeth L. Veal

XULON PRESS

Xulon Press
2301 Lucien Way #415
Maitland, FL 32751
407.339.4217
www.xulonpress.com

Edited by: Prophet Tammy Moore,
Elizabeth L. Veal

ISBN-13: 978-1-6628-1010-7

DEDICATION

I dedicate this book to *God the Father, His son, Jesus Christ*, my *Lord and Savior* and the *Precious Holy Spirit* who are the *True Authors* of this book.

> *"[looking away from all that will distract us and] focusing our eyes on Jesus, who is the Author and Perfecter of faith [the first incentive for our belief and the One who brings our faith to maturity], who for the joy [of accomplishing the goal] set before Him endured the cross, [a] disregarding the shame, and sat down at the right hand of the throne of God [revealing His deity, His authority, and the completion of His work]."*

> *(Hebrews 12:2 AMP)*

TABLE OF CONTENTS

Adulthood Years

FOREWORD

In these perilous times we are living in, we are encountering intense levels of spiritual warfare.

> *"Men are lovers of themselves, lovers of money, boaster, proud, blasphemers, disobedient to parents, unthankful, unholy, unloving, unforgiving, slanderers, without self-control, brutal, despisers of good, traitors, headstrong, haughty, lovers of pleasure rather than lovers of God, having a form of Godliness but denying its power. And from such people turn away!" (2 Timothy 3:1-5 NKJV)*

My Story is a right now book and is much needed for such a time as this. Apostle Prophet Patricia is a true Woman of God and has penned her life in such a way that you will not be able to put the book down. It is a page turner from the very beginning. Apostle Prophet Patricia Veal-Shannon is very transparent as she reveals every detail of her life; the good, the bad and the ugly. She holds nothing back. *My Story* takes us on a journey to see how Apostle Prophet Patricia faced and overcame many obstacles, trials, and tribulations in her life that has shaped her into the strong warrior she is today. Every reader will be touched in some way while reading this book. Apostle Prophet Patricia's skilled writing pulls you in and makes you feel as if you are right there with her. This is a MUST read!! As you read, you will reflect on your own life and will find a part of you in this book.

I, Tammy Moore, have known Apostle Prophet Patricia over a span of 18 years. I am a witness that she loves God and His people. She loves to see people free in every area of their lives. I highly recommend this book to all nationalities, men, women, young and old. You will be blessed!

INTRODUCTION

I, Apostle Prophet Patricia Veal-Shannon was inspired by God to write this book about my life and journey. My mission is to declare; despite, what you encounter in life, God's remarkable power will bring you through every obstacle that you could ever imagine. This book captures how God orchestrated and allowed me to undergo obstruction and trauma during my childhood, adolescence, teenage, and adulthood for a divine purpose. The Bible states, **"Many are called but few are chosen;"** therefore, while I was berth in my mothers' womb, God chose me to do a work for Him. I was chosen **to enrich the poor, to encourage the broken hearted, and to set the captives free**. Because of this, I was the target in the eyes of Satan. Satan's subtle, yet devastating avenues of destruction affected me mentally, physically, and emotionally. I have faced **child and domestic abuse,** as well as **neglect, rejection, molestation, abandonment, witchcraft, depression, oppression, poverty, and much more.** Satan's tactics came through a lineage of generational curses which derived from my ancestors. The men and women in my bloodline may have encountered or dabbled in the same things that bound me for so many years. Eventually, I concluded that there are some things I had no control over because I was born into them, but I heard God say,

"THE BREAKING OF GENERATIONAL CURSES STOPS RIGHT HERE! IN JESUS NAME", and **"NO WEAPON FORMED AGAINST YOU SHALL PROSPER."**

"My Story" will bless and encourage anyone who has fallen under generational curses believing that they can be set free from satanic strongholds. I assure you that while reading this novel, you will discern all the devices that Satan will use to attempt the obliteration of **God's chosen vessels**. You will learn that we do not have to undertake what has been passed down to us. God has given us the power to withstand all evil mechanisms of the devil. And we must know that God is with us, especially when we put our trust in him. **To God be the Glory!**

"For we do not wrestle against flesh and blood, but against principalities, against powers, against the rulers of the darkness of this age, against spiritual hosts of wickedness in the heavenly places." (Ephesians 6:12 NKJV)

THE DEVIL IS REAL!

Chapter 1
A Predestined Birth

"Before I formed you in the womb, I knew you; Before you were born, I sanctified you; And I ordained you a prophet to the nations." (Jeremiah 1:5 NKJV)

The scripture above has altered my perception of the Almighty God. He specifies that I was a notion in his mind before I was created in my mother's womb. While He anticipated my birth, God had **freed me from sin, made me whole, and set me apart** for his usage. He established his mark of approval on my life by anointing and appointing me in the office of a prophet. The call to decree and declare the Word of God to the nations before the foundation of the world [was created].

Jeremiah 1:5 has answered the many mind-boggling questions that I had as a child: **Why was I born?** I wanted to know the purpose of going through the adversities that I encountered. Why would God allow certain, horrific things to happen to me? I finally have found the answers to these questions through recollections of the significant people and events of my life. My life has been an inevitable beginning with an unexpected ending. Though the ending of our story may depict us as prosperous to the outside, our beginning may have been filled with pain, strife, and terror that can only be seen from the inside. The beginning of our story does not define our ending. Yes, we are going to undergo hardships and obstacles in our life, but we will press through, come through like pure gold if we faint not [persevere]. We will find ourselves in a better and glorious future with the Almighty God, leading and guiding us.

> *"For I know the thoughts that I think towards you, saith the Lord, thoughts of peace, and not of evil, to give you a future and hope." (Jeremiah 29:11 NKJV)*

This is an extraordinary outcome for an overcomer.

I began to visualize and explore, more so, the significance of my birth. In this exploration, I discovered how essential the occurrences in my life were to God's predestined plan. If I knew of this essentiality, I believe that enduring the calamities of the world would have been more bearable. Nevertheless, God knew that I would be born into a dysfunctional environment, and he also knew what I could and could not bear. The situations that I faced in my earlier life were not unfair punishments or the wrath of God, but they were preparing me for the greatness that I was destined for.

2

Now allow **"MY STORY"** *to begin.*

On the early morning of January 10, 1967, in Anderson, South Carolina, I was born to the proud, late Charlie and Shirley Crawford Jr. who were native of Anderson as well. When my mom gave birth to me, she was only the mere age of 14, while my father was 18 years of age. The age difference may seem odd and astonishing, but in their time, age was truly *just* a number.

I remember, before my dad's death, he told me that three weeks after my birth he had to rush me to the hospital because I was unable to breathe, due to respiratory problems.

"Girl, you gave us a scare. You would have died if I didn't get you to the hospital in time. You had respiratory problems where you couldn't breathe," he said while shaking his head.

These infantile respiratory problems would be the basis of the illnesses that I had encountered throughout my life.

"I shall not die, but live, and declare the works of the LORD." (Psalms 118:17 KJV)

After I was born, we stayed with my father's parents until they were able to move into our own home. Eventually, they move into our new home came the birth of my youngest sister the second born child, Denise Slaughter, in the summer of August 1968 on the 21st day.

Our lives are not solely lived by us, but they are also lived by the people who are there to witness it, the people that contribute to it, and the people that tell us the parts we weren't around to see. Just as my father told me something that I was not aware of, my mother would occasionally do the same. Sitting at the kitchen table with my mom, sipping on a boiling hot cup of coffee at age ten while eating butter toast just after midnight in our Brooklyn, NY apartment. She began telling me a little about her background. I listened to her go on about topics such as: her childhood, the separation of she and my father, and how she relocated to New York City soon after.

Mom was the "baby girl" the youngest child of seven children of her family. She also told me that two of her older siblings had different fathers from her. Significantly, I also learned that her childhood was not ideal.

"I couldn't go to school," she stated sadly.

At only eight years old, she and her siblings had to discontinue going to school and began working in the Anderson cotton fields to help provide for the family. The poverty they faced did not always ensure the luxuries that many of us take for granted. There were times they went to bed hungry, did not always have shoes to wear, and had to wear hand-me-downs. Despite her misfortunes as a child, my mom's impeccable imagination allowed her to envision herself in a better place in life as an adult. She had big dreams of being prosperous. I listened to her as she spoke of wearing the best clothes, having the finest jewelry, and living in a big, beautiful house. As she told my 10-year-old self these things at the kitchen table, I could see a bright glare in her eyes, as if she saw these things right in front of her. Unfortunately, the daydreaming did not cease *the mental, physical and emotional abuse that she encountered, but it only distracted her from it*.

"*Your grandma was very mean.* She would beat me with anything she could get her hands on," Mommy told me.

"How was her mom towards her?" I inquired.

"Your great grandma treated your grandma the same as well."

"You shall not worship them nor serve them; for I, the Lord your God, am a jealous (impassioned) God [[a]demanding what is rightfully and uniquely mine], visiting (avenging) the iniquity (sin, guilt) of the fathers on the children [that is, calling the children to account for the sins of their fathers], to the third and fourth generations of those who hate me." (Exodus 20:5 AMP)

"-keeping mercy and lovingkindness for thousands, forgiving iniquity and transgression and sin; but He will by no means leave the guilty unpunished, visiting (avenging) the iniquity (sin, guilt) of the fathers upon the children and the grandchildren to the third and fourth generations [that is, calling the children to account for the sins of their fathers]." (Exodus 34:7 AMP)

During our next coffee talk, she explained to me why she and my dad had separated. Their marriage was filled with many arguments that escalated into physical fights. Much of this escalation was attributed to my father's constant overindulgence in alcohol and the lack of spousal communication in their marriage.

"Your father was a **mama's boy**. He would go talk to her about everything and not involve me," she said in an angrily and annoyed tone as I just sat listening to her.

"He would stay out late **drinking, and he was cheating**," she told me knowingly.

"How do you know that he was cheating?" I asked curiously.

"I just knew. As a matter of fact, this is how your half-sister came along. He was such a ***big liar***," she emphasized. "I couldn't believe nothing he said, and Trisha, your father was some kind of stingy when it came to money," she chuckled to herself. I laughed as well, because of the way she said it.

"He was?" I just shook my head, but on the inside, I was in awe.

"He would p-- me off. When I would question him on Fridays about where his check was and his whereabouts, he wanted to fight me. I got tired of fighting and the lies, so I knew it was time for me to go," Mommy said.

"Why haven't you married my stepfather then?" I asked.

Being that I was only a child, I wanted to know why she had not married him. She left my daddy, so what was she waiting for? I just did not understand.

"I couldn't marry him if I wanted to. Your daddy won't give me a divorce," she responded. "And if he did, I wouldn't get married again."

"Why?" I asked.

"I'm not *in love* with him," she spoke honestly. I looked at her with a dry mouth and wide eyes. I was dumbfound-ed...I was in utter shock.

Our conversation transitioned to the time that she left my father. When she decided to truly leave him, I was one years old, and she believed that this was her only and best option. She called my Aunt Lola, her older sister who lived in New York City, to come and get her. When Aunt Lola arrived to rescue my mom in her distress, it was anything but an easy task-it was a struggle. My dad did not let go without a fight.

"*You* can go, but my *first-born stays*," he told her sternly.

Those words did not resonate well with her. She felt that he did not love her or want her, but he only felt these things for me. Regardless of how his words triggered her emotionally, I was going with her anyway. She repeatedly begged, and relentlessly tried to reason with him. The separation was a tug-of war, and I was the rope, literally.

"If I didn't leave, the fighting would have continued," she concluded.

The battle became so intense that Aunt Lola had to intervene on her sister's behalf. My Aunt Lola was not afraid of him, especially when her baby sister was involved. She swiftly snatched me out of my dad's arms while my mom was holding my sister, Denise.

"We all got into the cab went straight to the bus station that very same day heading to New York City where my aunt resides," she said. "I'll never looked back at Anderson, South Carolina, and I don't miss it. There was nothing there but hurt and pain. I wanted something better."

She was ecstatic about living in "THE BIG CITY" and moving there was a dream come true for her but for many future reasons, it would not be mine.

Chapter 2
Moments of Despair

Our coffee talks continued never on weekdays but only during the weekend midnight hour. She would awaken me with a motherly touch and a gentle whisper to my ear.

"Do you want to drink some coffee and eat some butter toast with me?" she whispered quietly so only the two of us could hear.

I awoke with an enthusiastic smile while nodding my head yes. There were times that she would tell me prior to her arrival. I would get so excited because I could not wait to hear what she had to tell me next. She placed a finger over her mouth as we tiptoed to the kitchen.

I remember her telling me, "I feel like I can talk to you about anything." That made me feel good because she trusted me. I felt...special.

During this coffee talk, she reminisced about what life was like in the city. She was a 16-year-old single mom having to care for my ten-month-old sister, Denise, as well as myself, a two-year-old toddler. While staying with Aunt Lola, she began seeking employment to provide for us. Because of my mother's *preferences*, she refused to clean the houses of white people as this was Aunt Lola's occupation. While my sister and I were with a babysitter, she spent time searching for other means of employment.

Finding a decent and ideal job was very difficult for her due to her limited educational background and illiteracy. Because of this, joblessness would follow her due to lack of qualifications.

"The jobs weren't for me," she stated plainly.

I accepted this reasoning then, but now I realize that this statement was her attempt to hide her illiteracy.

Soon after the many failed attempts of gaining employment, she had heard about another source of income and became a welfare recipient from the Department of Social Services. She was receiving food stamps, medical assistance and a monetary check every month. The monetary check was not much, but she was satisfied with it until something or someone else came along.

"How did you meet my daddy [stepfather]?" I asked curiously amid our conversation.

She shared with me that she walked passed him, and he took notice of her. My stepdad told me how he was so mesmerized by her beauty every time she would walk by him, as he sat on his Brooklyn stoop. He began to call her his *Black Beauty*. Though she found him obnoxious in his approaches, it was love at first sight for him.

She fancied the idea of him chasing after her, and after a week of his pursuit to win her, she finally agreed to a date with him. After several dates, she believed that it was time to introduce him to Denise and I.

"You didn't like me too much, as a little girl. You would try to get between us when we slept in the bed together," he once told me. "You wanted her all to yourself and was very protective over her," he said in a nostalgic tone.

"One night you slept in our room and we thought you were sleep, so we began to have sex," my mom told me. "I was making noises, and you sat up in the bed and said to him 'Don't you hurt my mommy!' All we could do was stop and laugh."

I laughed hysterically when she told me this.

Eventually, I came to know and love him as Willie McCoy Bazemore, born and raised in Lewiston, North Carolina. Before he came into our lives, he was a drafted soldier in World War II. Previously, he was married and had a son named kirk, but he and his wife separated when he returned from the war due to her infidelity.

Because my stepdad was not honest about the status of his relationship, my mom turned him away. He had failed to mention to her that his marriage was not fully terminated, despite her honesty with him about her prior marriage and still only separated.

> *"-but to the [a]married [believers] I give instructions—not I, but the Lord—that the wife is not to separate from her husband, [11] (but even if she does leave him, let her remain single or else be [b]reconciled to her husband) and that the husband should not leave his wife." (1 Corinthians 7:10-11 AMP)*

> *"but I say to you that whoever divorces his wife, except on grounds of sexual immorality, causes her to commit adultery; and whoever marries a woman who has been divorced commits adultery. (Matthew 5:32 AMP)*

"I was so angry at him," she said to me.

After his constant begging and pleading with her, she gave him an opportunity to expound and defend his actions. Besides, she understood that she could not be too upset with him.

"We both were still married," she said in realization with a chuckle.

"Oooh...okay," I nodded while looking at her, puzzled.

As a ten-year-old, I wondered to myself, *"Someone could actually keep you from marrying someone else?"* This was odd yet amazing to me.

Although, as a child, I lacked much knowledge of certain things she spoke about, I believed that talking was my mom's therapy. These coffee talks allowed her to get things off her chest. Regardless of not understanding many of the stories and experiences she shared, I was always eager to hear more.

After a year of living separately, they decided to cohabitate. Though, Denise and I were not his biological children, he raised and loved us as if we were his own. The great love and compassion he showed us is most likely the reason why we have never called him anything else but *Daddy.* He was a true dad. He was a great provider, and he never left us wanting for anything. He always spoiled my mom. Whatever my mom desired, my stepfather gave it to her. Her closest was filled with long and short fur coats, extravagant dresses, sharp pants suits, the finest jewelry, and the foxiest long leg boots and shoes. It was as if she had *Macy's* and *Lerner's,* her favorite stores, at the tips of her fingers. In this part of our lives, he ensured my sister, and I had the best apparel as well.

If you asked me, my mom was the best dresser around. Likewise, others felt the same way. Yet being on welfare, during those times, she had to change the way she dressed; after all, **we had to appear to be in need** in order to keep the resources coming in, especially the check.

> *"For such people do not serve our Lord Christ, but their own appetites and base desires. By smooth and flattering speech, they deceive the hearts of the unsuspecting [the innocent and the naive]." (Romans 16:18 AMP)*

> *"For not knowing about God's righteousness [which is based on faith], and seeking to establish their own [righteousness based on works], they did not submit to God's righteousness." (Romans 10:3 AMP)*

Anyway, Christmas was my favorite time of the year because I always had so many boxes to open. These boxes did not just consist of toys; there were clothes, beautiful skirts, blouses and jewelry.

I recall holding my mother's hand, at the age of 4, while we waited to cross the street. Gracing my arms was a beautiful long sleeve, white popcorn blouse under a crushed velvet pullover dress, white tights paired to black patent leather shoes, and a pearl necklace, that I kept twirling on my fingers with a big beautiful smile. I do not remember where I was going, but it was significant to me because I felt beautiful, rich, and excited in my heart. I promised myself I would *never* forget this joyful day.

> *"May the God of your hope so fill you with all joy and peace in believing [through the experience of your faith] that by the power of the Holy Spirit you may abound and be overflowing (bubbling over) with hope." (Romans 15:13 AMP)*

At the age of five, I remember standing in a chair in our apartment washing dishes. My mother was never hesitant in telling me to do household chores. The late birthday that I had did not permit me to attend school until I turned six.

My sixth birthday came swiftly, and I was finally able to begin the first grade. I loved school, and I was very intelligent, so it did not take long for me to learn how to read. In fact, reading was my favorite subject as a child. My teacher was also impressed with my excellence in all the other subjects. I was successful in school and a very fast learner; however, I rarely remember my mother ever assisting me in doing homework or reading a book with me. Nevertheless, the teacher recommended to my mother that I skip the second grade and enter third grade the next year. This excited me, but my mom was hesitant in this decision.

She notified the teacher that skipping the second grade would not be necessary because she wanted me to fully experience each grade. She did not want things to be complicated for me, so she had my best interest at heart. I did not understand the reason for her decision then, but I understand it now.

Though I liked school, there were other things that I enjoyed. My mom would take us to the park, the movies, or simply take us to visit Aunt Lola. I loved visiting my aunt and, especially, my two older cousins, Linda and Elaine. I looked up to them because they were older, and they protected my sister and I. Soon, we became neighbors when my mom, Denise, and I moved into the apartment building beside theirs. This was a convenient situation because when my mom needed a babysitter, Aunt Lola was right next door. The neighborhood was nice, but it was challenging to encounter *good* friends.

In the time I would spend with my aunt, I met a potential friend when I was seven, who lived a few houses away from my aunt's building. I would ask to play with her in view of the window so that my Aunt Lola would be able to see me. Our time together, on the weekends, consisted of us playing together, but I did not understand why she wanted to fight me, at times for no reason. I knew that when people liked each other, they did not try to hurt one another. Especially, when they are professing to be friends, but she insisted on attacking me and being obnoxious.

> *"For our struggle is not against flesh and blood, but against the rulers, against the authorities, against the powers of this dark world and against the spiritual forces of evil in the heavenly realms." (Ephesians 6:12 AMP)*

One day, Aunt Lola heard my loud cry for help from her front window of the apartment building, and she hurried down to rescue me. The first thing she saw was my arm in the girl's mouth. She had pulled my arm through the closed iron gate that was around her home, and sank her teeth in it. My aunt furiously pulled my arm away from the girl's mouth.

"Feed your child!" she screamed angrily, with the addition of a few other *choice* words, hoping the girl's parents would dare come and get a piece of her. The parents just fussed back while standing at their door.

Looking down crying in despair, I saw my arm, full of the girl's teeth marks embedded in my skin. When my aunt told my mom about the situation that had occurred, she was furious and forbade me to play with the girl anymore. However, you know how children are; they will fight, make up, and want to play with each other again as if nothing had happened. Despite the girl's meanness and savagery, I begged my mom, asking her could I play with the girl again because she was the only friend I had.

"No," she said dismissively.

"Do not even associate with a man given to angry outbursts; Or go [along] with a hot-tempered man," (Proverbs 22:24 AMP)

My mother had gone somewhere, and she left me with my Aunt Lola, so I took this opportunity to ask Aunt Lola if I could go outside, and she willingly said yes.

The girl and I playtime together started out as innocent, but once again, she grabbed my blouse and tried to bite me. To defend myself, I pushed her head back and bit her. As we began tussling and screaming, Aunt Lola and her parents hurriedly came to pull us apart from each other. Thankfully, my aunt did not reveal the situation, and my disobedience to my mother because she felt that my mom whacked me enough as it was. I got in trouble with my mom very often; therefore, she did not want to add fuel to the fire.

"What leads to strife (discord and feuds) and how do conflicts (quarrels and fighting) originate among you? Do they not arise from your sensual desires that are ever warring in your bodily members?" (James 4:1 AMP)

"God is our refuge and strength, a very-present help in trouble." (Psalm 46:1 AMP)

"Honor [esteem, value as precious] your father and your mother [and be respectful to them]—this is the first commandment with a promise— ³ so that it may be well

WITH YOU, AND THAT YOU MAY HAVE A LONG LIFE ON THE EARTH." (Ephesians 6:2-3 AMP)

Aunt Nellie, my stepdad's younger sister was another aunt whom I favored. She lived in Newark, New Jersey but would come to visit us often along with her husband, Uncle Buck. I became overjoyed when they would pull up in their long, shiny, black Cadillac. I thought Aunt Nellie was the most beautiful and kind person that anyone could ever meet. I wanted to go home with her because I just wanted to be in her presence. Truly, I used to wish that she were my mother because of the love she showed me. When she embraced me, I could feel the sincere love that she had for me radiating off her.

There was a time where Aunt Nellie had to beg my mother to allow me to spend the night at their home, but she would not let me go. Instead, she would insist that one of my other siblings go instead (during this incident my brothers were around). It was pathetic how protective my mother was over me, solely. She would even make excuses for why I could not go. "I need her here to help me with the children when I need to go out" or "She has chores to do around the house," she would say, but my aunt would stand up to her on my behalf.

"Well, that's not her responsibility; she is a child herself," she protested. Oh, my mother did not like this *at all*.

Finally, one weekend, my mother gave in: I entreated her to let me go. Humbly, she proceeded to pack my clothes and do my hair. Later that day, Aunt Nellie and Uncle Buck arrived to pick me up, and my visit with them would last for a week. What I enjoyed most about these visits was being with my cousins, Linda and Sabrina. Linda would take me everywhere as if I was her little doll baby, but Sabrina and I would play together. We all had so much fun together, and I hated having to leave them and return home.

Being free from the presence of my mother and sibling, was the most exhilarating feeling. Truth be told, I always felt like a hostage slave because I had so much to do at such a young age. It was no secret how I was treated, but no one knew what to do about it. In the opportune time of these visits, I had an outlet from my overwhelming responsibilities, the madness, the yelling, and the violence. Without these visits, I had no relief. **I felt alone**.

> *"Be strong and courageous, do not be afraid or tremble in dread before them, for it is the LORD your God who goes with you. He will not fail you or abandon you." (Deuteronomy 31:6 AMP)*

Please do not misinterpret the feelings I had; I loved my mother, yet I did not feel that this love was reciprocated. I had the impression that she only tolerated me because she birthed me. As a matter of fact, I do not recall my mother ever embracing me or showing me the affection that a mother would show her child. She had never given me a hug or said, "*I love you.*" In her eyes, everything that I did was *unsatisfactory*. Also, she was a disciplinarian. She said what she meant and meant what she said: when she said she was going to get you; you better consider yourself got. I just never knew when it was coming.

She was one of those parents that would give you what she promised even while you were asleep. She would say, "Pull down your pants and your underwear and you better not move." and if you did move, your whooping would be worse. In addition, accidents were prohibited in my mother's house. Constantly, she made me feel as if I needed to be the perfect little girl. I was very accident prone, but she would beat me as if I made the mistakes intentionally; I could never understand this. I was a very clumsy and unbalanced child, so I fell and dropped things a lot. Because of these mistakes, my mother would whack and punch me; she nearly paralyzed me (well, that's what it felt like). To make matters worse, she would ***bring up stuff from the past then use it to torture me repeatedly***. My whole being would become numb and disturbed to the mere fact that my mom was bringing up past issues. Issues, I thought were resolved through the disciplinary actions that had occurred prior.

> *"BE ANGRY [at sin—at immorality, at injustice, at ungodly behavior], YET DO NOT SIN; do not let your anger [cause you shame, nor allow it to] last until the sun goes down.* [27] *And do not give the devil an opportunity [to lead you into sin by holding a grudge, or nurturing anger, or harboring resentment, or cultivating bitterness]." (Ephesians 4:26-27 AMP)*

> *"For if you forgive* [a] *others their trespasses [their reckless and willful sins], your heavenly Father will also forgive you.* [15] *But if you do not forgive others [nurturing your hurt and anger with the result that it interferes with your relationship with God], then your Father will not forgive your trespasses." (Matthew 6:14-15 AMP)*

I was very skinny, nothing but skin and bones, and my little body took all her hits and harsh words. I can hear her saying things like, *"Seems like the more I teach you, the dumber you get. You're stupid. You cannot do nothing right."* Yes, I was far from perfect; I made mistakes, but there were times that disciplinary actions should not have occurred. Why couldn't she had sat me in the corner? Or, given me a warning or two? No, not with my mom. It had to be a straight beat down.

> *"Do not hold us guilty for the sins of our ancestors! Let your compassion quickly meet our needs, for we are on the brink of despair." (Psalms 79:8 NLT)*

> *"Train up a child in the way he should go [teaching him to seek God's wisdom and will for his abilities and talents], Even when he is old he will not depart from it. (Proverbs 22: AMP)*

Chapter 3
Lord, Please Help Me

It didn't take much to agitate my mother. I couldn't please her with anything that I did. For instance, she did not understand why I was so smart in school, yet I had a difficult time learning how to tie my shoes at age seven. In comparison, it was unbelievable that I was in the second grade and couldn't tie my shoes; whereas, Denise, who was six could tie her shoes. Every time I tied my shoes incorrectly my mother's fist went upside my head.

"The more I teach you the dumber you get," she spat.

"Death and life are in the power of the tongue, and those who love it and indulge it will eat its fruit and bear the consequences of their words." (Proverbs 18:21 AMP)

My little heart ached because of her harsh words and actions. She was cruel towards me because I could not tie my shoe; instead of being patient with me, she belligerently cursed me because I couldn't master and complete the task.

"A soothing tongue [speaking words that build up and encourage] is a tree of life, but a persuasive tongue [speaking words that overwhelm and depress] crushes the spirit." (Proverbs 15:4 AMP)

The way she raised havoc anyone who witnessed the scene would have thought that I had murdered someone or done something vicious; all because I couldn't tie my shoes. Her facial expression was absolutely frightening and too cold to glance at. Tears flowed uncontrollably down my face as I wiped them quickly without a word. If I had even made a sound, she would have continued to hit me. Consequently, she had given me until the end of that day to learn how to tie my shoestrings.

Denise had sympathy for me and repeatedly illustrated how to tie the shoe until I conquered it, but my mother had forbidden her assistance. I do understand that she only forbade Denise's help because she wanted me to learn independently. However, why did she do it in such a tyrannical way? Her scolding had become very obnoxious and deterring, and the constant strikes on the side of my head weren't imperative for me to understand her. In fact, the violent strikes frightened and dispirited me. Could she not have spoken to me with love and compassion? I just believed that I had the cruelest and most overbearing mother ever.

"For Christ did not please Himself [gave no thought to His own interests]; but, as it is written, the reproaches and abuses of those who reproached and abused you fell on Me." (Romans 15:3 AMP)

However, in the event of Denise and I running late for school was the only time my mother would allow Denise to tie my shoes. The next day had come upon us, and I was very nervous about having to showcase my ability to tie my shoes. Anxiously, I began to pray to myself: *"Lord, please help me. Please show me how to tie my shoes!"* Amazingly, **I had an open vision demonstrating step by step and** miraculously, I began tying my shoes in front of my mom.

"And He said, "Hear now My words: If there is a prophet among you, I the Lord will make Myself known to him in a vision And I will speak to him in a dream." (Numbers 12:6 AMP)*

"God is our refuge and strength [mighty and impenetrable], A very present and well-proved help in trouble." (Psalms 46:1 AMP)*

"It's about time. You are the oldest, and I expect more from you," my mother spoke after I had tied my shoes. I just looked at her nervously.

As quiet as its kept, there was an invigorating sensation that grasped my heart. Though this may seem silly to others, it put a smile on my face because I, with the vision that God gave me had conquered a difficult task. I felt like a *winner*!

"I can do everything through Him who gives me strength." (Philippians 4:13 AMP)*

"Just as it is written and forever remains written, For Your sake we are put to death all day long ;We are regarded as sheep for the slaughter."[37] Yet in all these things we are more than conquerors and gain an overwhelming victory through Him who loved us [so much that He died for us]." (Romans 8:36-37 AMP)*

My stepfather wasn't around when the scolding and beatings occurred because he would be at work. If my step-father had been around, surely, he would have handled things much differently. His temperament was more settled and calculated than my mother's abrupt one. When chastising my sister and I, his disciplinary action consisted of oral communication and non-physical punishments. We did not receive whippings from him until we were older, due to my mother insisting that he do so. These whippings would occur when he was in a drunken state, as if he would "hold" the urge to discipline us until he was drunk. Ever so rarely he'd beat us while in a sober state.

The eighth year of my life was a very memorable. For the third time in my lifetime, we moved into a new apartment. It appeared that every time I blinked my eyes, we were moving. During our coffee time, my mom revealed that the reason we moved often is because she didn't want anything to do with our other family members. She especially didn't want them to know where she lived because she felt they were too engrossed in her business, particularly concerning me. One of the last straws was when someone threatened to report her to Child Welfare Services for child abuse.

> *"For Christ did not please Himself [gave no thought to His own interests]; but, as it is written, the reproaches and abuses of those who reproached and abused you fell on Me." (Romans 15:3 AMP)*

Nevertheless, my mother desired a boy and tried until she eventually conceived. My two brothers were the first and only children that she and my stepfather had together. While enduring the trying conditions of my household, I had to mature quickly, and the responsibilities that I had increased with the two new additions to our family.

My first-born brother, Willie, was born September 4, 1972, and he was a handsome, curly haired baby, and resembled our mother. About two years later, in 1974, on December 23rd, there was the unplanned but welcomed birth of my youngest brother, Daniel. He was also a sweet, handsome baby, who resembled my stepfather. They brought him straight home to me; I was like his second mother. Thereafter, I noticed how **depressed** my mother looked after having Daniel. Overtime, she began to isolate herself from us. This left me tending to him. Later, Daniel constant wailing (possibly due to teething) at seven months old was unbearable for me; I was only a child myself. He was so attached to me that I couldn't use the bathroom in peace. At times, I believed he thought that I was his mother because he didn't see anyone as often as he saw me. Although I adored him, another thing that drove me crazy as a child, I was the only one that was able to put him to sleep. Daniel was incredibly spoiled **by me**; inevitably speaking, I did not have a choice in the matter.

With her being in a depressive state, I didn't have to worry about her being angry and using me as a verbal and physical outlet. As she began to change in her physiognomy [facial disposition and physical expression], I became very concerned about her; she was no longer in her content state.

> *"Finally, [a] believers, whatever is true, whatever is honorable and worthy of respect, whatever is right and confirmed by God's word, whatever is pure and wholesome, whatever is lovely and brings peace, whatever is admirable and of good repute; if there is any excellence, if there is anything worthy of praise, think continually on these things [center your mind on them, and implant them in your heart]." (Philippians 4:8 AMP)*

> *"You will keep in [a] perfect and constant peace the one whose mind is steadfast [that is, committed and focused on You— in both [b] inclination and character],*

> *Because he trusts and takes refuge in You [with hope and confident expectation]."(Isaiah 26:3 AMP)*

Due to her depression, she gradually began to overeat which resulted in weight gain. She had to visit the doctor on numerous occasions for herself and these visits left me watching over my three siblings after completing my homework.

Later in my mother and stepfather's relationship, they began to fight a lot. With suspicion, my father began to accuse her of having an affair, but he did not know who. He suspected this affair because my mom would do things out of the norm; such as, call him on his job to ensure that he was at work. She would also question him to ensure that he would not be coming home early. Her affection towards him had lessened, and this gave him more reasons to believe that she was being unfaithful. He would tell us to go into our bedroom before he began questioning her about her whereabouts, and then he would hit her. In hearing the startling commotion, we began crying and yelling at him to stop hitting our mother.

"Shut up before I come beat yawl a—too," he would shout. So, we did as we were told.

Though I tried to keep all my younger siblings quiet, it was difficult to do so as we watched our mom struggle in the fight. We silently cried while watching through the curtain that posed as a door to our room. He had gotten the best of her; his strength and forcefulness overpowered her efforts to defeat him. My father's drinking had become more intense; as a result, he became more violent. In rage, he dragged her across the floor and hit her in the face as she struggled to break loose from his grasp.

"Stop screaming or I'll kill you," he threatened as he grabbed a hold of her neck. She screamed for him to stop, but he did not stop.

"Wine gives false courage; hard liquor leads to brawls; what fools men are to let it master them, making them reel drunkenly down the street!" (Proverbs 20:1 LB)

Tirelessly, she kicked, maneuvered, and tried to block his hits with her hands and arms. Exhaustion ocurred, he finally stopped and apologized to her. In anger and hurt, she stormed into their bedroom, slammed the door, and locked it. In exhaustion, my dad went to sleep on the couch, and, on that horrific night, we all went to sleep that night in silence.

"for he will be great and distinguished in the sight of the Lord; and will never drink wine or liquor, and he will be filled with and empowered to act by the Holy Spirit while still in his mother's womb." (Luke 1:15 AMP)

One afternoon, my mom went out, and she took me with her. Unfortunately, that day, I learned that my father's suspicions were valid: my mother was having an affair. We had caught a cab to go to the man's place of employment. Truthfully, I did not want to be part of this deception; this was not fair to my dad nor was it fair to me. Once she disclosed who to ask for, I was stunned. Unbelievable! It was hideous. She wanted me to ask the receptionist, through the speaker, for him so that it would not look uncanny as opposed to her doing it herself.

The man with whom she was having an affair was my Uncle William, my stepdad's brother. What made me feel even worse was that she told me this was a secret between her and I. She was expecting me to keep such a consequential secret from my stepfather. Guarding the premises, I was so panic-stricken, and I remember thinking, *"What if daddy [my stepdad] finds out? What would happen? How would he feel? What would he do?"*

"He who walks in integrity and with moral character walks securely, but he who takes a crooked way will be discovered and punished." (Proverbs 10:9 AMP)

My mother had gone to see Uncle William so urgently because she was opposed to his desire to end the affair. He had realized the severity of the situation, the turmoil, the damage that it would bring to his wife, two children and his brother, my stepdad in the process. Personally, I was glad that he came to his senses because I loved him and Aunt Odessa, and I did not want the affair to jeopardize our relationship as a family. In overhearing, some more of their conversation, I learned that a romantic relationship was nonexistent, and they had only shared a kiss once. In fact, he was not in pursuit of her, but she had pursued him, and she held no shame in this. She had audaciously expressed her love for him with passion. Honestly, I preferred to be exempt from the situation because the less I knew the better things would be for me. I felt an unrest, and I was not sure why.

After the last meeting had taken place, we returned home. Walking through the door of the apartment, seeing the disposition of my stepdad, we could discern that he was furious. It was as if you could see the smoke coming from his nostrils. He began to wonder where we had been, and by his tone and stance, you could tell that he had been drinking.

On the inside, I was shaking in my boots and frightened for the sake of my mom.

The answers that she provided to his questions of her whereabouts, and who she had gone to see did not suffice; therefore, he began to interrogate me. The earlier feeling of unrest had begun to make sense: knowing of the affair and keeping the secret would only make me as guilty as she was. I wanted to be truthful with him, but my mom discreetly shook her head at me, signaling me to not disclose any information. The argument had heightened so much that I started screaming "Stop!" and began to cry. He knew she was lying, so he beat her relentlessly until she had finally told him the truth. I had never been so frightened in my life. After he beat her, he grabbed me and beat me terribly for being with her and for lying. I saw my mother's arm stretched out to save me, but she didn't have the energy to do so: she was hurt badly. In this situation, I was only a child, and she was my mother. What was I supposed to do?

I said to myself afterwards, "*I am just a child being obedient to her mom.*"

> "*Children, obey your parents [as God's representatives] in all things, for this [attitude of respect and obedience] is well-pleasing* [a] *to the Lord [and will bring you God's promised blessings].*" (Colossians 3:20 AMP)

My Uncle William wasn't spared from the intensified rage that fused the thoughts of my stepdad. My stepdad assaulted and cut him, but he didn't kill him. He lost it for a moment and out of control. The intoxication of alcohol didn't make it any better. I remember my mom trying to stop him as he stormed out the door. She knew where he was headed.

"For jealousy is the rage of a man: therefore, he will not spare in the day of vengeance. (Proverbs 6:34 KJV)

That same evening, my mom decided she did not want to live anymore; ***purposely***, ***she overdosed on prescription drugs***. When he returned, my father discovered that she was unconscious, he quickly called the ambulance, and they arrived just in time. After she arrived to the hospital, the doctors were able to pump her stomach, revive her, and save her from death. Though, they revived her physically, she was not revived mentally. Life began to look very dim for her as depression began to take a greater toll on her. She walked around lifeless as if she lost her best friend. She was very unstable.

"The thief comes only in order to steal and kill and destroy. I came that they may have and enjoy life, and have it in abundance [to the full, till it overflows]." (John 10:10 AMP)

Thereafter, my mother had a nervous breakdown: she cried depressively and uncontrollably without reason. I watched her hold her head and shaking it from side to side. This moment was something that I would never forget. As a child, it was the ***most terrifying position to observe my mom undergo such disturbance. She was struggling coping with life issues.***

"Cast all your cares [all your anxieties, all your worries, and all your concerns, once and for all] on Him, for He cares about you [with deepest affection, and watches over you very carefully]." (1 Peter 5:7 AMP)

"Therefore, I urge you, brothers and sisters, by the mercies of God, to present your bodies [dedicating all of yourselves, set apart] as a living sacrifice, holy and well-pleasing to God, which is your rational (logical, intelligent) act of worship.

And do not be conformed to this world [any longer with its superficial values and customs], but be transformed and progressively changed [as you mature spiritually] by the renewing of your mind [focusing on godly values and ethical attitudes], so that you may prove [for yourselves] what the will of God is, that which is good and acceptable and perfect [in His plan and purpose for you]." (Romans 12:1-2 AMP)

Due to her mental and emotional instability, she was in and out of the hospital which left me to care for my younger sister and brothers frequently. Once, she stayed for such a long time that we believed she was never coming home. When she did come home, I took notice to the many new prescription drugs that returned with her. These pills were to assist her in staying calm, but they made her slur so badly that we could barely understand her when she spoke. These pills also leveled her high blood pressure which had generated from her weight gain and eating habits. Although these pills were supposedly "helping" to maintain her health, I did not like how these pills made her look and feel. Along with the drowsiness and slurred speech, the medication slowed her pace of walking, and it even made her hallucinate. Specifically, *Volume,* a drug that relaxed her had caused a great share of the voices she heard and the hallucinations she had. The hallucinations scared me the most. I did not understand how a pill smaller than a mustard seed could be so powerful.

"God, when I grow up, please don't allow me to take any pills for sickness. Help me not to be sick," I prayed wearily.

"Do not be anxious or worried about anything, but in everything [every circumstance and situation] by prayer and petition with thanksgiving, continue to make your [specific] requests known to God. ⁷ And the peace of God

[that peace which reassures the heart, that peace] which transcends all understanding, [that peace which] stands guard over your hearts and your minds in Christ Jesus [is yours]." (Philippians 4:6-7 AMP)

My stepdad had become a total nuisance with all the arguing and fighting that he would initiate with my mother. There was no empathy for her mental state and sickness. As children, we were all helpless and just wanted it all to stop. I wanted him to stop and realize what was happening, but he did not and the domestic violence continued.

"So do not fear, for I am with you; do not be dismayed, for I am your God. I will strengthen you and help you; I will uphold you with my righteous right hand." (Isaiah 41:10 NIV)

Mom became fatigued and weary with the fighting, so she called the police, and they escorted him out of the apartment. Despite his departure, she had a strong inkling that he would return. To avoid this, she secured the front door by sticking butcher knives around the opening and along with the security bar that came with the heavy-duty metal door. As she predicted, every evening, for a few days after work, my stepdad would reappear with violent poundings on the door.

"Let me in!" he screamed loudly. He did this repeatedly until he became exhausted by his efforts. Eventually, he realized that he wasn't getting anywhere with my mom. She would not respond to any of his requests or threats.

"I do not want to see you again." This was the only reaction that she communicated through all his demanding.

"Please, Shirley don't do this," he said in a calm and pleading voice.

"No, you always say that you are going to stop," she replied.

"I will go get some help. I will do whatever it takes to get you back," he begged.

After months had passed, he had not been successful in his pleads to win her back apologetically, but they did stay in touch for the sake of Willie and Daniel, the sons that they had together. Eventually, my stepfather moved to Newark, New Jersey with Aunt Nellie to receive the help he needed. He knew that in order to have my mother back in his life, he had to gain self-control.

> *"It is not good to eat much honey, Nor is it glorious to seek one's own glory.*[28] *Like a city that is broken down and without walls [leaving it unprotected] Is a man who has no self-control over his spirit [and sets himself up for trouble]."* (Proverbs 25:28 AMP)

Henceforth, my mother had arranged for Willie, Daniel, and I to stay with a couple whom she was friends with, yet they were absolute strangers to us. She was traveling to take my sister to visit our biological father for about two weeks in South Carolina. Meanwhile, the couple treated us terribly and beat me like I was a demon out of hell. I had mistakenly walked in front of a moving car, so they took it upon themselves to give me a whipping. They told me to pull my pants down and proceeded to beat me as they forced me to stand. It felt like my mother never left. I started to wonder did she give them permission to do this.

When our mom returned, we discovered that she never gave them permission to discipline us in that way. Therefore, she was irate when we told her what had transpired, and she gave the couple a piece of her mind.

In the short time my mother was away, she met a man named Pete. When she returned from South Carolina, it was evident that she and Pete's relationship was becoming more serious and intimate. Sometimes, I overheard their conversations. They discussed how much they missed each other and how much they wanted to see each other. Sure enough, when she went to retrieve Denise from South Carolina, she made it her business to see Pete again.

When they had returned to New York, guess who was knocking at our door? Pete! His tall, slender frame complimented his fair-skinned complexion and manly- featured face, which was partially hidden by his enormous afro. He had a very deep southern accent that made him even more funny than he was. Despite how uncomfortable we were, my mother made us call him "Daddy," and as a nine-year old, I didn't understand why we had to. It bewildered me that we had to call this stranger daddy when we already had a *real* daddy. Due to our awkwardness, we would mistakenly call him by his first name anyway.

Nevertheless, Pete was kind towards my mom and most importantly, she was happy. However, he did have some habits of his own: he was a beer drinker and a marijuana smoker. What I can proclaim, he never showed signs of intoxication around us nor did he ever abuse my mom. He was very submissive to my mom. This could be because she had a way of *manipulating* people into doing what she wanted whether it was right or wrong, especially when it concerned her children.

"Love endures with patience and serenity, love is kind and thoughtful, and is not jealous or envious; love does not brag and is not proud or arrogant. ⁵ It is not rude; it is not self-seeking; it is not provoked [nor overly sensitive

and easily angered]; it does not consider a wrong endured."
(1 Corinthians 13:4-5 AMP)

I recall a time when my mother and Pete had gone out for a couple of hours, and our downstairs neighbors babysat us. While they were watching us, they asked us a couple of questions. "Did your mom cook?" they asked, and I had hesitated, but replied, *"Yes."* I was very curious as to why they were asking these questions.

"What did your mom cook?" they inquired, so I told them what she had cooked. I didn't see the harm in answering, but my mom didn't play about things like this. She would administer a rehearsal to ensure that we knew how to act when visiting with someone. If we were hungry, we couldn't ask anyone for anything. We were supposed to say, *"No, thank you,"* to anyone who offered us something. If were being offered candy, she said that we better ask permission to take it. Because of this, I always felt like I was walking on pins and needles with her. If I made one wrong decision, my head would get knocked or bitten off.

> *"Trust in and rely confidently on the LORD with all your heart*
> *and do not rely on your own insight or understanding.*[6] [a]
> *In all your ways know and acknowledge and recognize Him,*
> *And He will make your paths straight and smooth [removing*
> *obstacles that block your way]." (Proverbs 3:5-4 AMP)*

When she and Pete returned to pick us up from our neighbor's, they stayed behind to discussed how we were. I didn't know what was said exactly, but it was obvious through my mom's disposition of fury towards me that something wasn't right.

"*What did they say?*" I asked myself. I became very nervous and frantic, while holding my hands out wondering what had happened.

"Get your a-- upstairs!" my mom whispered angrily.

My stomach churned in nervousness for the maltreatment that was going to occur. Once we entered the apartment, she interrogated my siblings with questions concerning what was said downstairs. However, they didn't know much because they were playing when the neighbors asked *me* the questions. Receiving no answers, she told them to go to their room. Then, she began to ask me questions. I told her the questions that I was asked as well as my answers, but she didn't believe me: they had told her a different story.

> "*The* LORD *detests lying lips, but he delights in people who are trustworthy.*" *(Proverbs 12:22 NIV)*

"They said that you told them on your own," she said.

"Mommy that's not true," I told her.

"Someone's telling a lie, and I think it's you," she speculated.

I could not believe what I was hearing. I thought that my mom was making this up on her own just to beat me. Without hesitation, she told me to pull my pants down and lay on my stomach onto the table we had. I begged her not to beat me.

"Please," I cried, with tears rolling down my face "I'm telling you the truth."

"Shut up! You're only making it worse for yourself!" she yelled.

Then, she instructed Pete to get the jump rope and tie me down to the table, so I would not move and to make sure my hands were tightly secured, so they wouldn't be in the way. Although I saw the reluctance in his eyes, he did what he was told. With haste, he put a cloth in my mouth, so I would not holler, as she gave me the first two slashes with the extension cord across my buttocks. It stung so bad; I could not catch my breath. She continued to interrogate and beat me repeatedly until I confessed what she wanted to hear. My petite body was so exhausted from the squirming and efforts to resist the slashes that I suffered. I remembered crying out, "***Lord, Please Help Me***," internally, as sweat dripped down my face. Besides, I do not believe that Pete could take watching anymore.

> *"Save me, O God, because I have come to you for refuge."*
> *(Psalm 16:1 L.V)*

"Shirley, that is enough!" he shouted in a stern voice.

God heard my fervent, silent prayer: she had stopped. **She beat me for one hour**. When Pete finally untied me, I could barely walk. I was sweaty, feeble, and in excruciating pain from the welts that were on my behind. The slash of the cord had wrapped onto my vagina and left a bleeding, burning bruise. If I were bruised at any time, believe me I would be the only one that could see it- she made sure of that. The horrific act was so discreet that my brothers and sister had no idea it had occurred. They thought I left the house because I stayed in the room for so long.

> *"You have taken account of my wanderings; Put my tears in Your bottle. Are they not recorded in Your book?* [9] *Then my enemies will turn back in the day when I call; this I know, that God is for me." (Psalms 56:8-9 AMP)*

The beating replayed in my mind repeatedly, and I could not mentally recover from the repercussions of what transpired. It was terrifying and pure torture. "*She should have just killed me because here I am planning my escape,*" I thought.

I began to put my plan into to action. So, before it became dark, I told my mom that I was taking out the trash. I hurried and ran down the stairs, took off running never looking back while crying my eyes out. "*I would make life a little easier for my mother if I just disappeared,*" I convinced myself.

I ran to Aunt Lola's and told her what happened, but I knew that she would convince my mom to allow me to stay for a few days. Surprisingly, my mom when I returned home, she didn't scold me.

"Don't do it again," she simply stated.

Regardless of her statement, I did it again: I ran away from home again, and again, and again.

Before I proceed, I would like to recall an incident that occurred, prior to this, before my stepdad and mommy had separated.

At age nine in the fourth grade, my mother would patiently wait until my father left to go to work before she would beat me, though he told her that she needed to stop. The whippings occurred for various reasons: not washing the dishes, not doing my sister's hair correctly, or forgetting to dump out the trash. I became overwhelmed with many responsibilities while she lounged around watching television, and cooking. One thing for sure, I was glad I didn't know how to cook because she would have added that to my workload.

She was very consistent in her lounging, and she never switched up. I felt like my mom was lazy and loved to give me orders. It was as if it was a crime for me to enjoy sitting down. I always had to keep busy, and when I wanted to nap, I had to sneak. She utilized me in every area of the home including with my siblings. Also, I was tired of getting whipped and not being shown any affection. I never received a compliment from my mom. The only time I was happy was during school hours, and I dreaded going home. I had my work cut out for me.

> *"Then [Ezra] told them, Go your way, eat the fat, drink the sweet drink, and send portions to him for whom nothing is prepared; for this day is holy to our Lord. And be not grieved and depressed, for the joy of the Lord is your strength and stronghold." (Nehemiah 8:10 AMP)*

One day, I was weary of going to school with blue and red bruises on the back of my left hand. This was the location of the bruises, so it would not be obvious or in view, since I am right-handed. However, the swelling and color caused them to be quite noticeable. It looked like there was a mountain forming, and I made sure someone saw it.

My teacher asked, "What happened to your hand?"

"My mom beat me with the back of a hairbrush," I openly told her.

Surely, the teacher reported it to the principal, and they wanted to have a meeting with my mom; therefore, they called her, and she came.

She stayed after the meeting to pick us up, so while we were walking, she tightly grabbed my arm. "Wait until I get you home," she gritted through her teeth.

Quickly, I broke away from her and took off running. She soon caught up to me and yanked my wrist back. I had no knowledge she could run that fast. Struggling, I continued to pull away from her as she held an expression of rage; I was terrified. When we returned home, it was only she and I, so she secured all the locks on the door. A couple of minutes later, there was a knock at the door.

"Don't make a sound or I'll kill ya," she threatened with her hand around my neck.

"You shall not commit murder (unjustified, deliberate homicide)." (Exodus 20:13 AMP)

They continued to knock, but she didn't answer, so they left. She made me strip naked. She pushed my face up against the wall with her arm pressing down to restrain me. I tried to stop her, but I couldn't escape the clutches of her strong hands. "Please, Mommy. No, no, no!" I repeated but to no avail my screams for mercy were unrecognized by her. She was in a zone while I was petrified, as she swung that thick, leather belt. She beat me like I was a Hebrew slave, as she declared I was no longer her daughter. She continued until she got tired.

Thereafter, she smacked me and said, "Don't you look at me. I cannot stand to look at you. I'm taking you down south to your lying tail daddy," followed by other choice words.

"You are just like him," she spat.

She told my stepfather that she and I were leaving tonight because she did not want me to spend another night around her. She packed our suitcases and got in touch with my biological father. He had agreed to me coming, yet I noticed that my mom didn't mention what happened, but she expressed to him that she'd inform him when she arrived.

In the meantime, she gave explicit instructions while we were on our way to the subway, telling me that she did not want me to look or talk to her. During the time we were waiting for the train to arrive, she asked me why I reported her to my teacher.

Afraid to tell her the truth, I simply said, "I don't know," while shrugging my shoulders.

"If you shrug your shoulders one more time with that stupid look on your face, I'm going to push you onto those train tracks," she threatened.

In fear, I told the truth. "I just wanted you to stop beating me all the time," I said to her while apologizing.

"You are sorry, a sorry a--, and I'm not going to forgive you for what you did," she said obnoxiously.

My mother had a way of saying things that made me kneel over as if she punched me right in the stomach. As tears began to form and trail down my face, I sat there fearful of her next move. She made me horrified.

"Death and life is in the power of the tongue;" (Proverbs 18:21 AMP))

"He heals the brokenhearted And binds up their wounds [healing their pain and comforting their sorrow]." (Psalm 147:3 AMP)

On the train ride, there was silence between us. Finally, we arrived at the bus terminal where we boarded the

Greyhound bus and sat in our seats without conversing with one another. The journey was lengthy and boring. I began to drift off to sleep as my head slowly rested on my mother's arm. However, the nudging of her arm would awaken me to notify me that she didn't want me to rest on her. Her closed off posture always made me feel unloved, disparity, and rejection. I was a little girl longing for the love of her mother.

Amid our journey, we had to switch buses. During the switch, my mother offered me something to eat. I accepted. She bought the food and carried it on the next bus where we sat and ate while riding to our destination.

As we were getting closer to Anderson, South Carolina, I took notice of how her attitude shifted towards me. She became mysteriously nice to me and even allowed me to lay on her arm. While making small talk, she mentioned that she didn't want my biological father to know what had transpired. Plus, she wanted me to inform him of a different story about her reason for bringing me to him. "Hmmm, that's why she's being so kind to me," I said to myself. She just didn't want my dad to know what had occurred, but I didn't care as long as she was happy, I was happy. I was just happy that she was speaking to me.

Being with my biological father was quite an experience; I spent more time with my grandmother and my Aunt Anne because he worked. He would always peep in to see how I was doing and always bring me treats. He would whisper and tell me not to share, but I would share with Aunt Anne anyway. I stayed very close to her. She took me everywhere she went, and I loved it. I enjoyed being with them for the weeks I was there.

"Instruct them to do good, to be rich in good works, to be generous, willing to share [with others]" (Timothy 6:18 AMP)

One day, my mother called to see how I was doing, and I told her that I loved it here. However, as soon as I said that I loved it, the arrangements changed. Suddenly, I had to return to New York because it was the middle of the school year, and there were some people becoming suspicious of my whereabouts. She would have been in serious trouble if she didn't bring me back. There was a deadline for my return, and she had to prove I was still living with her since I was a part of her household for Social Services. For a minute, I felt important because someone cared about me. More so, I became very valuable to my mother since Social Services would have decreased her resources if they knew that I wasn't living with her.

"Children are a heritage and gift from the Lord, the fruit of the womb a reward" (Psalm 127:3 AMP)

When my mom arrived to pick me up, I was happy to see her, but I wasn't happy about returning to the same environment. Despite my feelings, everyone was glad to see me back.

Returning to the incident of me running away, I was able to speak to my stepfather, and he was furious about everything, especially the part Pete played in it. Regardless of what happened between him and my mother, I loved him, and my siblings and I wanted him back home. Yearning for his return home, we didn't know that arrangements were being made for his return until we seen Pete bags packed and said his goodbyes. He also apologized for participating in the despicable act with my mother, and I openly accepted.

However, I disliked the mere fact that he contributed to my mother's new marijuana addiction. My mother fancied smoking weed and the cravings for food it gave her especially, the junk food. It was obvious that the potency of this drug made her happy to a certain extent. It also made her laugh constantly. Marijuana was a short-term antidote for a long-term problem and used for the moment to appease her with laughter.

> *"But now I am coming to You; and I say these things [while I am still] in the world so that they may experience My joy made full and complete and perfect within them [filling their hearts with My delight]." (John 17:13 AMP)*

Also, the marijuana played the instrumental part of becoming my enemy. I remember my mom making a spectacle out of me in front of my sister and brothers. This episode transpired when our next-door neighbor, Pastor Peartree asked our mom if we could go to church with her. Her store front holiness church was just around the corner from where we lived, but this would have been our first time we saw the inside of a church if she allowed us to go.

My mom didn't say yes right away, but Pastor Peartree didn't give up on us. At random times, she asked my mom if we could go with her to church. She even promised my mom that if she allowed us to go, she would make sure we were fed. My mother then reconsidered and said yes. We were excited about attending church services, as we began going often, and we joined the choir.

> *"Let us seize and hold tightly the confession of our hope without wavering, for He who promised is reliable and trustworthy and faithful [to His word]; 24 and let us consider [thoughtfully] how we may encourage one another*

to love and to do good deeds, ²⁵ not forsaking our meeting together [as believers for worship and instruction], as is the habit of some, but encouraging one another; and all the more [faithfully] as you see the day [of Christ's return] approaching."(Hebrews 10:23-25 AMP)

We stayed all day Sunday, and we were able to eat during intermission between the two services. After second service, we would pray, and **I loved to pray**. We knew a little something about praying because my mom would pray with us every night before going to bed. We would watch her attentively. She also taught us a couple of prayers. **Now I lay me down to sleep, Our Father,** and **The Lord is my shepherd** were her favorite.

"Then shall you call upon me, and you shall go and pray unto me, and I will hearken unto you." (Jeremiah 29:12 KJV)

"Train up a child in the way he should go [teaching him to seek God's wisdom and will for his abilities and talents], even when he is old, he will not depart from it." (Proverbs 22:6 AMP)

During prayer service, people were excited about Jesus, and we were excited too. Pastor Peartree had asked if anyone would like to be saved and to please come to the altar. My sister and I didn't know too much about being saved, but we wanted to be anyway; therefore, we walked up and accepted Christ into our hearts that night. When we returned home, my sister told our mom about her experience of getting saved.

"I did too," I said in a soft low tone.

Just by my mom's body language, I was not accepted. Her countenance changed, and she got quiet. I was heartbroken because I didn't understand why she wasn't happy for me like she was for Denise. I wanted my internal instinct to be wrong, but sadly, I was proven right the next day.

> *"That if thou confess with thy mouth the Lord Jesus, and shalt believe in thine heart that God hath raised him from the dead, thou shalt be saved." (Roman 10:9 KJV)*

My mother smoked her weed and began making jokes about me being saved. At that moment, my stomach began to twirl like a whirlwind because she chose me out of the four children to belittle and humiliate for no apparent reason. She told me to get in the closet and sit in there. I started crying and banging on the door for her to open it. It was so dark and scary in there. Then, she opened the door while voicing discriminative and derogatory remarks towards me.

> *"Let there be no filthiness nor foolish talk nor crude joking, which are out of place, but instead let there be thanksgiving." (Ephesians 5:4 ESV)*

"Yawl look, that's the devil right there. Look at those gray eyes," she said tauntingly as she smoked her weed. "She's different. She doesn't look like none of you," she said with laughter.

She had created a clear distinction between our skin colors which showed how she truly felt about me. I'm a lighter brown complexion while my mother, Willie, and Denise were dark skinned, and Daniel and my stepdad were light skinned. I was wondering what our skin color had to do with anything when she gave birth to me. How could a mother be prejudice against her own child?

"She ain't nothing, but the devil," my mother said annoyingly. "I believe your sister is saved, but you're not."

They all began to laugh at me. I knew my sister and brothers did not know any better because they were only following our mom. Regardless, my heart was pierced with unexplainable pain and torment. The ridiculing lasted for a few hours, and what I did believe about me being saved-she killed it. I didn't understand why **I was picked out to be picked on**. I felt like the black sheep out of my siblings, and what made it worse was that my mom showed no remorse whatsoever.

> *"A good man out of the good treasure of his heart bringeth forth that which is good; and evil man out of the evil treasure of his heart bringeth forth that which is evil: for of the abundance heart his mouth speaketh." (Luke 6:45 KJV)*

> *"A soothing tongue (speaking words that build up and encourage) is a tree of life, but a perverse tongue (speaking words that overwhelm and depress) crushes the spirit." (Proverbs 15:4 AMP)*

Although, she made a mockery of me and my belief in the truth about God's Word, I continued to *PRAY. "LORD, PLEASE HELP ME!"* I asked.

Chapter 4
School Daze

Not only did I deal with the bullying at home, but I also had to endure it from my peers at a new school. While minding my own business, two girls began to pick a fight with me over a boy that had his eyes on me, and I didn't even know this. I was ten, and I wasn't even thinking about boys especially, after what happened when I was 8yrs. old. Back when we were staying with Aunt Lola, a boy named Tooley, that was nine years old had started to pursue me as his "girl-friend". One time, we were caught kissing while humping each other with our clothes on. Whoever had caught us it had gotten back to my mom and Aunt Lola. Back at Aunt Lola's apartment, my mom asked me where I learnt or where I had seen this sexual act.

"I saw yawl (she and stepdad) doing that," I spoke innocently.

Boy, Aunt Lola laughed so hard at my mother, but my mom wasn't laughing at all. She was embarrassed and furious at me. I had gotten the beating of my life, and she didn't allow me to live down the incident for a whole year. She kept throwing it in my face to torment me for what I had done. All I did was imitate what I saw, but that didn't matter to her. She even brought up the fact that Tooley was fat: this is the part she couldn't get over. Therefore, because of this past incident, there was no way I was thinking about the boy that the two girls picked at me about. My mom didn't have to worry about me and boys after the drama she put me through.

One of the girls who wanted to fight was named Beatrice, who had beautiful, gray eyes, yet she was still jealous because the boy she liked had his eye on me, the new girl, the girl with *hazel* eyes. Seriously, could I help that he liked me? I didn't even know him, let alone like him. It was only the first day of school, and I was minding my business. This was absurd.

> *"You are still worldly (controlled by ordinary impulses, the sinful capacity) for as long as there is jealousy and strife and discord among you, are you not unspiritual, and are you not walking like ordinary men (unchanged by faith)?"* (1 Corinthians 3:3 AMP)

Well, I understood why he wasn't attracted to her. It was not her appearance: it was her attitude. She was conceited and had a nasty mouth: she was always cussing. I was standing in line waiting to enter the school while being **picked out to be picked on**, AGAIN! Unbelievable! Her bullying probably made her look bad in the boy's eyes. It appears every time I turned around someone wanted to fight me over something stupid.

Before proceeding with the situation with Beatrice, I would like to recall two other instances where I found myself in predicaments with girls that wanted to fight me: Emerald and a girl in my neighborhood.

At the previous school I attended, a girl name Emerald wanted to fight me. Every week, she would harass me and pick a fight; instead, of trying to get to know me. Oftentimes, there was someone always there to intervene and get her out of my face. However, this one time, there was no one around but her "crew". Emerald provoked me to fight her and to throw the first hit, so I did.

"LORD, HELP ME BEAT THIS GIRL because I'm not a fighter. I don't like fighting," I prayed internally.

Boy, did I let her have it. After I gave her a good beat down, someone came out of nowhere and broke us up. People were cheering me on, but if only they knew that I was scared out of my wits, and the strength came out of nowhere.

> *For our struggle is not against flesh and blood [contending only with physical opponents], but against the rulers, against the powers, against the world forces of this [present] darkness, against the spiritual forces of wickedness in the heavenly (supernatural) places." (Ephesians 6:12 AMP)*

All I could see was her face in my hand, and how I got the best of her. I was so happy on the inside that I won thinking "maybe this is the end of that," but not by a long shot. Emerald wanted a rematch, and I truly thought she was crazy.

After a few other fights with her, both wins and losses, she finally wanted to be friends. Why would I befriend her? I did not trust her because she would tell lies about me to others to keep them from befriending me. Her problem was that she could not control me like she did her crew. How ridiculous was this? It was hurtful, but I did not allow it to bother me. Emerald was about confusion and drama which was something I did not want to be a part of. I handled her with a long spoon, and I had no choice because she moved right out of the way-literally. She and her family moved to a new neighborhood; therefore, I was a happy camper, but she left a stink bomb behind her. Others listened to lies she told about me, and she was able to destroy friendships I had with others in her absence.

> *"Telling lies about others is as harmful as hitting them with an ax, wounding them with a sword, or shooting them with a sharp arrow."(Proverbs 25:18 NLT)*

I felt this way about it: if anyone could tell you that I gossiped about you, and you believed them, **you** were never my friend in the first place. I just couldn't figure out what her vendetta was. What did I ever do to Emerald? I considered myself to be friendly and never bothersome to anyone. I was not a fighter, yet others wanted to fight me.

> *"Let God arise, let his enemies be scattered: let them also that hate him flee before him." (Psalm 68:1 AMP)*

> *"Faithful are the wounds of a friend [who corrects out of love and concern], But the kisses of an enemy are deceitful [because they serve his hidden agenda]." (Proverbs 27:6 AMP)*

The second situation was a time when my mother had to make me fight this girl, who lived in the same building as us. The girl was taller and a couple of years older than me. While my siblings were playing outside, they overheard the girl talking about our mother and ran to tell me what she said. So, I confronted her and told her to stop talking about our mother.

Bickering back and forth, then she pushed me, but I didn't retaliate, so my sister and brothers ran upstairs and told our mother that I did not push the girl back. They loved to tell on me, and it was pathetic how they couldn't keep anything to themselves-unless you bribed them. My mother told me that if I did not get downstairs and beat that girl, she was going to beat my a--. Honey, I ran downstairs, and jumped on that girl like my life depended on it. The girl didn't have a chance to throw one lick. My mother and her mother had to get me off her, and then, later, my mother felt kind of sorry for her and told me to apologize to her. Because she found out the girl was an only child, and she didn't have any friends. "What!" I said to myself, "I didn't want to fight the girl in the first place." I was totally out done but I apologize. The girl accepted my apology, and she apologized to me as well for talking about my mother. We became friends.

In conjunction with fighting that girl, this act is what stopped my mom from calling me a coward. I did not hear that word from her anymore. She now looked at me in a different way- as a *WINNER*.

> *"Bear with each other and forgive one another if any of you has a grievance against someone. Forgive as the Lord forgave you." (Colossians 3:13 NKJV)*

> *"But thanks be to God, who gives us the victory (conquerors) through our Lord Jesus Christ." (1 Corinthians 15:57 AMP)*

Back to Beatrice, the grey eyed girl that wanted to fight me over a boy I didn't know. I had an opportunity to talk to her alone when she called me over to her while we were at school. She told me that she really had nothing against me and how she was being pushed to fight and wanted to befriend me

"Really, but why were you being pushed to fight me?" I questioned.

"For no reason. Because you are pretty, and you are the new girl in school," she confessed.

"But you are pretty, and the other girl who was pushing you to fight me is pretty," I pointed out.

"We thought the boy was going to like you over us," she explained

"I don't even know the boy. I had no clue yawl thought that," I exclaimed.

"Well you don't have to worry about it anymore," she assured.

After the conversation, I had noticed that she was afraid of the other girl even though they both had made me *afraid* to come to school. Before leaving, we exchanged numbers and addresses.

The last time I saw Beatrice, I had visited her home to let her know that I was moving the next day. When I was there, she apologized to me again.

"I wish I would have gotten to know you," she said regretfully.

"Me too," I agreed.

We said our goodbyes and hugged each other, and I left. I remember leaving her doorway while smiling at the thought of my fighting days being over. I wondered what was it about me that made my peers want to fight me. It was mind boggling because I never started anything. Also, I didn't understand why Beatrice had wanted to befriend someone that she was afraid of? These were my thoughts as I walked home.

"If possible, as far as it depends on you, live at peace with everyone." (Romans 12:18 AMP)

"A peaceful heart leads to a healthy body; jealousy is like cancer in the bones." (Proverbs 14:30 NLT)

Although I made a friend, I was glad to be moving, so I wouldn't have to face the other girl who had started this whole mess.

"Soon as I make a friend, it's time to move again," I sighed to myself. We hadn't even lived there a good two months. I did not even know the exact reason for the move, but I did know that my mom couldn't stay in one place for long; this was weird to me as well.

Behold, You have driven me out this day from the face of the land; and from Your face (presence) I will be hidden, and I will be a fugitive and an [aimless] vagabond on the earth, and whoever finds me will kill me." (Genesis 4:14 AMP)

Chapter 5
Pandora's Box

Not long after we moved into our new apartment, we took a trip to see my mother's brother, Uncle Hustle, and his wife, Aunt Giva (Give-uh), in Anderson, South Carolina. Aunt Giva also had a niece down there who was around seventeen, while I was about eleven during the time. She introduced all of us to her. I liked her because she treated me as favorable than my other siblings. I loved the attention that she gave me, and I gravitated towards her. We asked Aunt Giva and Uncle Hustle if she could spend the night. They said yes, but there was an issue because all my siblings wanted to sleep with her. But I ended up being the one who did, and I was glad.

While I was asleep, I felt her caressing me, but I did not move- I did not care. I was aroused, and it felt good to me. She started kissing me and the external parts of my body that had awaken something that I thought was buried. Meaning, these sensual sensations weren't new to me because it brought back a recollection of my first encounter when I was eight years old.

At age eight, my relative who was seven that came back from the south had introduced me to this seducing act. We woke up one morning, and she asked me if I wanted to play "house".

"Yes," I answered.

"You be the wife, and I'll be the husband," she said and I nodded my head in agreement.

She wanted to kiss, so we did. We went a little further and took off our panties, and she started fumbling me. My eyes got wider because I could not believe what I was feeling. My mother had called our names to get up, and we responded with an okay. We were scared out of our wits as we heard her walking towards the room door. Hurriedly, we tried to pull up our undergarments before she opened the door, but it was too late. She stood there waiting for us to get up; however, the only problem was that our panties were off. Apparently, the wait was too long, she pulled the covers back and saw that our undergarments were down. At the same time, we were trying to pull them up. She was ecstatic and cussing while running to get her belt.

"What were yawl doing?" she asked.

"Nothing," we lied.

"Yawl were doing something," she spat.

That day, she beat us like we stole something, especially me, because we wouldn't tell her who really started this. I refused to especially after the way my relative was looking me with frightfulness in her eyes, so I took the blame.

Years later, my relative shared with me that she had been molested by our male relative. This encounter with her **had opened a can of worms** because it did not stop right there; it kept happening between me and other girls my age that I knew. We were young and **curious** not knowing any better. I found myself addicted to this stimulation. When there was no one around, I would **masturbate** using couple of things that rekindled the sensation. I would take my hands and rub them against my vagina or lay on top a piece of clothing and rub my body against it to get aroused. I did this as if they were natural things to do and okay.

> *"So put to death and deprived of power the evil longings of your earthly body [with its sensual, self-centered instincts] immorality, impurity, sinful passion, evil desire, and greed, which is [a kind of] idolatry [because it replaces your devotion to God]." (Colossians 3:5 AMP)*

Returning to the situation with my aunt's seven-teen-year-old niece, she did something new that I never experienced: she went down my body and began to stimulate my vagina with her tongue. I did not stop her. Surprisingly, she wanted me to return the favor, but I couldn't partake in what she wanted. This part turned me off because I really didn't want to participate in that way. She sensed that I was inexperienced, so she settled with me caressing and kissing her. Truthfully, I just wanted someone to love and pay attention to me.

"Don't tell anyone," she said.

"I won't tell," I said.

When it was time for her to go, I hated to see her leave. I did not know if this should have happened because over the years, I struggled. I began to look at girls in a different way, and it started to feel uncomfortable. I didn't want to be attracted to girls. I would look at their backsides as if I was a male. I would catch myself and shake it off. I tried to ignore and alter these feelings, but it became a little strong and difficult to resist.

Despite this addiction, there was something on the inside negating that this act was detestable. I should not be attracted to girls. Therefore, **I remembered praying, asking God to take this form of thinking away from me**.

"LORD, HELP ME," I prayed.

I would have dreams of having relations or being attracted to my friends or girls that I did not know. I would wake up abruptly, shake it off and saying out loud "*I LIKE BOYS*!" I would do this repeatedly every time those thoughts and dreams surfaced. **As I continued to resist, it left me**. Thereafter, my thoughts change towards girls and the dreams, and the attraction for girls had ceased.

> *"For this reason, God gave them over to degrading and vile passions; for their women exchanged the natural function for that which is unnatural (a function contrary to nature)."* *(Romans 1:26 AMP)*

> *"Submit yourselves, then, to God. Resist the devil, and he will flee from you." (James 4:7 AMP)*

> [21] *After leaving there, Jesus withdrew to the district of[a] Tyre and Sidon.* [22] *And a [b] Canaanite woman from that district came out and began to cry out [urgently], saying, "Have mercy on me, O Lord, Son of David (Messiah); my daughter is cruelly possessed by a demon."* [23] *But He did not say a word in answer to her. And His disciples came and asked Him [repeatedly], "Send her away, because she keeps shouting out after us."* [24] *He answered, "I was commissioned by God and sent only to the lost sheep of the house of Israel."* [25] *But she came and began to kneel down before Him, saying, "Lord, help me!"* [26] *And He replied, "It is not good (appropriate, fair) to take the [c]children's bread and throw it to the [d]pet dogs."* [27] *She said, "Yes, Lord; but even the pet dogs eat the crumbs that fall from their [young] masters' table."* [28] *Then*

> *Jesus answered her, "Woman, your faith [your personal trust and confidence in My power] is great; it will be done for you as you wish." And her daughter was healed from that moment." (Matthew 15:21-28 AMP)*

On the grounds of us visiting South Carolina, my mom wanted Uncle Hustle's opinion on moving to California. She expressed that a different scenery and a new environment would be good for her, and that the fast-paced life of New York City had taken a toll on her. Sad to say, another move was in the making.

Chapter 6
Encountering Unfavorable Forces

When we got back to New York, she finally made the decision that we would be moving soon due to the activity of evil forces or voodoo, meaning **witchcraft**. My mom believed that someone had put something on all of us, and I believe this is the reason she did not allow us to eat everyone's food. She also expressed that this was something that heavily happened in the south. Once, my mom took us to a woman whom she paid to reveal who was working against her and how to defuse the problem. She tried to verbalize her perception of the visual concept; in which, I could not see because she was, supposedly, seeing beyond what meets the natural eye.

"Look at your brother. Do you see how his shoulders are lopsided?" she asked me. I responded with a simple no.

"For the gifts and calling of God are without repentance.[30] For as ye in times past have not believed God, yet have now obtained mercy through their unbelief:" (Romans 11:29-30 KJV)

My mother told the woman what she was encountering, and the woman confirmed the culprit of her demise. She gave my mother a few bags of purple powder, bible verses and instructions along with it.

*"Whoever gives heed to instructions prospers and blessed is
the one who trusts in the LORD." (Proverb 16:20 NIV)*

When we returned home, my mother was eager to get
started. We followed the steps thoroughly: first, I undressed
the boys and put them in the tub of water mixed with the
powder, washed them down in it, and **quoted the scrip-
tures** as the woman had instructed. Thereafter, my mom,
Denise, and I had to do the same. My mother saw a difference in us all after the ritual. **She knew that the curse was
demolished**. I did not understand it all, but I was obedient.

*"Children obey your parents in the Lord [that is, accept
their guidance and discipline as His representatives], for
this is right [for obedience teaches **wisdom and self-
discipline**]. ²HONOR [esteem, value as precious] YOUR
FATHER AND YOUR MOTHER [and be respectful to them]—
this is the first commandment with a promise— ³SO THAT IT
MAY BE WELL WITH YOU, AND THAT YOU MAY HAVE A LONG
LIFE ON THE EARTH." (Ephesians 6:1-3 AMP)*

*"No weapon formed against you shall prosper; and every
tongue that shall rise against thee in judgement thou shalt
condemn. This is the heritage of the servants of the Lord,
and their righteousness is of me, saith the Lord." (Isaiah
54:17 KJV)*

*"I will destroy the cities of your land and tear down all your
strongholds. I will destroy your witchcraft and you will no
longer cast spells." (Micah 5:11-12 AMP)*

When it was time, my mom had sold all her furniture
and had us pack all our clothing to move to Los Angeles,
California. We were sad about having to leave our church
home; we loved Pastor Peartree. Before we left, she embraced
us with her love and joyful smile. She had been an angel to

us, and we were truly going to miss her. I would never forget her persistence and eagerness to bring us to church.

> *"Bless the LORD, you His angels, you mighty ones who do His commandments, Obeying the voice of His word!" (Psalm 103:20 AMP)*

When we arrived in Los Angeles, we stayed with my mother's second brother and his wife who resided there. Something I remember about L.A. is that it rained a lot. Also, I remember riding through Las Vegas in my uncle's car. It was exciting watching all the bright lights that night. Due to my mother's indecisiveness we only stayed in Cali for a month. She decided to move back to New York because she was home sick, but I believe it was more to it than that. I could not believe she was ready to return already; but I admit, she barely scolded me in California. When she did scold me, my uncle and aunt would intervene on my behalf. I was grateful for that, but she didn't like it. In fact, she did not like anyone defending me nor did she like anyone telling her how to raise her children.

The whole time I was there, she wanted me to watch my baby brother, but my uncle intervened and said, "No. You should let her go play with the rest of the children. You need to watch your own baby," so I believe that this left a bad taste in her mouth.

Of course, I overheard the vigorous conversation, since I was nosey. I listened as they proceeded to tell her that she was too hard on me. The next thing I knew, we were packed and ready to depart on the next bus back to New York. Once we arrived, we stayed with a friend of my mother's until we found a place of our own. Although, this was probably an inconvenience for her friend, she loved my mom and wanted to help.

While we were staying there, we fell on some hard times, especially while having to wait for the first of the month, so we could eat. There were times we had to eat grits with no butter, no salt, and no sugar. It was hard to digest it. I would have rather not eaten anything, but I did not have a choice. Every time we took a spoonful, we would nearly vomit. But If *I*, Patricia, had vomited, she would have given me more grits. "*What is it about me she doesn't like?*" I would ask myself.

Even while living there, I could not do anything right. She'd find a way to catapult her anger and frustration towards me. If I didn't hear what she said, she would smack me right on my ear. I was her punching bag. If I looked at her the wrong way, she would punch me in my eye with no hesitation. All at the same time, I would hold my eye while crying and trying to catch my breath. I was always walking on eggshells because I didn't know when her fist was heading my way. It was frustrating and bothersome to live like this most days. Every time she called my name, I would jump wondering what I had done now. If anything went wrong with my sister or brothers, *I* was the one at fault because *I was the oldest*.

I was afraid to even talk back under my breath because she had good ears. When I did attempt this, she would catch me every time, and her fist came knocking me on the side of the head. You're probably wondering if the people we were staying with ever saw it, and the answer to this is no. She was very discreet in what she did and how she did it. It really didn't matter where we were or what it was;

I got it. Even if I had gotten my clothes dirty, she would come upside my head. *"How can I not do that if I am playing outside?"* I said to myself. Though I didn't understand her logic, I tried my best not to get dirty, but I wasn't always successful; therefore, I had it coming.

> *"For you have need of endurance, so that when you have done the will of God you may receive what is promised." (Hebrews 10:36 ESV)*

Chapter 7
A New Start

My mom had been looking for a place for us to live, and she was determined to not reside in the same neighborhood we left before we moved to California. She went out every day faithfully until she found something, and eventually, she did. She told us we were moving to the Flatbush area of Brooklyn, New York. She stated that it was a very nice neighborhood and great schools for us to attend.

Simultaneously, there was more fantastic news. Remember my stepfather, who was residing and working in New Jersey? Well, my mother was ready for him to come back home. Prior to this, they had been conversing with each other for some time. We were so excited to hear he was coming back because we missed him so much, and I guess my mom did too. She wanted him to remove himself from everything and return to New York. She told him that if he resigns from his place of employment, she will take care of him. This is the part I did not like. I didn't know why I was disturbed about this arrangement, but I felt an insecure feeling on the inside.

"If anyone fails to provide for his own, and especially for those of his own family, he has denied the faith [by disregarding its precepts] and is worse than an unbeliever [who fulfills his obligation in these matters]." (1 Timothy 5:8 AMP)

He pondered the offer; then agreed to the proposition that was presented by my mom. However, he also had a few stipulations for my mother. He told her that *she needed to stop smoking weed because he did not indulge in it.* He was only a Budweiser beer and Vodka drinker, so he told her that she could drink what he drunk or drink something else. Also, she had to agree to become stable at our new location. He told her that there shouldn't be any more moving; she agreed. With her agreeance to this, he couldn't tell his family members where we lived. Once, they both agreed to each other's stipulation, he was set to officially come back.

Because of her final contingency, we went years without seeing our aunts and uncles, and we missed them, but my mom was steadfast in her decision. My mom didn't want any parts of Aunt Lola nor did she want any dealings with my stepfather's family. They were all just memories in our heart.

Our new residence was located on the block of Bedford Avenue and Avenue D. I was now in the fifth grade and rode across town on a yellow school bus to P.S. 236. The elementary school was in the *Kings Plaza* area, a predominantly white neighborhood. It was different than the other schools that I had attended before. There were students of various cultures but mostly Caucasian students. Though this adjustment was challenging, I liked this change because it gave me the opportunity to intermingle with others who were different from me, and what I was accustomed to. This transition took me out of my comfort zone.

It was an interesting year, especially while trying to make new acquaintances. However, there was a pair of best friends that I observed closely and wanted to become friends with: Carolyn, an African American girl and Mindy, a Caucasian girl. I knew them because Carolyn rode on the yellow bus with me, Mindy was in some of my classes, all three of us were in the same homeroom. I admired their friendship, and I knew I wanted to be apart of it, so I chose to gravitate to them more than anyone else. The two girls had been friends since first grade, but it had never crossed my mind to break up the friendship; I only wanted to become part of it.

> *"The righteous man is a guide to his neighbor, But the way of the wicked leads them astray." (Proverbs 12:26 AMP)*

> *"Faithful are the wounds of a friend (corrects out of love and concern) But the kisses of an enemy are deceitful (because they serve his hidden agenda)." (Proverbs 27:6 AMP)*

We had only lived in the Flatbush area for three weeks, when I had encountered a horrific atrocity. While, coming home from the store, happy go-lucky, skipping and hopping through my wonderful neighborhood, I entered the first door of the three-family building. My key was tied around my neck and tucked in my blouse (we were called latchkey children). As I was about to open the second door with my key, a strange man opened the first door that was behind me and entered in. We both were standing there looking at each other, and I took in his tall, dark, and handsome stature. He was dressed up, and I could smell the cologne he had on. Then, he began to ask if I knew the certain person that he was looking for. He believed that they may have lived in one of the apartments. At that very moment, I began shaking in my pants because it was just him and I in this small hall area. *"What am I going to do?"* I thought.

"No, I don't know anyone by that name who lives here," I told him.

While not displaying any fear, I proceeded to answer his questions, boldly. I didn't feel the need to mention the first and second floor apartments being vacant and me living on the third floor. Therefore, I spoke as if they were occupied and only answered what he had asked me, being sure to not give him extra information.

So, I replied, "No, that person doesn't live here."

"Do not forsake wisdom, and she will protect you; love her, and she will watch over you." (Proverbs 4:6 NIV)

"For God hath not given us the spirit of fear, but of power and of love and of a sound mind." (2 Timothy 1:7 NJV)

Then, he put his hand in his pocket, took out a quarter, bent over to kiss me on my lips, and placed the quarter in my hand. At that point, I was devastated.

"Don't you tell anyone," he said to me.

"Okay," I responded.

I was so in shock from what just had happened. My mind and body were in distress, and I had a feeling of numbness. It was unbelievable. Once he left, I opened the door and walked upstairs, as I reminisced on what just occurred. I began to think about what could have happened if I had not listened to the voice within my head.

"The sheep that are My own hear My voice and listen to Me; I know them, and they follow Me." (John 10:27 NKJV)

"Answer only what the stranger asks. Do not show any fear and stay calm. Don't allow him to know that you're the only tenants that live in the building," the voice told me. I followed those instructions, but the events ran repeatedly through my mind. The nasty kiss from a grown man was terrifying, but I had decided not to tell my parents. Because I thought, *"What is the use, no one could catch him now?"* This experience taught me a valuable lesson: **never be naive when it comes to people.** I also became more aware of my surroundings and waited until people walked by before entering my building.

> *"It is better to put your trust in the Lord than to put your trust in man."* (Psalms 118:8 NIV)

The next day, I boarded the school bus and sat in the back, *as I* was still traumatized by what had happened. This incident must have caused me to show an external countenance of worry and fear which caused Carolyn to ask me what was wrong. I began to cry and tell her about the strange man who startled me the night before. When we arrived at the school, she told Mindy and they both consoled me. As you can see, we became friends. They embraced me for a little while until they got tired of me hanging around them (well, that is how I perceived it). Sometimes they were my friends, other times, they were not. To me that was not enough; therefore, I had to do something about it. I was obsessed with associating myself with them, and I know that sounds a little crazy, but I could tell they were good people to have as friends. I decided to come up with a plan that would stabilize our friendship, permanently. My mind began to brainstorm; I knew that they liked candy and bubble gum because they would bring bags to share with each other and, sometimes, even me. It was embarrassing to continue to take from them when I never had anything to offer back.

Though it was not much, my mom would give us an allowance. It was just one dollar a month and only enough for one person. If we had asked her for more any other time, her answer was always no. Being that she did not give it to me when I asked, I took it upon myself to take it. The first time I took money from her, it was twenty dollars which was a lot of money back then and I could buy plenty of candy. I calculated how many packs of Bubble Yum and Bubblicious that I could purchase. Each pack was only twenty to twenty-five cents, and I had twenty dollars... OH BOY! That was a lot of candy to take to school, and I would be able to share with them. They loved it! It put a smile on everyone's face, including mine because I did not know that giving felt so rewarding. It brought a joy that was incredible. It felt good to give for a change.

> *"Jesus, how?' He said, 'It is more blessed to give than to receive." (Acts 20:35 NKJV)*

After sharing with my friends, I had left over candy that I had to hide until the next day. Every time I replenished the stash, I bought something different: Snickers, M&Ms, Now & Later's, etc. To stock up, I kept stealing from my mom until she had noticed money missing from her wallet. I became one of the suspects under her surveillance. When she asked me about it, multiple times, I continued to lie. I knew then I had to come up with another plan, so I began to steal from my stepfather starting with $20.00. I took out of his wallet and hid it in my drawer under some clothes. I was waiting to spend it for school, but my plans were interrupted; he went in his wallet to pull the money out and saw that it was missing. He called me and my siblings.

"Who took $20.00 from me?" he asked us.

"We didn't take anything," we all answered.

"Someone took it, and we are searching the whole house until we find it," he demanded. "I am going to find who did it. I got something for him or her," he said promisingly.

"Trisha, did you take the money?" I knew he had asked me because of suspected history of stealing from my mom. I looked him dead in his face and told him *no*, but he did not believe my answer and went to my room.

"You have not gone out the house, so it is still here," he said. He pulled my drawer out, frantically searched under my clothes, and found the $20.00. Although, I knew I had put it there, I told him that I did not know how it had gotten there.

"So, it walked into your drawer by itself?" he asked sarcastically. I just shrugged my shoulders, while playing dumb.

He pushed me into the room and took off his belt. He whipped me so bad, that **I did not steal anymore from him**.

"Thou Shall not steal." (Exodus 20:15 AMP)

"You do not steal, nor deal falsely, nor lie to one another."(Leviticus 19:11 AMP)

When I ceased to bring Carolyn and Mindy candy, to my surprise, they told me that I never had to buy their friendship in the first place. They told me that they were distant at times because they needed their space and did not want to tell me, so they ignored me. Nevertheless, I respected their truthfulness. Also, they let me know that there was no love lost which put a smile on my face. Well, instead of a twosome, we were a threesome (when it was convenient for us to hang together). After all, everything happens for a reason. Later, Mindy relocated to a new school, and Carolyn and I became closer.

In the closing of my 5th grade year, I met more new friends of diverse backgrounds: both Caucasian friends and African American friends. Overall, I loved my last year in elementary school. I had learned how to sew, cook, and took a woodshop class for the first time. My favorite memory was the talent show where Carolyn and I did *the Hustle*. It was funny when our Caucasian friends would ask Carolyn and I to teach them our moves, and being that I was a friendly person, I didn't mind sharing what I knew.

> *"And do not forget to do good and to share with others, for with such sacrifices God is pleased." (Hebrews 13:16 AMP)*

There were times that I would have rather been in school than at home. School is where I had fun and a lot of laughs. I dreaded going home because I knew what was waiting for me: chores and more chores. Getting up for school was a bonus and anticipation for what the day was going to bring. I had a great year at P.S. 236 Elementary School. It was my last year before beginning middle school.

Chapter 8
Inherited Sins

The next school year, I looked forward to beginning middle school, and the experience of taking the city bus by myself with my fellow students without my siblings. While most students liked riding the city bus because it made them feel mature and "grown up." I was just excited to ride with adults. Also, because my parents couldn't keep their eyes on me like they did before when the school bus pulled up directly in front of our building. It was very annoying and embarrassing for me because they were always yelling out of the window as soon as I stepped off the bus.

"TRISHHHA! I need you to go to the store for me!" My mom would yell out of the window, as if she could not wait until I had gotten upstairs. She would throw the money down to me with the list, and she would tell me to put my books on the inside of the hallway until I came back. What else could I do, but go?

The school that I attended for sixth grade, Roy H. Mann Middle School, was also out in the Kings Plaza, a predominantly Caucasian area. I had never seen so many white people in my life until I went to this school. There were so many white people, you could smell the stench of prejudice in the air. At a new school, I would once again be meeting new students, but this time I would be interchanging between different classes. I loved to change classes because I was able to see students that I had never seen before. In addition, this was another good year of me getting A's and B's on my report card.

Everything was not always good, though. Once when my friends and I stopped to a corner store that all the students would go to, I was tempted to steal because I did not have any money to buy some Macaroons (this was something that I had done numerous times before). As usual, I would look around to see if anyone were looking, sneakily take the pack of Macaroons, and cautiously place it in my jacket pocket. I began to walk towards the door, and suddenly, I was startled because I was stopped by the storekeeper's voice.

"Give me what you have. I saw you through the mirror," he said.

Guiltily, I handed him the item and begged him not to call anyone because he had threatened to call the police. All I could think about was what would happen if my parents found out. I knew that my mom would have killed me-that is for sure.

I cried and I begged until the man came out and said, "Don't come to my store anymore."

"I promise and I won't steal anymore," I said worriedly.

"But God, who is rich in mercy, because of His great love with which he loves us" (Ephesians 2:4 NKJV)

Having recollection, we had a couple of weeks left before the end of my sixth-grade year. My classmate, Charlotte, and I were asked to be monitors in classrooms while the teachers and students were out of the class. Our duties included washing the board, checking papers, and wiping the desk. While everyone was gone, we became hungry; we wanted a snack, but we did not have any money to buy anything.

"Let's check their coat pockets to see what we can find," I suggested to Charlotte.

"Okay," she responded. Charlotte's face lit up. "I would have never thought of that."

Boy, when we started digging in the pockets, she was speechless and could only laugh.

"How did you know?" she asked me.

"One day a teacher told me to pick up someone's coat, and when I picked it up, I heard the sound of change. So, that is how I knew. Plus, white folks always keep money."

Every pocket we checked had money, and there was enough for us split. Every day, we visited classes, until we started feeling bad about what we were doing. So, before we stopped, we checked the coat pockets one more time, and they were empty. We knew, then, that they were on to us; so, we stopped doing it and realized that stealing was wrong.

> *"If we confess our sins, he is faithful and just to forgive us our sins and to cleanse us from all unrighteousness." (1 John 1:9 AMP)*

> *"Treasures of wickedness and ill-gotten gains do not profit, But righteousness and moral integrity in daily life rescues from death." (Proverbs 10:2 AMP)*

Also, students began to talk about how money was missing from their pockets, and this scared us; therefore, I was glad that we decided to stop.

Though I stopped stealing from the students, I did not completely stop. I wanted to stop, but I could not. It was as if something had a hold on me, and I could not shake it. I would go to the grocery store, made sure no one was looking, then, I would confiscate the king size Hershey bar with almonds and sneak it my pocket. On the way home, I would eat every bit, leaving no evidence. Maybe I believed it was okay to do because my mom would open a pack of her favorite cookies and eat them before she got to the cashier. Afterwards, she put the wrapping in another isle wherever we were walking and never mentioned the cookies to the cashier.

> *"Train up a child in the way he should go (teaching him to seek God's wisdom and will for his abilities and talents), Even when he is old he will not depart from it." (Proverbs 22:6 AMP)*

When my mom and I had our coffee talks, she stated that my aunt would shoplift in the stores by hiding clothes in her girdle. Because she was a full-figured woman, this went unnoticed. It seemed that stealing ran in the family. Every time I went to the store, I promised myself that I would not steal anymore, but it was so tempting; the weight of stealing was strong.

> *"He stretched out his hand over the sea, he shook the kingdoms: the LORD hath given a commandment against the merchant city, to destroy the strongholds thereof." (Isaiah 23:11 KJV)*

"When He arrived at the place [called Gethsemane], He said to them, "Pray continually that you may not fall into temptation." (Luke 22:40 AMP)

Chapter 9
Cinderella Moments

During the summer before my seventh-grade year began, at the age of 13, my usual leisure consisted of playing outside with my neighborhood friends, but this was contingent upon my parents' specific rules for the summer. We could not go into the street, we had to be visible, and we had to be in the house before dark. However, I was not always allowed this privilege because I always had to do chores. If those chores were not done, I could not go out- I felt like Cinderella...like I was the stepchild or something. My mother always found an excuse for me to stay inside, and do not let a friend ask if I could come outside-her answer would be no. The chores and my mother, often, were stumbling blocks in my summer.

In some instances, she was two different people, Dr. Jekyll and Mr. Hyde. I didn't have to do or say anything, but my presence alone agitated and aggravated her; despite this, she wanted me in her view. At times, I was so nervous around her, especially when she called my name. I had to consider her tone, words, and actions to determine her mood at that moment. Perhaps, it was my lying and stealing that contributed to the animosity she had towards me. Also, due to this animosity, she didn't trust a word that I said.

> *"Lying lips are extremely disgusting to the Lord, but those who deal faithfully are His delight." (Proverbs 12:22 AMP)*

> *"Providing honorable things, not only in the eyesight of the Lord, but also in the sight of man." (2 Corinthians 8:21 NKJV)*

When she sent me to the store, I had to practically run because she timed me. Timing me was probably her way of making sure I didn't go anywhere that I was not supposed to. She didn't even consider that I might have to go to a completely different store, if the store she sent me to didn't have the item. On the upside, going to the store was another form of freedom for me. It gave me an opportunity to think and dream about different things. I daydreamed frequently: this was one of the reasons that I was slapped so much. When my mother called my name, I was envisioning myself somewhere else and didn't hear or respond right way.

> *"Where there is no vision, the people perish: but he that keepeth the law, happy is he." (Proverbs 29:18 KJV)*

There were times when she wanted to have "mother and daughter talk." My mom instilled in me that I could get pregnant from boys just by holding their hands. I believed my mom so much, that in second grade, I told the teacher that I had to hold a girl's hand in line. Unbeknownst to my teacher, I was scared that I would get pregnant if I held hands with a boy because of what my mom told me. Later, my mom told me that when you receive your menstrual cycle, you can become pregnant and once it appeared, I had to be sure to tell her. I was so confused and afraid to ask my mom questions about anything because of her tone and her persona. Knowing my mom, she would jump to conclusions because of the questions I ask. She didn't recognize that I was a little girl who still played with dolls and boys were not on my agenda.

My mom was unpredictable; she would say anything out of her mouth. Because of what I was going through with my mom, I could not begin to state how many times I ran away thus far. Despite how many times I ran away, I always ended up back home and she always managed to find me. I just wanted an opportunity to express to my mom how I felt without backlash or fear; instead of keeping it bottled up.

Well, my opportune time had manifested: she asked me a question during one of my punishments. I was picking lint, by hand, and trash off the living room carpet, as tears rolled down my face. Before I began, she had ripped my clothes like a mad person while everyone one else was outside. It looked like I was wearing rags.

My mom sat on the ledge of the window frame looking at me and she asked, "You sometimes feel like you are Cinderella, don't you?" My mouth flew open when she said this.

"How did she know what I was thinking?" Cinderella was my favorite childhood story, and I felt just like her.

"Sometimes I do," I spoke honestly while wiping my tears as they fell.

"Why do you feel that way?" she asked me.

"I am tired of you spending the welfare money only on yourself buying nice expensive clothes. You don't buy us the latest clothes and shoes. It's all about you. As our mother, you're supposed to make sure we have what we need, and you act like you don't love me. You're always beating me and sometimes for no reason," I spoke boldly.

"You think you are so smart, but you are not. You're dumb," she spat. I continued to cry and pick lint off the carpet.

"Don't sit over there thinking you are *Cinderella*. *Cinderella* is prettier than you," she taunted.

I cried so hard that my head began to hurt while snot flowed out of my nose. I was so angry because of her attitude towards me that I could have screamed. After a while, she thought about what I said in that moment, and suddenly, there was a turn around.

"Sorry that you feel this way about me," she spoke. "Go wash your face, put on some clean clothes, and go outside with the others."

> *"Moreover, if your brother sins against you, go and tell him his fault between you and him alone. If he hears you, you have gained your brother." (Matthew 18:15 NKJV)*

I don't know what happened, but I was glad to express what was on my heart.

Another thing, I couldn't wait to be employed, so I could buy my own clothes- the things that she would not get for us but only for herself. I knew in my heart that she wouldn't take care of us the way she took care of herself.

My mom was a fanatic, maybe even an addict when buying the newest and latest apparel. Despite, her shapely figure, she would buy clothes that wasn't her size. Her closets were full of clothes with tags on them because her plan was to lose weight to be able to fit into them. However, my mom had one hang up-she loved to eat.

She would take me shopping with her and put three to five outfits on layaway for herself. She paid on them every month until she got them out. This was very upsetting to me because we had to wear cheap sneakers and clothes that weren't the latest fashions. She could have got them with the money she chose to spend on herself. Because of my apparel, I was picked on at school all the time, and it was embarrassing. She just didn't know.

Nevertheless, my 7th grade year started off great; I met new friends and embraced old ones. It was always a pleasure to be back at school. Unfortunately, this year, I was not receiving the best grades because I had a lot going on at home. I had to help my sister and brothers with their homework and do my own homework. But I could not finish it because I was exhausted. Also, I had to make sure we all had clean clothes for school. If there weren't any, I had to wash them by hand because we could not afford to go to the laundromat. If they weren't acceptable to my mother then I had to redo them. This chore ruled out the option of going to bed early, so I would fall asleep in class. My grades were dropping every quarter, so I made changes to my report card before I gave it to my parents. They expected a lot from me when it came to my grades, and I didn't want to get whipped because of failing grades.

When I received my report card for the last quarter, it was terrible. I was going to be held back from entering the 8th grade. I cried like a baby, but I wiped my tears from my face and pulled myself together. I knew I couldn't go home with this report card; therefore, I threw my report card away and thought about the lie I was going to tell my parents. When I arrived home, that was the first thing they asked me for.

"I couldn't find it, and I lost it," I said lying.

My stepfather had a hard time believing me and kept questioning me about it. He finally gave up, as he proceeded to pick his teeth with a toothpick trying to determine whether I was telling the truth or not.

"When the summer is over, you had better bring me something that says you are in the **8th grade**," he spoke in a serious tone.

$\int hapter\ 10$
Believing for a Miracle

I ran to my room, got on my hands and knees, and **prayed, asking God to forgive me for lying.**

> *"God, I need Your help. I really need a miracle. God please, if you do this for me, I will do better in school. Lord, if I could just have a second chance, I would do better. In Jesus' name, Amen."*

For days in my heart, I cried to the Lord, hoping that he had heard me. I reminded him of what my parents were going to do to me, if he didn't. I had no way of knowing if he heard me or not, but I just had to believe that he had.

> *"Now faith is confidence in what we hope for and assurance about what we do not see. This is what the ancients were commended for." (Hebrews 11:1-2 NIV)*

Over the summer, I had no worries of the situation. I can't explain it! I did not allow it to bother me because I believed that God heard my prayer. I carried on and enjoyed my summer as if nothing ever happened, but it felt like the summer ended too quickly. I wasn't ready to return to school.

> *"If you can?" said Jesus. "Everything is possible for one who believes." (Mark 9:23 NIV)*

"And the peace of God, which passeth all understanding, shall keep your hearts and minds through Christ Jesus." (Philippians 4:7 KJV)

The first day of school my father couldn't wait to remind me about the report card.

"Don't you forget, or you know what's mine? (my behind was his)," he said.

"Okay," I responded happily.

In the meantime, on my way to school, I was asking myself, "Who am I going to speak to? What am I going to say?" I just didn't know what to do. Once I got inside the school building, there was a call for all 7th graders to report to the auditorium (which meant me since I was held back). When everyone became quiet, the Principal stated that students who didn't get promoted to the eighth grade, would have an opportunity to undergo a second chance to get moved on.

He announced, "We are going to have two 7th grade classes: **7A** and **7B**. **7A** is the regular 7th grade class, and **7B** is the intermediate class for students who weren't promoted with their 8th grade class this year."

In order to be promoted I had to meet this requirement: I needed to pass all my classes in the first half of the school year. If I did, then I would be promoted to the eighth grade in the second half of the year. I was in awe. I couldn't believe my ears.

"Oh My God!" I said to myself while simultaneously **laughing and crying**.

I knew that **God did it just for me** and gave me a second chance. **My miracle!** All I could say was "*Thank you, Lord!*"

My heart was full of joy. It was unbelievable. I dared not tell anyone about this miracle because they wouldn't believe me.

> "*In my distress, I called to the Lord; I cried to my God for help. From His temple he heard my voice; my cry came before him, into His ears.*" (Psalm 18:6 NIV)

> "*If you ask anything in my name, I will do it.*" (John 14:14 NKJV)

> "*I will give you thanks, for you answered me, and you have become my deliverer.*" (Psalms 118: 21 NET)

However, I went to the office to ask for a copy of my original report card, and the secretary gave me one. Once I read it, I saw that I needed to make a few changes. I had to remind myself that my stepfather was very smart; therefore, I had to be smarter. After school let out, I went straight home to face my dad. I prepared myself to tell a lie to my father about my *original* report card

"Do you have it?" he asked me.

"Yes," I responded. He took it, observed it, and started asking me questions about it.

"Why some of the grades look traced over?"

"The teacher did it; they made a mistake." I was sweating bullets when I told him that. He just looked at me.

"Alright as long as you got promoted, I am okay," he spoke.

Thus, I walked away, while under my breath, asking the Lord to forgive me for lying. I felt bad, especially, after what He had done for me.

> *"It is better to say nothing than to make a promise and not keep it."* (Ecclesiastes 5:5 AMP)

Keeping my promise in this area to God was no problem, I was maintaining A's and B's in my intermediate class. I loved English literature, and I learned how to recite poetry. Amongst other things, I also had a crush on my teacher, Mr. C, which motivated me to get to school in a hurry, so I could gaze at him. He resembled the teacher on the T.V. show called **Welcome Back Kotter**. In addition, I enjoyed Mr. C's teaching and how he cared about us, his students. He was also very comical and made me laugh; there was never a dull moment in his class. I had my share of laughter in that class when I didn't have to deal with being bullied (this time by boys).

James, John and Leroy made my days at school a living nightmare. It was bad enough going through it at home, and now I had to deal with the humiliation of being called out of my name at school as well. They called me names such as *Skinny Minnie*, *Grandma*, and *Bones better than Bones* because of the clothes I wore, and they also picked at my shoes. As I previously mentioned, I didn't have the most fashionable clothes nor shoes, so every day I had to hear cruelty. They would say that they were *just joking*, but those jokes hurt me. I would only be at peace when they weren't at school.

> *"Let there be no filthiness and silly talk, or coarse (obscene or vulgar) joking, because such things are not appropriate (for*

believers); but instead speak of your thankfulness (to God)."
(Ephesians 5:4 AMP)

Leroy's tactics were different from the others. His bullying didn't just entail jokes; he would push me around physically. For instance, if I were standing around in the classroom, he would purposely bump into me for no reason and dare me to say something. I tried my best to avoid him, but he always happened to show up where I was just to taunt me.

Fortunately, Drew, one of my classmates came to my defense. I remember that he called me *"pretty eye or cat eyes."*

"She has those hazel eyes, so you only pick on her because you like her," Drew told him.

"No, I don't!" Leroy exclaimed defensively.

"Well, that's not how you treat a girl that you like," he said angrily.

"Shut up! You need to mind your business," Leroy spat as he got in Drew's face and pushed him.

"I'm not scared of you," Drew assured while pushing Leroy back.

A fight erupted between the two, and the teacher came just in time to break them apart. Leroy walked out of the classroom in rage and looked back at me.

"I'm gonna get you," he said, angrily.

I was so afraid. **Every day I would pray that he would not attend school**. One day he did not come to school for a long time, and I didn't care why. I was ecstatic; my prayers were answered.

One day, I saw Leroy in a crowd of people, but he didn't see me-I made sure he didn't. He was such a nuisance. The last time that Leroy saw me, he approached me differently. He was nice when he asked me a question. His attitude amazed me so much, I didn't hear what he had asked. I don't remember what I said, I just know that he walked away nicely. However, I did notice there was a scar under his eye. Whatever happened to him, I'm glad that it happened because it brought about a change in Leroy.

> *"Ye shall not need to fight in this battle; set yourselves, stand ye still, and see the salvation of the Lord with you Oh Judah and Jerusalem." (2 Chronicles 20:17 NKJV)*

As for James and John, who were fraternal twins, I thank God that I didn't see them all the time. The only time I bumped into them was in the hall.

John had sickle cell disease, and I really felt sorry for him. He was much skinnier than I was due to his sickness. He never knew, but I admired him because he always laughed and had fun although it was on the expense of hurting me by his way of "joking". While enduring the hurt and pain of people picking and laughing at me, I promised God that I would never laugh or partake in any gestures or activities that would humiliate others. After all, I knew what it felt like.

> *"Do to others as you would have them to do to you."*
> *(Luke 6:31 NIV)*

My progression and time in the intermediate 7th grade were quite an experience, one I would never forget. I succeeded the requirements that were needed to enter the 8th grade in the second part of the school year. When I received my report card, I didn't have to change that 7 to an 8-it was already there. I was the happiest student in the world. I cried tears of joy because I made it, and I was able to show my parents my true, untampered report card. Later, I graduated with my 8th grade class, and I was so happy, and my parents were happy as well, especially my stepfather.

> *"Yet grace (God's undeserved favor) was given to each one of us (not indiscriminately, but in different ways) in proportion to the measure of Christ's (rich and abundant) gift." (Ephesians 4:7 AMP)*

Unfortunately, my mom and dad didn't come to my graduation. All that I had accomplished **with the help of the Lord**, and there was no one there to support me. I felt so alone and unloved as I waited in line watching other graduates with their parents.

> *"And the Lord, He is the One who goes before you. He will be with you; He will not leave you nor forsake you; do not fear nor be dismayed." (Deuteronomy 31:8 AMP)*

I tried to be very discreet in how I was feeling and appear to be unbothered but deep inside, my heart was broken.

Withholding my tears, I asked God in a quiet voice, *"God why me? Why did you give me this set of parents?"*

There were times when I just wanted to die; I didn't want to live any longer. As a matter of fact, I tried to kill myself once by taking six or seven pills. These made me sleepy and numb to the beating my mother promised me that day. Well, committing suicide must not have been meant to be because I'm still here. Something always made me see things in a positive way, and I never knew what it was, but it would put a smile on my face.

> *"Therefore, you now have sorrow: but I will see you again and your heart will rejoice, and your joy no one will take from you." (John 16:22 NKJV)*

> *"And the peace of God, which passeth all understanding, shall keep your hearts and minds through Christ Jesus." (Philippians 4:7 NKJV)*

Despite it all, I was excited for the summer because I would have my first, real summer job. In the past, I did sporadic jobs such as going to the store for my elderly neighbors or shoveled snow for the neighbors. I would get paid for these jobs, but my summer job would pay more money. As a disclaimer, I appreciated every monetary pay I received from these small jobs, but it was just time for a promotion.

Chapter 11
Puberty Hits

Although, I was now working, the summer of 1981 wasn't all that great. At the age of fourteen, puberty had begun for me. Painful knots that were the beginning stages of breast development began to sprout out on my chest. Boys began to pay attention to me when they did not before. Speaking of boys, there was a boy who lived on my block that I really liked. Brian, he had already graduated and attended high school a year ahead of me. All the girls liked him. I would introduce my friends to him, and he would fall for them, but he never paid any attention to me. This may be so because my parents were strict, and I was skinny and flat chested with long, sandy brown hair during that time, but now, puberty had a way of drawing people and the people that you don't want. I felt funny and embarrassed because the nubs of my breast poked through my blouse. I had no bras yet, and I didn't like the fact I was filling out.

On top of that, my mother was harassing me because my menstrual cycle had started, and she wanted to know when my period came on every month. She threatened by saying what would happen if I had missed my period. I didn't know what in the devil she was talking about; she spoke in riddles. If I wanted to find out what she was talking about, I had to read books to get my information. I would read about romance and love, and in some of those books sex was mentioned, so I received a clear picture.

Regarding puberty, my mom didn't mind sharing my business with her favorite sister, Nancy, who was also one of my favorite aunts, and I was her favorite niece. She would call Savannah, Georgia in a heartbeat just to tell Aunt Nancy everything about me. They would be chuckling and carrying on, over the phone. They discussed me, as well as my cousins, Aunt Nancy's children. Sandy, Aunt Nancy's oldest daughter, and we were the topics of many of their conversations. It was like they were comparing notes. My mom didn't care if I heard what she was saying or not; she would tell my aunt everything. So, when my breast began to grow and my menstrual began, she knew as well. I was so embarrassed by my mother's lack of discretion. They also began to talk about my cousin, and her dealings with boys.

"She bet' not come in here pregnant; she is gettin' out," my mom told her while on the phone. Aunt Nancy would say the same thing about Sandy.

"She betta' stay a virgin too," she added. "*What is a virgin?*" I asked myself curiously.

> *"For this is the will of God, that you be sanctified [separated and set apart from sin]: that you abstain and back away from sexual immorality;" (1 Thessalonians 4:3 AMP)*

One day, I just happened to be walking along with some friends, and they were picking on me about if I was a virgin or not. I was absolutely dumbfounded because I had no idea what a virgin was. Therefore, I tried to deviate from the question because I didn't know what to say; they were looking for a yes or a no answer. I was so embarrassed because I didn't know the answer. Eventually, they became distracted by something else and forgot about what they were asking me. I was happy about that. It gave me time to find out the meaning.

I tricked one of my other friends into telling what a virgin was. "Girl, I bet you don't know what virgin means!" I said to her.

"Yes, I do!" she exclaimed, "It's somebody that never had sex before."

"My mother never told me the meaning." I said to myself. Again, she always spoke in riddles when it came to our puberty development, so I never understood what she meant. Instead of telling me, she would take me to the movies to see *Shaft, Foxy Brown* and other African American Rated R movies that had sex scenes.

When watching these movies, not only did I see what sex was, but I began to get aroused. I remember these familiar feelings through the exp**erience I had with the relative, my Aunt Giva's niece in South Carolina, and others.** I had received this same stimulation from just watching a man and a woman have sex. This sexual sensation had me moist between my legs; I thought I urinated on myself. It was truly embarrassing.

My mother continued to take me to see these vile movies, and I would have dreams about them. There were times, I had to put my hands between my legs to keep from having an orgasm, and I knew what this was from reading the romance books. **Books and movies are how I figured out what was happening to me.** To avoid these *feelings* when we went to the movies, I would cover my eyes when the sex scenes came onto the screen. I felt embarrassed and violated through the visual non-discretion of the movie. I wished that my mom would have felt comfortable enough to talk about those important matters, then I would not have had to do the research and find the answers on my own.

> *"Run away from sexual immorality (in any form, whether thought or behavior, whether visual or written). Every other sin that a man commits is outside the body, but the one who is sexually immoral sin against his own body."* (1 Corinthians 6:18 AMP)

I continued to read books to enlighten me on sexual intercourse and what could be a possible outcome of doing so. I became more curious about sex, and my mother was on high alert because I was becoming older and who knows what she thought I was doing.

My stepfather wasn't any better in controlling the thoughts of what I could have been doing behind closed doors; because of this, he was reluctant in allowing me to go to a house party that was just around the corner from where we lived.

He questioned me, "Are boys going to be there?"

"Yes," I told him honestly.

"No," he said without hesitation.

Then, I asked, "Why?"

"Because I said so," he told me dismissively.

Since he had told me no, I went to ask my mother and at first, she said no, but after I persistently asked her, she finally said yes. The only contingency was that I would have to take my sister. Now, I didn't want to take my sister, but it was the only option, so I agreed to take her. Also, she was able to convince my father to allow me to go, but he gave us a curfew which was midnight. The only issue was that the party didn't "start" until midnight. After being at the party for a little while, we went back home and asked if we could stay longer, and luckily, they said yes. Denise and I had a great time, but in my mind, I thought "*The next house party I go to, my sister will not be going with me even if I have to bribe mommy.*"

Shortly after, my opportunity to go to another house party came around again, and once again, my stepfather expected me to be home by midnight-*humph*. I told him previously that people started coming at midnight. Honey, twelve' o clock came and went while I partied hard, drenched with sweat, until my stepdad came and got me at three o'clock in the morning. As we were walking home, I was laughing to myself saying, "*I don't care if I never get to go out again.*" I was so engrossed in my own thoughts that I didn't hear anything he was saying. I was reminiscing on how I threw down on the dance floor which was something that I loved to do.

If I do say so myself, I was a great dancer. I knew all the latest dances. You named it, I did it. Back then, Michael Jackson was one of my favorite dancers of all times. The reason I loved dancing because it kept my mind off things, and it made me very happy. When I danced, I felt a sense of freedom and liberation. I dreamed of being a dancer and among other things such as a teacher, a business administrator, a wife, and even a mother. I dreamt of these things all the time; despite my circumstances, I continued to dream of the things I could be and do.

Walking back home, my father kept talking to me as everything went in one ear and out the other. I was truly fed up by his lecturing, but overall, all that mattered to me was that I had a goodtime. When we got home, I was surprised that my mother didn't say anything, so I just walked past her and went to bed. Although, my mother didn't do or say anything, my father punished me for my failure to correspond with the curfew he had given me.

Chapter 12
Epiphany

Eventually, I yielded to the fact that my mother **didn't trust me.** I knew that I had brought this upon myself due to the countless lies that I told over an extended period. I desired her trust and her belief in me; therefore, I decided to make a vow to God that I would not lie to my parents any longer.

I had epiphany that my dishonesty was hindering my mother's love towards me. I wanted her attention but not in the negative way that she was giving. Trying to win her love and attention was not only difficult but painful in the process. I accepted that it was too late and had to suffer the consequences of my actions.

Also, I had run away about eight times within four years, so it wasn't just my lying that took a toll, but also me running away and the numerous times that I had stolen from her. Eventually, I lost interest in stealing and it had gotten old, so there were no more consequences for me, at least not because of stealing. She still knocked me around but for other reasons.

As I recall, I was shown love twice by my mother: when I had bronchitis pneumonia and menstrual cramps. When I was ill with bronchitis pneumonia, she thought that death was knocking at my door. We were snowed in, and we couldn't get to a doctor. At first, they thought that I was lying about being sick, so I could get out of doing my chores. When my mom took my temperature, it revealed that I was truly sick. My legs buckled under me, and while I tried to do my chores, I ached all over my body. My father picked me up and carried me into my bedroom, since I couldn't walk. All I could remember was that my mother stayed near me and tried to keep me awake until the fever broke. She put plenty of blankets over me because of the chills I had encountered through the fever. I truly felt her love for me during my sickness.

Every month, around the same time, I would have the worst cramps because of my menstrual cycle with symptoms that consisted of back pain, cold sweats, and vomiting. The pain was so unbearable for me that she had to keep me home from school. When I stayed home, she showed her love towards me by ensuring my comfortability by giving me hot tea to drink, pain relievers, and allowing me to sleep at the bottom of her bed. I laid there balled up into a knot, as I cried until I fell asleep. In those moments, I felt her motherly love and compassion.

> *"The Lord is good to all and has compassion on all He has made." (Psalms 145:9 NET)*

That night I had an encounter that made it a night that I will never forget. A beautiful, huge angel with widespread wings stood looking and smiling at me through my mother's living room beads. He shined bright like a light with long, curly hair. With fear, I frantically pulled the blankets over my head. I said to myself, *"What am I going to do?"* with my hand over my mouth. When I removed the blankets from my face, he was gone. I remained amazed at his majestic beauty. At that moment, I knew then that an angel was watching over me and his presence reassured me of that. I smiled to myself. For those few seconds, I felt special.

> *"For He shall give His angels charge over you, to keep you in all your ways." (Psalm 91:11 NKJV)*

> *"They said to her, "You are out of your mind!" But she kept insisting that it was so. They kept saying, "It is his angel!" (Acts 12:15 AMP)*

> *"Are not all the angels ministering spirits sent out [by God] to serve (accompany, protect) those who will inherit salvation? [Of course, they are!]" (Hebrews 1:14 AMP)*

There were times that my mom showed her care for me, and there were times where she was fickle. She would change her persona and actions towards me in a heartbeat, especially when she needed me, in order to take care of important business that affected her. For instance, she would keep me home from school to assist her in filling out her forms at Social Services, so she could continue to receive resources.

"Trisha fill these papers out. It's my eyes; I can't see the words. My eyes hurt; I need glasses," she said while handing me the paperwork.

"Okay, mommy," I said not thinking anything of it.

She also used me as a medium to lie to our landlord when she couldn't pay the rent on time or had come up short. Mrs. Bradford, our landlord was very fond of me, and my mom knew this, so she used it to her advantage. I liked Mrs. Bradford; she was very pleasant to talk to despite her Jamaican accent which many people could not understand...

well except for me. But her kindness could not be taken for weakness because she was a smart cookie, and my mom couldn't pull anything over her head.

Mrs. Bradford offered me a job to keep the inside and outside steps clean for her, and she would pay me. My mother would give me the rent to pay Mrs. Bradford, and I had to tell Mrs. Bradford that she wasn't home even though, she was. When Mrs. Bradford questioned me about the amount that I had given her, I had to tell her that this is all she had for the rent. I hated lying to Mrs. Bradford especially after **I told God that I was going to stop lying**. However, Mrs. Bradford could look into my eyes and know that I was lying for my mother. She would tell me that the only reason why our family was not evicted, some time ago **was because of me.**

"I am sorry. Thank you," I told her humbly with tears in my eyes.

"No need to say anything...**your eyes tell everything,**" she said while smiling.

She hugged me and gave me my pay right out of the rent money. The way she treated me left me marveled and speechless. *"What did I do to deserve such a liking to?"* I asked myself, *"I just lied to her."*

In my heart, I was so grateful for her response. I thanked the Lord and asked Him to forgive me for the lie I told her for my mom.

> *"Let the favor of the Lord our God be upon us, and establish the work of our hand upon us; yes established the work of our hands." (Psalm 90:17 ESV)*

"I have not come to call the righteous, but sinners to repentance." (Luke 5:32 NET)

"Be merciful (responsive, compassionate, tender) just as your [heavenly] Father is merciful." (Luke 6:36 AMP)

After Mrs. Bradford made her rounds to collect rent, she then thanked me for doing such a marvelous job on the steps. Unfortunately, every time she paid me; my mother would take my money. Although I was upset about it, there was nothing that I could do. I had to comply whether it was right or wrong. Besides, I certainly knew what would happen if I didn't give her the proceeds.

"Honor your father and your mother: that your days may be long on the land which the Lord your God gives you." (Exodus 20:12 AMP)

My mother believed that I should receive compensation for the things that I did for others even when I wanted to do them out of the kindness of my heart. If I baby-sat for one hour, I would have considered doing it for free, but she said that they had to pay me or else and with no delays. If there was any discrepancy upon this agreement, I had to hunt them down. Anyone who had met my mother knew that it wasn't me at the root of these demands. My mother wanted the money; that is what she wanted. She would give me and the customers an ultimatum: no money, no babysitting. I wanted to do this out of the kindness of my heart because people don't always have the money to pay because other things come up. Maybe my mother felt that I was naïve because of the way I think. When I had expressed this perspective to her, she paid me no mind.

"Blessed are the pure in heart: for they shall see God."
(Matthew 5:8 KJV)

Therefore, I had to continue harassing people that owed me money by going to their house every few hours until they returned home. Doing this, chasing down people for money made me feel desperate. I had empathy for others and their struggles; whereas, my mother did not care, nor did she play when it came to money.

"For the love of money is the root of all evil: which while some coveted after, they have erred from the faith, and pierced themselves through with many sorrows."
(1 Timothy 6:10 KJV)

Another incident, I recall concerning money was on picture day at school. I had found an envelope with $200.00 in it and was sure that someone had lost their picture money. It was in my heart to do the right thing and return it to the office, and when I did, I felt good about it. Overwhelmed with excitement, I couldn't wait to tell my mother about the good deed I had done, believing that she would be so proud of me for doing the right thing. To my surprise, she was furious about what I had done. She told me that I should have kept the money, and how stupid it was of me to seek that the money be returned to its proper owner. After yelling at me, she told me to get out of her sight. As I walked away, I still had a good feeling in my heart, knowing that I did something right.

I believe it was a small voice inside of me that directed me to turn in the money. If I didn't turn it in, I would had been stealing, something that I did not do anymore. Plus, the name was on the envelope, and if I had ignored this, I would have been doing something that I knew was wrong.

In closing, the student was happy to get it back, and I was happy that I gave it back.

> *"Samuel said, "Has the Lord as great a delight in burnt offerings and sacrifices as in obedience to the voice of the Lord? Behold, to obey is better than sacrifice, and to heed (is better) than the fat of rams." (1 Samuel 15:22-24 AMP)*

> *"So, whoever knows the right thing to do and fails to do it, for him it is sin." (James 4:17 ESV)*

Chapter 13
Summer Job Experience

No matter what I did, I could never satisfy her, and she was always difficult to please. It appears I had to walk on eggshells all the time. When she called my name, I would say to myself, "*What have I done now?*" There was always something, and I could never get a relief.

"Trisha's name is the only name you know out of all the of the children," my stepfather would say to her, in my defense.

She had three other children, and seemingly, she didn't know their names. For example, my mother's bedroom was right near the kitchen; regardless of the proximity she would shout and wake me up, in the middle of a school night, to get her a glass of water. Mind you, my room was on the other side of the kitchen. I could never understand why she would take me through useless periods of grief and headaches. During the summer, I had to get up early in the morning to make it to my summer job without falling asleep on the train, after a night of her shenanigans. I had to pray that I would not miss my stop each day.

I loved my summer job which was in Harlem, NY at the Congress of Racial Equality, known as C.O.R.E, where I was the youngest youth worker there that summer. The skilled employees taught us, the inexperienced youth workers, how to answer phones, type on the computer, and file different paperwork. In addition to doing desk work, we beautified the communities in certain areas of Harlem. Before having this job, I heard terrible things about Harlem from violence to crime, but these things weren't the case. The people seemed to be friendly and watched out for one another, from my perspective.

Like school, going to work gave me a break from my homelife and peace of mind. I was never in a rush to get home because there were always more chores to do. I never really felt like a child or like I had a childhood. At work, I felt free and appreciated. When I came through the door, people were happy to see me, and I never was in a conflict with anyone. In the beginning, I met Melissa, a young lady who was older than me and deaf. Though, her deafness affected her speech, I comprehended every word that came out of her mouth along with sign language. Melissa was a unique, kind, and humorous person, and I was sure to spend time with her at work. Also, she treated me as if I were her younger sister. I admired how she didn't allow anyone to vex her and her abilities because of her hearing-impairment. She embraced her disability, handled the insults, and jokes made towards her maturely. I don't remember too many people, but Melissa was worth remembering.

"Above all, taking the shield of faith, wherewith ye shall be able to quench all the fiery darts of the wicked." (Ephesians 6:16 KJV)

As I stated previously my mother would time me when I went to the store, and she would also time me coming home from work; it was ridiculous, but I brought it on myself. She was incognizant of my feelings and extremely annoying with the notions that she accrued in her mind about me. Yet, I still loved her, despite the ill- mannered attitude that she had towards me.

Chapter 14
Dreams of Future Events

I always had this internal instinct that I was beyond my years, and this feeling caused me to believe that I was special. I may have felt this way because of the dreams I had at night. These dreams would manifest into reality, and it was scary when they did. Also, I would know things before I saw them or before I was told, as if I had seen the future or read minds. However, I had never expressed this to anyone because they would have thought that I was weird. For some odd reason, I kept dreaming about the same thing for a couple of years, and I would be in awe because it seemed so real. I constantly dreamt that while coming home from work, and I happened to look up, there was residue of smut around the window and broken glass from our apartment which alluded a fire had taken place.

> *"He said, "Listen to my words: when there is a prophet among you, I, the LORD, reveal myself to them in visions, I speak to them in dreams." (Numbers 12:6 NIV)*

Daydreaming kept me occupied, and it gave me something to look forward to in the future. One of my dreams was that I would finish high school, go to college, and live in a big house with a white picket fence. Escaping reality in my mind, became natural to me and what probably kept me sane.

Another common daydream of mine was having *super*p*owers,* so I could zap people out of my life who were doing me harm. I became interested in books that talked about the *supernatural* which led me to desire the ability to erase obstacles that laid before me. Of course, witchery was out of the question (too scary), so being a superhero with superpowers was my best bet. This is also where my love for *Wonder Woman*, my favorite superhero, fostered from. She was smart, beautiful, clever, and strong. Her open visions and strength always allowed her to catch the enemy. Unfortunately, I had to come to the realization she wasn't real, but I liked the idea that *Wonder Woman* could be me. You could say that I had a very hopeful and creative imagination.

> *"I pray that God, the source of hope, will fill you completely with joy and peace because you trust in him. Then you will overflow with confident hope through the power of the Holy Spirit." (Romans 15:13 NLT)*

> *"You know of Jesus of Nazareth, how God anointed Him with the Holy Spirit and with power, and how he went about doing good and healing all who were oppressed by the devil, for God was with Him." (Acts 10:38 NASB)*

> *"Listen carefully: I have given you authority [that you now possess] to tread on [a] serpents and scorpions, and [the ability to exercise authority] over all the power of the enemy (Satan); and nothing will [in any way] harm you."(Luke10:19 AMP)*

Sometimes, I wonder how I didn't lose my mind during the early stages of my life. Home was a disoriented place for me, a place that I hated to return, a place where I didn't feel loved. If anyone mentioned the word "*home*" my stomach became flustered, and the anxiety of what awaited me was truly agonizing. It was like a horror movie. I was scared out of my wits on the inside of what could happen next. My stomach boiled wondering if she forgot about the beating that she promised me when I got home from school. This was a miserable feeling. Who wants to come home to this? I didn't.

> *"Anxiety in a man's heart weighs it down, but a good (encouraging) word makes it glad." (Proverbs 12:25 AMP)*

> *"For God has not given us a spirit of fear, but of power and of love and of a sound mind." (2 Timothy 1:7 KJV)*

I used to ask myself, *"Why did I have to be born to a mother who didn't love me? Why does she take her frustration and anger out on me? What have I truly done for her to act as if she hated me?"* I believed her resentment towards me went deeper than what was on the surface. *"God, she never shows any affection towards me. She does not embrace me or get close to me for some reason,"* I told **Him**. When I tried to hug her, she would push me away. I truly believe that my daydreaming is what kept me going when everything else made me want to give up.

As a child, I could not understand the vice that was behind the rejection and why it was there. At times, she didn't show any remorse, and when she did come back to her senses and realized she'd gone overboard in disciplining me, she would say she's sorry. Of course, I willingly accepted her apology. I took what I could get when I could get it.

> *"Then Peter came up and said to him, "Lord, how often will my brother sin against me, and I forgive him? As many as*

seven times" Jesus said to him, "I do not say to you seven times, but seventy-seven times." (Matthew 18:21-22 ESV)

Chapter 15
My First Kiss

At times, it was like my mom wanted me all to herself, and I could never put my finger on what was truly behind it.

> *³ But the Lord is faithful, and He will strengthen you [setting you on a firm foundation] and will protect and guard you from the evil one." (2 Thessalonians 3:3 AMP)*

I had one friend that thought something was wrong with the way that my mother treated me. **Let's just call** my friend, Ms. C. Anytime Ms. C ask if I could come outside, she had to bribe my mother, and because she had to do this, she felt that something wasn't right. I was truly embarrassed by my mother's behavior and words in these instances. We would have to persuade her with food (since she loved to eat) for me to go outside. Thankfully, Ms. C never held this against me, and I believe she had sympathy for me. She didn't allow these issues to stand in the way of our friendship. She was very understanding of my situation and very aware of my home circumstances.

Ms. C and I had known each other for a long time-since elementary school. She was my best friend whom I did many things with. Before she had moved to the south, we rode the same bus and lived on the same block. A couple of years later, she moved back to New York, and I was glad about that; she was my girl. From there, we spent a lot of time together, and I loved hanging out with her. She was sweet, though she could be a little obnoxious but in a funny kind of way. She wasn't stingy but very generous. The first thing she asked me when I came to her house was *"Are you hungry?"* If I told her yes, we would sit down and eat breakfast together. Ms. C kept money, more than I could say for myself, and she treated me though I couldn't return the favor. I would feel so guilty about it, but she didn't care if I had anything or not; she was always there for me and I loved her for that.

> *"The man of too many friends (chosen indiscriminately) will be broken in pieces and come to ruin, But there is a (true, loving) friend who (is reliable and) sticks closer than a brother." (Proverbs 18:24 AMP)*

Ms. C wasn't scared nor intimidated by anyone; in fact, she would fight male or female; it didn't matter to her. She made sure no one messed with me, so much that people we encountered would mistake us for sisters. Since people thought we were sisters, we decided to adapt to this idea. Another thing that I can say about her is that she was very confident. She knew she was beautiful, and no one could tell her otherwise. If someone gave her compliment, her response was *"I know,"* and then I would bust out into laughter because of the way she said it-without blinking an eye. She meant it. She would laugh as well and say, "What? What? I mean it"

Boy, she knew how to make me laugh and thought I was hilarious as well. In our time together, we would play dress up and put on makeup, although we didn't need it. Ms. C was pretty without it, and I would complement her by telling her she could be a model. She would respond by telling me that I was as well, but I didn't believe it because I was called ugly all my life by my mother. When someone like your mother, the woman that birthed you, tells you that you are ugly, you begin to believe it. My perception of myself was influenced by my mother and my fellow classmates that picked on me and called me names.

> *"I will praise thee; for I am fearfully and wonderfully made: marvelous are thy works; and that my soul knoweth right well..." (Psalm 139:14 KJV)*

One day, I decided to introduce her to Brian, remember the boy that I had a crush on since elementary school. He lived right across the street from me, and he was sophomore football player and very well-mannered. When I saw him, I daydreamed about being his girlfriend. Though he didn't know that I liked him, I could still dream. Ms. C was very interested in meeting him, so I set it up because we were good friends even though I liked him. One thing that I didn't understand was why Brian couldn't keep a girlfriend for no longer than six months. He had a different girl on his arm every time I turned around. He was a smart and attractive guy with a six pack, so I could not understand why he couldn't keep a girlfriend.

The time and day were set for Brian and Ms. C to meet, and I was excited for them. When Ms. C saw him, she agreed that he was indeed fine. After the introductions, they began to become acquainted with one another. Due to the success of the first meet up, we decided to schedule a second meet up. When the next meet up came, they walked with me to The Projects because I had to pick up money that was owed to me for doing hair. That day, I had my first real kiss with

Brian, and it happened because they both convinced me to practice, so I would have had some experience in the future. Though, this was not my actual first kiss, IT WAS CRAZY.

First, Ms. C would kiss him while I stood outside of the project building. After her one minute was up, it was my turn, and I was so nervous, but when he looked into my eyes, and I gazed into his...it was magical. The French kiss was so pleasant my foot went up in the air, as I envisioned us in a romantic scene of a movie. I hoped that he would never forget this moment because I surely would not. We took so long that Ms. C had to stop us. I heard from other girls that he was a great kisser, and now I knew that they were telling the truth.

Then, he walked us home, but I had to detour because I couldn't risk getting caught walking with him. All I could think about was *that kiss*. One day during my travels, I bumped into him

"You are a great kisser," he said as we greeted each other and he walked along beside me.

"So are you," I said while blushing, he gave me this long-lasting smile.

"How is everything between you and Ms. C?" I asked with concern.

"I don't know. I'll see her later," he said nonchalantly.

"Okay," I said not wanting to pry.

Ms. C and Brian had dated for a little while, but I believe he was afraid of Ms. C, due to her aggression. You always had to come correct and be correct with her. She didn't have time for games or tricks as she would state, "*Tricks are for kids.*" I would laugh hysterically at her little sayings; she was truly a character. Though her personality was very upfront and aggressive, I was more passive-aggressive. Regardless, of our differences, we still clicked. Withal, our summer was coming to an end, as well as my summer job. Now, I was preparing to go to South Shore H.S. whereas, Ms. C would be attending a different high School since she lived in a different district. Even though we were going to different schools, she would always be my girl.

Chapter 16
A Different Vibe

South Shore High School was a multicultural school, but the neighborhood was predominantly African American. South Shore High School wasn't anything like my prejudice middle school, Roy. H. Mann in the *Kings Plaza* area. At Roy H. Mann, there were riots every Friday in the area, and black boys were attacked by huge white boys, who graduated and came back to start trouble. There were many times where the bus would take off and leave a crowd of us stranded, purposely. We would have to walk until we could see our destination; in which, we called it our territorial line (the area where we "belonged" in the eyes of the prejudice. We all walked together and never apart, to avoid the white people that drove by and harassed us by calling us "n------". The young men that drove by never directly harassed the black girls, and we didn't have any problems with the white girls.

Halloween was the scariest: they would put on mask, running and waiting to aim the eggs at the black boys. We were frightened for them and tried to pull them on the bus before the bus driver closed the doors. The white boys would be hanging from the window as the bus took off, and some would run after the bus. I would have never thought that I would ever experience or witness racism and prejudice. Television is where I had seen terrifying situations like this happening.

Richard, a classmate of mine who was thick, tall, and quiet, was the main target. He never bothered anyone. The white boys would wait until after school and chase him while hitting his back with chains and sticks. He tried hard to escape the terror that he faced every Friday, but the boys remained persistent in the harassment. A crowd of students would shout and cry out telling them to stop harassing, assaulting him, but they proceeded to do as they pleased. It was a nightmare of hatred and sadness. Thereafter, we started seeing the police patrolling the area. I guess the principal alerted the police, especially after Richard's parents came up to the school. The police started patrolling the school grounds every day, and the riots began to calm down. It was a relief from the violence, and we were excited about it. We were able to ride the bus peacefully.

Because there was none of this chaos at South Shore, my high school years were of a different caliber than my middle school years at Roy H. Mann.

"Let the peace of Christ rule in your hearts, since as members of one body you were called to peace. And be thankful." (Colossians 3:15 NIV)

Entering high school, I was excited about meeting new students, cute boys, and reconnecting with my friends from middle school. Also, I was interested in seeing how huge South Shore High School was; I had never been to a large school.

This year was different than any other school year because I was looking my best and was able to wear the latest clothes and shoes, due to the money I made at my summer job. My mother and I agreed that I would purchase my own school clothes, and I didn't mind this at all; honey, I felt and looked brand new. The different color Lee Jeans and the Devil Jeans were *in*; we would turn them into **straight leg** (skinny) jeans. I would pair the stylish jeans with a cute blouse and my favorite sneakers, Nikes. My hair was pressed and curled into a Shirley Temple. I was brand new and a happy camper. I didn't have to worry about people calling me out of my name anymore, as if God wiped away my enemies. It was like *a **breath of fresh air**!* Those students who tortured me every day weren't friends of mine-they were my enemies.

> *"Revive me, O Lord, for Your name's sake! For Your righteousness' sake bring my soul out of trouble. In Your mercy cut off my enemies and destroy all those who afflicted my soul: For I am your servant." (Psalm 143:12 NKJV)*

Boys were now starting to notice me but wouldn't get close to me or approach me. I used to wonder and ask myself, *"What is wrong with me?"* I just thought I wasn't attractive enough, but then again, my parents were probably what kept many boys away, but not all of them. Brian became attracted to me and showed interest in me, but I wouldn't give him the time of day because he went out with a couple of my friends. Aside from Ms. C, he had messed with a friend of mine named Denise, who was from Jamaica. At times, I didn't like the way she treated him, but he really liked her. After a year, their relationship ended, and she moved back to Jamaica. Another friend of mine he dated was Heather, but that didn't last long.

Although Brian had liked me, the other boys in school were very distant towards me, and I didn't know why. This left me with low self-esteem because of the rejection- rejection that I also faced at home

> *"Come to Him [the risen Lord] as to a living Stone which men rejected and threw away, but which is choice and precious in the sight of God." (1 Peter 2:4 AMP)*

There are some girlfriends of mine from high school that I want to tell you about. Firstly, Veronica, who was a Trinidadian girl that I went to middle school with. Back in middle school, we had a friend group of our own: there was Jane, she very sweet and funny, and Denise, whom I mentioned earlier. Denise and I would walk to the bus stop together, since she lived right around the corner from me before she moved back to Jamaica. Heather, a beautiful Jamaican girl, came along, and then there was Judy. Honestly, I never knew what Judy's problem was. She always used sarcasm with Veronica and I, but we didn't pay her any mind. When she would say something hurtful to me, Veronica always defended me. Anyway, after middle school, everyone scattered and went their separate ways except for Veronica and I- we stayed in touch.

Veronica was also one of my best friends. What I liked about her the most was her comical persona, intelligence, and the many laughs we had together. She was a warrior, and like Ms. C, she would fight anyone that she had to; it didn't matter that she was petite. She was a friend who stuck closer than a sister. No one better not had bothered me, or it was *"on and poppin"* with Veronica.

The group of friends that Veronica and I were a part of in high school was composed of girls, who were older than us, smart and that didn't mind fighting. When I felt that a fight could break out, I would pray *"God please don't allow a fight to break out,"* because I didn't like fighting. I also prayed this because in some crews (group) that I knew of, you had to jump in when they were fighting, and if you didn't, they would fight *you* (this arrangement reminded me of my mother). But they never pushed me to fight. If I happened to be around, I was the one who held their coats and bookbags while they kicked some butts. I guess they saw me and my desire for peace, but it wasn't that they *wanted* confrontation in their defense. Someone else always started the fight with them first. Regardless, of their fighting, **they were the older sisters that Veronica and I wished we had.** Veronica was the oldest of four siblings *like me,* and they knew both of our moms and their parents were strict. The older ones discovered a way to hangout; in spite of, especially on the weekends, since their parents worked at night.

Porsha, the first girl I met out of the older girls lived down the street from me. She was so kind to me, and I hated when she had to leave to go to Jamaica for one year that seemed like forever. When she returned, her accent was different. She wasn't the same Porsha I knew and met, but I loved her anyway.

Also, there was Cathy, her tall sister Rachelle and our other friend, Desiree, who was very funny. I loved them all, and I think we laughed more than anything. We had our ups and downs, but we were sisters; no one could break us apart.

> *"If possible, as far as it depends on you, live at peace with everyone."* (Romans 12:18 AMP)

We deeply cared about one another; however, they all had a special concern for me-***the runaway child***. They would hide me in their parents' home for a little while although I couldn't stay. The point is that they welcomed me in which I truly appreciated it. Not only did they sneak me in, but they would make sure I was fed and had clothe when I ran away. We even had an opportunity to go to house parties together. I still cherish them in my heart for all the laughable times that we had together and the things that they did for me.

Two girls that I also cherish are Nicole and Wanda. Nicole introduced me to Wanda, who was her best friend. Wanda was a junior at South Shore High School that took me into her parent's home. Her family was willing to help me, and I believe I stayed with her for maybe a month; her parents adored me. I cleaned and did whatever needed to do during my time there, but when it was time for me to vacate, I left. They always hated to see me leave, but her parents were cautious which I understood. I was someone else's child who ran away, and they didn't want conflict. Both Nicole and Wanda did all they could to help me. This is what I will always cherish in my heart.

Because I was a people person, you couldn't help but to get along with me. I was friendly with everyone no matter their ethnicities, culture, or race. I had met so many people from different backgrounds in my lifetime such as: Hispanics (specifically Panamanians), Puerto Ricans, Jamaicans, Haitians, Trinidadians, to African Americans, and Caucasians. Many people thought that I was different from others that they encountered. They treated me as if I were a part of their family, and we loved each other. It was such a privilege to meet so many diverse people from whom I could learn new things, and they could learn things from me.

> *"This is how we know what love is: Jesus Christ laid down his life for us. And we ought to lay down our lives for our brothers and sisters." (1 John 3:16 NIV)*

> *"A man who hath friends must shew himself friendly and there is a friend that sticketh closer than a brother." (Proverbs 18:24 KJV)*

Instantaneously, the attacks of emotional and physical abuse that I had encountered changed once I attended high school; it was extraordinary. During my elementary school years, my peers wanted to fight me and my middle school peers wanted to bully, tease, and joke about me. However, my high school years were the opposite; they had a different vibe in the atmosphere. There was compatibility and normality with peers who cared about me, and they dared someone to mess with me. They were willing to protect me. This was the strangest thing, but I loved it. These were like stages of growth, so to speak. It wasn't fun going through this, but the result was worth it. At first, I had problems comprehending this thing we called life and had questions in my mind that I didn't have the answers to. This was frustrating to me. I would always ask God, but he never answered me. In the end, I was glad that I finally had some peace, and I didn't have to be afraid at school anymore.

> *"So shall they fear the name of the LORD from the west, and his glory from the rising of the sun. When the enemy shall come in like a flood, the Spirit of the Lord shall lift up a standard against him." (Isaiah 59:19 KJV)*

> *"But the Lord is faithful, and he will strengthen you and protect you from the evil one." (2 Thessalonians 3:3 NIV)*

Nevertheless, there was home that I still had to contend with.

Chapter 17
Feelings of Worthlessness

Ninth grade was pretty consuming because I started cutting class. I had eyes on boys, and I began to hang out with other students. Thankfully, ninth grade was a plus since they didn't leave you back unless you were in the tenth grade. Meaning, they would promote a student no matter what grades they had-good or bad. This was perfect for me I had a **"I don't care" attitude** that allowed me not to do any work. My workload at home had canceled out my homework because I was always exhausted afterwards. What was the use? No one else cared if I had homework or not; therefore, doing homework and going to class wasn't an important task to me anymore. **I gave up.** The enthusiasm about school was no longer there. I just wanted to hang out and have fun.

> *"But as for you, be strong and do not give up, for your work will be rewarded." (2 Chronicles 15:7 NIV)*

At the age 15, my mother was constantly becoming upset with me for being late from school. She didn't believe that my tardiness was due to the bus running behind schedule; instead, she had *other reasonings*.

"I am taking you to the doctor to see if you are a virgin," she told me.

"I haven't been doing anything," I tried to assure her.

"We will see," she told me in a disbelieving manner.

My story was always that the bus broke down, or the bus never showed up. Regardless of my attempts to convince her, it didn't matter-she didn't believe me. She took me to the doctor anyway.

Once he finished examining me, I asked him, "Am I ok? Am I a virgin?"

"You know what that means, don't you?" he asked. "Your mother wanted to know if you were having sex with a boy."

When the doctor told me that, I was so hurt and embarrassed although I knew the meaning for virgin I just wanted to hear it from the doctor.

"Your mother doesn't trust you, but you are a good girl," he said to me.

"*I am going to fix her*," I said to myself. I was so distraught by her actions, so I began to organize a plan that would deliberately overturn her false allegations as the truth; this is how disgusted I was.

> *"Do not take revenge, my dear friends, but leave room for God's wrath, for it is written: "It is mine to avenge; I will repay," says the Lord." (Romans 12:19 NLT)*

Then, my mother had the audacity to state, "I am going to get you checked next year too. You and your sister aren't going to bring any babies in my house. If either of you ever get pregnant, this is not your home anymore. I will kick your a--out!"

She thought very little of me. I wasn't even thinking about having sex with boys - I was too scared. All I had were innocent little crushes on boys and nothing more.

After everything, I asked my dad if I could have a boyfriend.

"No!" he proclaimed quickly.

"Why not? You know I'm not doing anything wrong," I told him.

"Yes, we do know; therefore, we would like to keep it that way, and plus you are too young," he explained to me.

"Even if you meet him and he comes here?" I tried to bargain.

"Nope. Too young. You have plenty of time for a boyfriend. You need to focus on school. You're already under suspicion with your mother thinking you're going to mess up," he replied.

I told him, "That's not going to happen, Daddy. What about when I turn sixteen?" I inquired.

"I will think about it." He said and with that response, I walked away hopeful.

Observantly, when my stepfather was sober, he was a completely different person. He was sweet, soft spoken, and a man of few words which was the opposite of his loud, repugnant, and unbalanced persona while drinking. His drinking made me resemble that of a stone alcoholic. In addition, every day he would venture out and find him a drink with neighborhood friends on the corner early Friday and Saturday mornings.

"Woe to those who rise early in the morning that they may pursue strong drink, Who stay up late in the evening that wine may inflame them!" (Isaiah 5:11 NKJV)

One fall day, he came home and told us that we were invited to one of our friend's house for a celebratory gathering. Two days before the celebration, my father began to tell me about this young man who wanted to meet me and wanted to take me out on a date. The gathering was for his nineteenth birthday celebration. Apparently, he had asked my dad if he could take me to the movies. I hadn't even met him, but my dad had told him yes on my behalf. This bewildered me because my father had just told me that I couldn't date.

"Daddy, I don't want to go out on a date with him. For one, I didn't even know him, and you just met him." I spoke.

Also, I was surprised that my mom was okay with it too.

"Just meet him. You might change your mind," my step-father said convincingly.

"Okay," I gave in.

"I like him. His name is Tory, and he's visiting from South Carolina. His family owns a garage business, and he has a car," daddy informed me.

This information didn't impress me. "*So, what!*" I said to myself.

We went to the gathering, and Tory was sitting with the adults that drank, while I was with the children since I didn't drink. Later, we were introduced to one another, and I came face to face with Tory's tall, skinny, light skinned frame and well-groomed with Jerry curls. He looked *okay* in the face and he smelled good too.

The host needed some things from the store, so Tory volunteered to go and asked me if I would like to accompany him. My dad said it was okay, so we were on our way.

While we were driving to the liquor store, our conversation consisted of us learning about each other, but it then deviated to the topic of sex. I was uncomfortable talking about it because I was against doing it at the age of 15 and wasn't ready. After we picked up what he came for, we headed back to the party. While we were walking upstairs to the apartment, the next thing I knew was that my back was against the wall. He slapped me, grabbed my face while pressing my cheeks together, telling me to not talk about sex like it was nasty.

"You don't know what you are talking about," he spat.

Well, he was right; I didn't know, and I didn't want to know. I believe he was offended by me opposing sex. I was so petrified by his actions, that I began to cry. He told me to be quiet and that I better not say anything or else.

"Your step-father doesn't care nothing about you" he told me. "I wanted to take you out and he said '*no*!' at first, but he changed his mind when I offered to buy him a bottle of vodka and not just any size; he wanted a gallon. He told me I could have anything I wanted," he smirked.

My heart was broken. A gallon of liquor was the motive that my father wanted me to go out with him. I felt like he sold my soul and body to the devil. My stepfather made me feel cheap, dirty, and worthless.

"Now as to the matters of which you wrote: It is good (beneficial, advantageous) for a man not to touch a woman (outside marriage). v.2 But because of (the temptation participates in) sexual immorality, let each man have his

own wife, and let each woman have her own husband."
(1 Corinthians 7:1-2 AMP)

"Wine is a mocker, strong drink a brawler, and whoever is
intoxicated by it is not wise." (Proverbs 20:1 NASB)

"Be alert and of sober mind. Your enemy the devil prowls
around like a roaring lion looking for someone to devour."
(1 Peter 5:8 NIV)

I was afraid of Tory but furious with my father. I didn't want to go out with this maniac, but I pretended to be interested. The whole week, I couldn't comprehend what my father had done; it was mind boggling. I was nervous and dreaded the day that Tory had to pick me up. The next weekend was our movie date, and he had to have me back home at a decent time. It appears that Friday came faster than usual. Afterwards, we went to the store since the movie ended early, and he asked me if I drank, and I said no, so he got me a soda and himself a beer. Then, he took me to his one room apartment where we sat and talked until he asked if he could kiss me. I said yes due to my fear of him, but I made it very clear to him I wasn't ready to have sex.

"Please don't push the issue. If you continue, I'd rather you just take me home," I told him honestly.

I didn't mind the kissing, but anything else was a no, so he didn't push the issue after that. After a couple of kisses, he began to tell me that in two weeks he was returning to the south. Oh my God, I was so glad since I was only entertaining him because I had to. After that, he asked if he could rub against me, and I allowed him to lay on top of me. Thank God I was wearing pants.

"Girl, you ain't nothing but a tease," he said while sucking his teeth.

"Call it what you want, but I am not giving up anything," I scoffed. "*Especially not to you,*" I thought to myself.

While he was rubbing against me and kissing me, I felt numb on the inside. I became aroused by the feeling of his erected penis through his pants, but he didn't know this. When I got home, my panties were wet with evidence of hormonal secretion. After that day, I continued to be life-less and standoffish towards him, and I showed no interest whatsoever. He would try to put his hand on my breast, but I swiftly move it. When we were together, I had boundaries: Tory couldn't touch me on my private areas or caress them. He could only see me on the weekend, so these activities could not have occurred that many times, anyway. Moreover, he started making plans for his next visit to New York City. "*This negro really think that I want to see him again. We'll see about that.*" I said inwardly.

Eventually, all *despicable* things must come to an end. His last night in New York had come, and we said our good-byes. I could not believe that I had fooled him, but then again, I'm a good actress. I simply played the game and came out the winner because, unbeknownst to him, it was all a front. I didn't lose my virginity, and he didn't gain a thing but a cold shower. I was in control.

> "*For this is the will of God, that you be sanctified (separated and set apart from sin): that you abstain and back away from sexual immorality; v.4 that each of you know how to control his own body in holiness and honor (being available for God's purpose and separated from things profane)."*
> *(1 Thessalonians 4:3-4 AMP)*

"Thank you, Jesus! It is over," I said as I got out of his car.

When it was over, I felt so hurt and betrayed by my parents. Every weekend when I left him, I would go into the bathroom to scrub myself because I felt dirty after having him all over me. My parents had allowed this. In disgust, I **prayed and asked *God,*** *"Did **YOU** mistakenly give **me** to the wrong parents? Why did I have to grow up in an unloving home? I always feel like an outcast."*

"God, are you sure I belong here?" I questioned.

But **HE** never answered me.

"Now we know that God heareth not sinners: but if any man be a worshipper of God, and doeth his will, him he heareth" *(John 9:31 KJV)*

Chapter 18
Games People Play

"And we know (with great confidence) that God (who is deeply concerned about us) causes all things to work together (as a plan) for good for those who are called according to HIS plan and purpose". v.29 For those whom He foreknew (and loved and chose beforehand), He also predestined to be conformed to the image of His Son (and ultimately share in his complete sanctification), so that he would be the firstborn (the most beloved and honored) among many believers." (Romans 8:28-29 AMP)

I had enough of other people's rules and expectations of me, so I started *doing me*. I began sneaking around to see guys that I had crushes on and those that were attracted to me. **These were guys I never had sex with**. First, it was Jose. He was tall and very sweet to me, and I was his girlfriend for a short period of time and in that time, all we did was kiss. He would walk me to class and hold my books. At some point, I broke up with Jose not in a malicious way but for two reasons: I was afraid that my parents would find out, and his brother got on my nerves. I believed that he had a crush on me because he would always pick at me; however, when we broke up, his brother left me alone, so maybe he didn't have a crush on me. Jose was heartbroken, but he understood due to how strict my parents were.

Another boy was Mike, a senior football player who was dark skinned and very muscular-six pack and all. My friend Iris a classmate of mine introduce me because he begs her to introduce him to me. Iris was my girl when I wasn't hanging with my crew. They lived in the same project building. Anyway, Mike would always pick me up by my waist, due to his strength and masculinity. I was a little shorty, so this was no challenge for him. I remember that when his ex-girlfriend found out about us messing with each other, she became very jealous, but we didn't pay her any mind. I would cut school to see him sometimes and this wasn't hard because he lived across the street from the school. When we were together, he wanted more than just kisses, but he didn't pressure me to do anything else. It wouldn't have mattered if he did because I was steadfast in my decision to not have sex. After a while, I began to wonder why I hadn't seen Mike. I soon found out that he was incarcerated, so that was the end of Mike and me.

At the end of the summer, I had met Michael, a fine-looking senior from another high school. When Ms. C and I were walking one day, he introduced himself to us and we told him our names. I didn't learn until later that he wasn't only interested in me but in Ms. C as well.

After we first met, some weeks passed, I would stop by to see him when my mom would send me to the store. Once, when I visited, we talked and kissed but out of curiosity, I decided to ask him a question.

"Would you wait to have sex with me?" I inquired.

"Sure. No problem. I can wait," he said

One Saturday while I was going to the store, guess who I bumped into? Michael and Ms. C were just yapping away. I was feeling some kind a way, but I remembered that I had never hinted to Ms. C that I liked Michael, so I kept my anger on the inside. Later, on the phone, she told me that after they had sex, he called and told her that she had given him a STD. *"Good for him. He got what he deserved."* I laughed to myself after we ended the phone call.

Though I found his karma to be hysterical, I was still heartbroken because he lied to me and played the both of us. I wanted to know what possessed him to do such a despicable act. He hid himself from me for weeks, until I finally bumped into him and had the opportunity to ask him why he played me.

"It was a mistake-it just happened. She was giving it up and you weren't. I didn't mean to hurt you. I am sorry," he said apologetically.

I could see the shame on his face, and I accepted his apology, but Ms. C had no remorse. She had laughed when she was telling me. After this situation, I felt life must go on.

"Be not deceived; God is not mocked: for whatsoever a man soweth, that shall he also reap." (Galatians 6:7-9 KJV)

Fortunately, my ninth-grade year at South Shore High School was amazing up to the very last day of the school year. I felt that I had met the love of my life.

"Hello, you have some pretty eyes," he said as he stopped and looked me straight in the eyes.

"Hello," I said and smiled.

Then, I said to myself, "Wow, who is that?" I knew he didn't attend here because I had never seen him. He just appeared out of nowhere. I continued about my day, but I was determined to find out who he was.

However, days passed and a young man with dreamy brown eyes, smooth brown skin, and beautiful curly, wavy hair approached me at the pizza shop. I learned that his name was Prince, and his name sure did fit his looks and personality. He was drop-dead gorgeous, as well as the perfect gentlemen. He was indeed a young man, due to the slight mustache on his face and mature features. You would have thought he was eighteen years old, but he told me that he was only fifteen. I didn't believe that a sophomore in high school could be as fit as a senior. I asked to see his I.D and when he gave it to me, I learned that he wasn't lying about his age. He proceeded to tell me that he wanted to get to know me. I took this to heart and gave him two weeks of hardship in chasing me down.

Finally, I gave in and answered his questions because I wanted to get better acquainted with him as well. When I was sent to the store, I was eager to see him because I knew that he would probably be at the pizza shop, and those times he would walk me there. When I had my summer job again that summer, he walked with me to my job every morning, and he walked me back home every evening. After weeks of this, Prince invited me to his home, and I accepted the invitation. I had started walking him back to his home to avoid getting caught by my parents. When he picked me up from work, we would take the back way of the city. Prince was very kind to me and lovely to be around. Looking at his beautiful smile and long eyelashes that sat above his beautiful brown eyes, was enough to make me weak at the knees. I believe it was the same for him when he looked into my eyes.

I remember when he first asked if he could kiss me, and of course I allowed him to do so. As we made out, I could feel his penis pressing against me. "*He would kill me*" I laughed to myself thinking about his *size* being inside of me. Boy, did we *kiss* in the hall of his apartment building, but I knew in my heart that I couldn't allow it to go any further. Although I liked him, I didn't allow my feelings to change how I felt about sex. By being very observant and wise, I learned from Michael that if a person has already experienced having sex, there is strong possibility that he will not have the willpower to wait; therefore, I wasn't going to set myself up to be heartbroken again.

Later, Prince had ended up telling me about his ex-girlfriend, who had found out about me. Well, he assured me that things were over between them, but did I believe it? Hmmm… yes, but I had my suspicions.

Nevertheless, one Monday morning, Prince and I were walking together because I had to go pick up my paycheck on the other side of town. As we turned the corner, we surprisingly bumped right into my stepfather. Oh, I had so much fear running through my body at that moment.

"Uhhh, Ha! I gotcha! You didn't think you were going to see me this morning, did you? " my stepfather taunted. Boyyy, I didn't know what to say.

"And you, I bet' not eva' catch you around my daughter again," he threatened as he told Prince to get away from here.

I had to stand there and watch Prince go a different way. I couldn't stop him.

"This is why we don't trust you," my stepfather said to me.

"Daddy we haven't done anything, and I am not going to do anything. You and mommy need to trust me," I stressed.

"I just want you to stay away from that boy," he said.

"Okay" I said, with my fingers crossed behind my back. I wasn't going to.

The place where I was heading to pick up my check was far, so I had to catch the train. Surprisingly, as I continued to look down the street, standing by the subway station was Prince. I had such a big smile on my face overwhelmed with joy because he hadn't allowed my father to scare him way.

"Your father didn't scare me," he told me as he took me by my hand, "I wasn't going to let you go all the way there by yourself." This made my heart glad.

Somehow, I knew that the day would come where sex would be the main subject of our conversation. Well, the day came and Prince was expressing to me how much he *wanted* me.

"Can't you tell?" he asked while pulling me closer to him, so I could feel the bulge in his pants pressed against me.

"Prince, I am not ready to have sex," I told him in an annoyed tone.

"I don't know how long I can hold out. It's hard" he said.

"Maybe you need to find someone else because I am not going to do anything," I shrugged.

"No. We'll see," he said.

"Okay." I didn't care.

He stressed saying that he had to take a cold shower.

Later, he told me that his ex-girlfriend came to see him. She told him that she was pregnant, so they decided to work things out because of the baby. Before the pregnancy, I had reason to believe that he still had some feelings for her, so I was okay with the decision. He was honest with me, yet ashamed of his weakness for sex. **I was just glad that I didn't allow him to talk me into losing my virginity to him.**

> *"I am jealous for you with a Godly jealousy because I have promised you to one husband, to present you as a pure virgin to Christ." (2 Corinthians 11:2 AMP)*

The summer was ending; therefore, my summer job for the year was coming to an end. I spent the last days helping to beautify the community and distribute food to the elderly.

My sophomore year had begun, and unfortunately, I had just agreed to being Tommy's girlfriend. This wouldn't had happened if I weren't peer pressured to do so by Veronica, but I knew she meant well. Of course, my parents knew nothing about Tommy being my boyfriend-they would have killed me. Moreover, Tommy was a kind, handsome gentleman, but he looked very young and had a babyface. He was brown skinned with beautiful, black, thick curly hair. All the girls loved them some Tommy, but he just wasn't my type. I wasn't at all attracted to him as much as he was attracted to me.

In fact, I was more intrigued and attracted to the young man that caught my attention by complimenting my pretty eyes on that very last day of school before I met Prince. His complexion was of a lighter tone, and he possessed a tall stature. He had a manly, hard core appearance with a strong, deep voice that matched his looks. Another thing that I liked about him was that he not only looked older, but he actually was older than me. I had done a little investigation of my own and found out who he was and learned that his name was Shaun.

As for Tommy, he was such a nice guy. He had my class schedule, so he insisted on carrying my books and walking me to my classes. I would wonder why he never asked me for a kiss or even tried; I was getting worried. This may sound silly, but I was used to guys expecting me to do this. Veronica told me that he was being respectful, but I thought something was wrong. I mean, we knew each other for a long time, since middle school. Then, I began to wonder why I wouldn't I expect someone to be respectful towards me; however, Tommy just didn't do it for me. I had to find a way to break up with him. He hadn't done anything wrong, but I just wanted who I wanted and didn't want to keep stringing him along. Breaking his heart wasn't my intentions, but I had to do something. I knew that my tenth-grade year was going to be very interesting, and this was proof of that. It was the hardest thing that I ever had to do up to this point in my life.

"I don't want to be girlfriend and boyfriend anymore," I said sadly.

"Why? Did I do something wrong?" he asked in a panicked tone.

"It had nothing to do with you, but it had all to do with me," I honestly told him.

You could see the sadness upon his face. I started crying because it hurt me to do it. "We can be friends," I told him softly.

To my disappointment, he didn't even want to be my friend, and I didn't blame him. I didn't push the issue. I gave him a soft kiss on the cheek and left.

Once upon a time, I was curious about why boys weren't drawn to me. Now, they were drawn to me like flies, yet I had no interest in them. There is only one person that caught my attention, and it was time for my manhunt. I found out that Shaun did attend *South Shore High School* but only came when he felt like it. After chasing him down for months, I finally caught up with him. We had many conversations, but one subject came up that I wasn't very fond of. He came clean and told me that he had a girlfriend, who was from a Christian home, and he really liked her. After hearing this, I was heartbroken; however, this didn't deter me from liking him. I knew where he lived and where he hung out at, and I even knew where his girlfriend lived.

"Can we just be friends?" he asked.

"Yes," I told him with sadness.

This sounded so *familiar*, and I remembered saying the same thing to Tommy. Oh, how the tables have turned.

> *"Be not deceived; for God is not mocked: for whatsoever a man shall sow, that also shall he reap." (Galatians 6:7 KJV)*

Though we agreed to be friends, I couldn't shake the feelings that I had for him. We never had sex, not yet anyway, and we never kissed...we were *just* friends.

On one of our walks together through the school hall, he busted out stating, "Pat, I would never date you."

"Why not?" I questioned in a curious yet offended tone.

"Because I am afraid that you'll break my heart," he responded. "You are beautiful and with those beautiful eyes, I would have to hurt somebody over you."

This increased my liking towards him even more. Boy, did he put a big smile on my face. Though he had his flaws as a weed smoker and drug dealer, this didn't change how I felt about him. He was very kind to me, he never disrespected me in anyway, and he was always honest. During the conversation, he proceeded to tell me that he wanted us to hang out on my sixteenth birthday.

"We could do it during school hours," I suggested.

"What do you want me to bring you?" Shaun asked me.

"Pink Champale and a pack of cigarettes," I told him with excitement.

"Pat, I didn't know you drink or smoke" he said in a surprised tone.

"We are celebrating my birthday, right? You asked me what I want, and this is what I want," I told him honestly.

"Okay," he said with a bewildered expression.

Little did he know, my mother turned me on to Pink Champale because that's what she drank from time to time.. I would ask her if I could taste it, and she would allow me to. One time she bought me my own bottle, and I was feeling good. I had learned how to smoke in the school bathroom; I would share several puffs off a friends' cigarette. I would choke on the smoke until I became an expert. There's an old saying: *practice makes perfect*, and what I asked for was relevant to the occasion. Shaun and I made plans around December, since my birthday was the following month. All I could think about was what I wanted to wear. I had a picture in my mind, and I was wondering how it was going to come about.

Coincidentally, my mom asked me was it okay if she only bought Christmas gifts for the other children because she couldn't afford to purchase for all of us.

"Sure, as long as you get me something for my birthday," I told her.

"In that case, you could pick anything you want," she told me.

"I already knew what I wanted: a skirt suit with a nice blouse and a pair of shoes to match."

"Deal," she agreed.

That day couldn't have come any faster. Surprisingly, my mother was also excited. I really believed that she appreciated me for giving up my gifts for Christmas, and the fact that I didn't make a big deal out of it. She was truly determined not to let me down. She kept her promise even if she had to borrow the money. I really wanted her to surprise me. I pictured myself dressing conservative but beautiful at the same time. I wasn't one to wear mini-skirts or mini- dresses; I was more of a classy type of girl.

Chapter 19
Sweet Sixteen Revenge
16-17 yrs. old

The big day had come, my birthday sweet sixteen. I did my own hair into my infamous *Shirley Temple curls*, and I was dressed in a rust skirt suit with a cream blouse, cream stockings, and shoes to match my suit. It was very cold that day, but I didn't care because I was dressed to impress. When I got to school, I received so many compliments and birthday wishes. Shaun had met me at the school as he promised with the bags in his hand.

"Let's go! We're taking a cab to my homeboy's crib," Shaun told me.

"Okay," I replied

"Dang Pat, you look nice," he complimented nicely, "You make me look like a bum."

"You look pretty nice yourself," I blushed. He always wore designer clothes, which was something that I observed about him.

When we arrived there, we sat around talking and listening to Reggae music as Shaun rolled a blunt, and I drank *Champale*.

"When you start smoking?" Shaun asked.

"I puff here and there. I am sixteen today, so I'm doing it up." I responded.

"Cigarettes is bad for you," he told me.

"Well, why do you smoke?" I asked inquisitively.

"Well, you're a young lady, and you don't need to smoke," he said to me.

"Well, I do," I said dismissively. He just shrugged his shoulders.

"I'm going to leave it alone," Shaun responded.

"Good," I said smartly.

"Is it okay to kiss the birthday girl?" he asked while we were left alone in the living room.

"Sure," I nervously responded.

Oh my God, I've been waiting for this moment. He kissed me and immediately started laughing.

"Why are you laughing?" I asked.

"You never been kissed before?" he said.

"What made you ask that?" I asked.

"Because you're stiff. You have to move your head when you are French kissing," he said.

"Oh, I can do that," I responded.

What he didn't know was that I'm a great kisser; he just made me so nervous.

I showed him that I indeed knew how to kiss which led to him saying, "Wow, you were holding back." We both started laughing.

Shaun was also very respectful. He didn't try to touch me or anything; we were just two friends hanging out. I knew that I could never lose my virginity to him because I would fall in love, and eventually, he would break my heart. That day, I had such a wonderful time with him; it was a birthday to remember.

I reminisced on how my birthday went, and when Shaun had asked me about my smoking and drinking. I didn't occur to me to tell him the real reason why I had taken up those habits. I started smoking and drinking as a part of my rebellious attitude towards my parents. After my mother revealed that she was going to take me to the doctor to see if I was a virgin when I turned sixteen. ***"She is going to be very disappointed when she takes me to the doctor this time. I won't be a virgin any longer,"*** *I smirked to myself.* In accomplishing losing my virginity purposely, I was waiting and seeking for my prospect. It needed to be someone that I wouldn't fall in love with but attracted to.

It didn't take long into the school year for me to find my prospect; he had his eyes on me. He would chase me down every time he saw me. In his pursuit of me, I detected that he was a *player,* an *eye wanderer*, and since I was no fool, but a clever observer, it wasn't hard to figure out. It was also good to know a little about who I was planning to lose my virginity to, and what I had to be prepared to deal with. At the beginning, I played hard to get, but he remained persistent. Finally, he had asked me my name, and I told him while asking him what his was. Born was a junior in high school, and a part of the *Five-Percent Nation*, or *Nation of Gods and Earths*, which was a movement founded in 1964 in Harlem, New York. I remember the heated discussion that we had about our differing beliefs and his attempt to convert me to the Nation.

"I don't care what you show me or what you say. There is a true God that I believe exists, and you will never change my mind about that," I told him sternly.

"Are you saved or something?" he inquired.

"No, but if I were, I would believe in God and his son, Jesus. I would never bow down to you and think that you are my god. And no, I will not change my name to be your girl." I said with conviction. Then, he left me alone and stopped pressing the issue.

> *"You shall have no other gods before Me. [4] "You shall not make for yourself any idol, or any likeness (form, manifestation) of what is in heaven above or on the earth beneath or in the water under the earth [as an object to worship]. [5] You shall not worship them nor serve them; for I, the LORD your God, am a jealous (impassioned) God [[a]]demanding what is rightfully and uniquely mine], visiting (avenging) the iniquity (sin, guilt) of the fathers on the children [that is, calling the children to account for the sins of their fathers], to the third and fourth generations of those who hate Me." (Exodus 20:3-5 AMP)*

"Wait a minute, wait a minute, calm down shorty," he said, "You got a lot of spunk!"

"Thank you...I think," I said with a smile.

> *"For I am persuaded, that neither death, nor life, nor Angels, nor principalities, nor things present, nor things to come, nor height, nor depth, any other creature, shall be able to separate us from the love of God, which is in Christ Jesus our Lord." (Romans 8:38-39 AMP)*

He was playing right into my hands, and he probably thought that I was doing the same in his. After that discussion, Born invited me to his home and following my acceptance of his invitation, we checked into each of our homerooms, and we left.

Born was very attractive, so it's very easy to be stimulated by him. We stopped to the store on the way, and he bought my favorite drink. I drank my *Champale,* and he smoked weed, cigarettes, and drank beer. We had to have those elements there because it calmed my nervousness. He told me that he lived with his father, but he was usually at work. I visited his home twice, but we didn't do anything because I didn't want to rush into it; I was scared and did not like pain. I heard that having sex for the very first-time hurts, and there is some bleeding involved. Thankfully, he was very patient and understanding with me, and I was glad of that. When I left his house, I would go home as if I had just left school. No one knew what I was planning or doing; besides, it wasn't anyone's business anyway.

My mom and I were the same: nothing changed. I was still getting smacked and punched; it didn't matter. I would wash clothes in the tub just about every night by myself, since my mom didn't want my sister to help because she didn't do a very good job. When I didn't do up to her expectations because of exhaustion, I would get hit and had to re-do the clothes. There were times where my sister, and I were supposed to take turns washing dishes, and all my sister had to say to me was that she had done the dishes, or she isn't going to do them.

"Well, somebody better get the dishes done," my mother spoke while looking at the both of us.

My sister would take her stand, and I would take mine, but guess who ended up doing the dishes? Me! I wasn't looking forward to my mom smacking me upside my head, so I had to. My mother blamed me for everything and wanted me to do everything. Remember, I am the oldest of four siblings, so I always had a lot on my plate. Everyone needed help with their homework, and by the time I got to mine, I would lose interest in doing it. The only thing I wanted to do was sleep.

After years, school was still my escape goat, but now I anticipated getting there for one reason: to see Born. We'd meet up at school then leave to go to his house.

While we were lounging around, drinking and smoking cigarettes, he brought up his religious beliefs again, tried to talk me into changing my name, and becoming his *little goddess*.

"Born, I am not changing my name. I told you what I believe in," I said irritably.

"Alright, alright calm down," Born spoke while laughing. "It was worth a try." I just rolled my eyes.

Anyhow, I planned on ending things between us at the end of the month, but first things first: losing my virginity. One Saturday, my mother allowed me to go to a friend's house, but this was a cover up to go to Born's house. Boy, he couldn't wait to see me. When I arrived, his dad was there, so he introduced me to him as he was on his way out the door. Once, we were alone, we smoked and drank for a while, before things heated up, and we started kissing. After a few minutes, he took me by the hand and led the way to his bedroom.

"Are you ready?" he asked me softly.

"Yes," I uttered nervously.

"Don't be scared. I'm not gonna hurt you. I'm going to be very gentle," he said.

"Okay," I nodded. "Do you have a condom?"

"Yeah," he said.

We started out kissing as he caressed my body, and he entered in me slowly. I screamed and cried at the feeling of his size slowly pushing into me. "*What is so good about this?*" I thought. It was so painful. Afterwards, I went into the bathroom and noticed that I was bleeding like I was on my menstrual cycle. When I got home, I tried to keep my composure and tried to walk as normal as possible. "*Maybe I need to do it one more time after the pain goes away,*" I convinced myself.

It took almost a week for the pain to go away, and once it did, I was determined to see him again, so that we could do it the second time without the pain. But even when we did it for a second time, it wasn't all what I expected it to be. Then, I thought that maybe it would have felt different if I was in love with him. Yet, the reason that I did not allow Shaun to be my first was because I was already in love with him.

> "*It is God's will that you should be sanctified: that you should avoid sexual immorality; that each of you should learn to control your own body in a way that is holy and honorable, not in passionate lust like the pagans, who do not know God.*" (1 Thess.4:3-5 NIV)

My plan had been executed, so it was time to do one last thing. I approached Born in school, and pulled him aside, asking if he could talk for a minute.

"What's up?" he asked.

"I think it would be best we go our separate ways," I said.

"Okay, if that's what you want," he shrugged.

"Yes, that's what I want." I nodded.

"It was easier than what I thought; he didn't put up a fight or anything. He probably didn't care about me anyway," I scoffed to myself as I walked away puzzled.

Later, that school day, Born walked up to me and took me by the hand.

"Thank you for allowing me to be your first," he whispered in my ear and kissed my cheek.

I walked away smiling because my curiosity of wondering if he had cared about me, was now satisfied. My mission was accomplished as I planned.

I just wanted revenge against my parents. They didn't trust me when I told them that I was a virgin before, so I went and fulfilled their accusations, since they claimed that I had done anyway.

"Do not say, "I will repay evil", Wait (expectantly) for the Lord, and He will rescue and save you. (Proverbs 20:22 AMP)

Once before, **my parents** had told me that if my sister got pregnant, the blame would fall on *me*. I couldn't believe my ears. What could I have said to something like that? How could I be held responsible for her actions? This just made me angrier and more disgusted with them; therefore,

I was glad that I had taken matters into my own hands. Now, they could say I had sex, and it would be true- not an accusation.

> *"Keep your behavior excellent among the [unsaved] Gentiles [conduct yourself honorably, with graciousness and integrity], so that [a]for whatever reason they may slander you as evildoers, yet by observing your good deeds they may [instead come to] glorify God [b]in the day of visitation [when He looks upon them with mercy]." (1 Peter 2:12 AMP)*

Finally, the day that I anticipated had come upon us. Out of the blue, my mother said, "I made an appointment to take you to the doctor to see if you're still a virgin."

"There isn't any need to take me to the doctor. I'm not a virgin anymore," I said boldly but bluntly.

"Okay," she spoke. I was flabbergasted at her plain response.

"Well, I am going to take you anyway to make sure that everything is okay. Did he use protection?" she asked.

"Yes," I told her.

"Good," she spoke. "Are you still talking to the boy?"

"No," I told her plainly.

"If you ever feel like this is going to happen again, ask me for some birth control," she told me.

"Okay," I responded.

"I'm going to have to tell your father," she warned.

"Okay," I responded.

I thought that maybe he would be lenient towards me, since I didn't get pregnant, like my sister did. Denise was pregnant, and I wasn't even aware of the fact that she was seeing anyone in the first place. She had hidden her personal affairs very well. Later that evening, my father came home, and it was clear he had been drinking. I knew that my mother had told him, by the way he called me into the room.

"What is this that your mother is telling me about you not being a virgin no more? Who is this f------ boy? What's his name? Where does he live?" my father stated furiously, demanding answers to these questions.

His abrupt reaction was not one that I was prepared for as I stood there dumfounded. They had flipped the script on me; my mother was supposed be irate, not my stepfather.

"Take your a-- into the back room and take off all your clothes," he yelled.

I did as I was told and was naked with not a stitch of clothing on. He stormed backed there and beat me angrily until he got tired. I believe he had beaten me for my sister as well. My mother hollered out my stepfather's name for him to stop and took her time getting to my rescue. Though she got there eventually, I really believed that she didn't want to intervene. When my stepfather first found out about my sister's pregnancy, he cried; that's all he did.

My stepfather changed after that and started believing what my mother had been telling him. He now believed that I wasn't going to be anything in life, but a woman with a house full of babies. My mother spoke about how worth-less my life was going to be, and my dad believed it. He couldn't even stand to look at me.

"For I know the plans I have for you, "declares the Lord, "plans to prosper you and not to harm you, plans to give you hope and a future." (Jeremiah 29:11 NIV)

"For so is the will of God, that with well doing ye may put to silence the ignorance of foolish men..." (1 Peter 2:15 KJV)

Chapter 20
Promiscuity

Despite the awful things that my parents believed, I still had dreams embedded on the inside of me. I dreamed of finishing high school, graduating from college with a degree, and become a teacher or business administrator. I couldn't forget about having children and living in a big house. These were *my dreams and plans*.

> *"We make our plans but God has the last word."*
> *(Proverbs 16:1 GNT)*

> *"You make your plans, but God directs your actions."*
> *(Proverbs 16:9 GNT)*

Just like my stepfather couldn't stand the sight of me, I couldn't stand to look at him either. All the negative and demeaning things that they spoke about were hurtful. My rebellion and resentment towards them heightened. I **TURNED UP THE VOLUME ON PURPOSE.** I no longer cared about what they thought or what I did. Life goes on!

One day, while walking with my friend, there were two guys behind us who were trying to get our attention. One of them was very tall, and his height gave away that he was a basketball player as well as the basketball in his hand. I assumed that they were coming from practice. After a few minutes, we stopped walking and faced them. Looking at the two guys, I thought the tall one was cute. He was brown skinned with matching pretty, brown eyes and a curly top. James, or Jimmy as people called him, was polite but shy. His friend, Tony, asked me if I would give Jimmy my number. I told Tony that I couldn't give Jimmy my number, but he could give me his. Jimmy agreed and gave me his number, so I could call him on the pay phone when I went out to the store. In our conversation, I learned that he wanted to get to know me better as did I.

"Are you willing to meet my parents?" I asked him.

"Yes," he said, timidly, at first, but in realization, he changed his answer to no.

Jimmy was a little scared, but I told him that I needed him to meet my stepdad, so we could stop sneaking around. Jimmy went to *Erasmus High School*, a predominantly black school, but we didn't live far from each other. If we wanted to see each other, we could just walk since city transportation wasn't necessary. In the meantime, I thought back to when my mom mentioned birth control, and how I needed to ask for it if I had sex again. After going back and forth with myself, I got the guts to ask her for it.

"Mom, I think I'm going to need birth control because I want to be protected just in case," I explained to her.

"I'm glad you came to me," she stated. "When I discussed this with your stepdad, he was totally against it. He said, that's like giving you permission to have sex, but I told him that if we don't give you the protection you need, you are going have sex, regardless."

My mom was right; I couldn't stop. I was becoming very promiscuous, even though I didn't love having sex itself. **I just wanted to be loved,** so I equated sex with love and affection. Eventually, I had sex with Jimmy too, who was a virgin and I knew this because I had to guide him. We were protected since he used a condom, and I was on birth control. I was an expert now after only having sex twice.

We all barely went to school: Jimmy, Tony, Rebecca, and me. Rebecca, Jimmy's eighteen-year-old sister, would hang out with us sometimes. I found out that she was a virgin but a tease like I used to be. One time, we skipped school together and went to one of her male friend's house. When we arrived, he had a bottle of scotch waiting for her, and she shared it with me as well. I thought I was going to die; I was as drunk as a skunk, vomiting all over the place. Fortunately, they made sure that I was sober before I left to go home.

"Girl, *Scotch* is not my drink. Never again. It made me so sick," I told her as we rode the train home.

When I got home, I needed to be able to function naturally, so no one would notice my drunkenness. I tried to sneak a nap, but it didn't work because my mom kept my name in her mouth. She would never call anyone else to do anything for her. I was having such a bad hangover, but I had to push through. That day, I learned to never drink alcohol on an empty stomach. *Red* liquor was not my thing, so I chose to stick with my beer from there on out. Now, I drank *Millers* or *Old English* beer because *Pink and White Champale* was beginning to taste like water. I had become tolerant of it, and it wasn't strong enough. I wanted to feel high and numb, and it didn't give me that feeling.

The four us would meet up every day, until one day, Jimmy and Rebecca were punished and couldn't come outside; therefore, Tony and I were left alone. I shouldn't have embraced the idea of hanging out with Tony alone because one thing led to another, and we ended up having sex in the hall of his building. He was okay looking and made me laugh. He was also more mature than Jimmy, and this turned me on. What did I know? I was just a teenager who wanted to be loved and saw sex as an equal to being loved.

Did Jimmy and Rebecca ever find out? Of course, they did. One day, I was so drunk that I accidentally called Jimmy, Tony. It happened numerous times, and Jimmy became very suspicious. I knew I had to come clean because the guilt was eating me up. When I told Jimmy the truth. He broke up with me and called me a *wh---*. I knew that my actions were wrong, so I took his harsh words. I hadn't meant to hurt him or anyone else, but it just happened. I didn't think about the consequences of my actions. Prior to this, Rebecca had also liked Tony and allowed him to be her first. I had not only hurt Jimmy, but also Rebecca. I wasn't a good friend and brought havoc, so I decided to move on from them.

> *"Be sober-minded; be watchful. Your adversary the devil prowls around like a roaring lion, seeking someone to devour" (1 Peter 5:8 ESV)*

> *"8 The one who does not love has not become acquainted with God [does not and never did know Him], for God is love. [He is the originator of love, and it is an enduring attribute of His nature.]" (1 John 4:8 AMP)*

I thought about Ms. C and how I hadn't seen her in a while, so I decided to call her on the payphone.

"Hey Ms. C, its Patricia. What are you doing this morning? Are you going to school," I asked her while leaning against the payphone?

"Nope. Come on to the house, and we could leave from here," she told me.

"I'm on my way," I told her before hanging the payphone on the post.

Once I arrived at her house, we left out and went about our day. In our travels, we saw the love of my life, Shaun, and his brother, E. When they drove up, Shaun had introduced us to E and asked us, curiously, what we were up to.

"Just walking. What is yawl doing?" I asked.

As we conversed, someone brought up the idea of playing cards.

"Speaking of cards, what about a game of strip poker?" E suggested.

"I'm down," Ms. C said while smiling.

"I'm down," Shaun nodded.

Then, everyone looked at me, waiting for my answer.

"What about you Pat? You down?" Shaun said with an endearing look.

"I'm down," I gave in while looking at Shaun smiling.

Once we all agreed, they invited us to ride with them, and we stopped at the store for some beer and chips. After we grabbed everything, we went back to Shaun and E's *crib* (slang for house). Once we settled in, we sat on the floor around the living room table and began preparing to play the game. Shaun gave me a blanket just in case because he didn't want anyone looking at my body. There was this look in his eyes that revealed that he secretively still cared for me. I appreciated this, but I would have probably still asked him for one, due to my shyness and the insecurities I had about my body. E had also given Ms. C a blanket. It had become clear that the two had hit off well, though all they did was talk smack to each other about the poker game. I guess in their own way, they liked each other.

Ms. C and I's garments were coming off, and I couldn't believe we were losing. Now, I was glad that Shaun had given me the blanket because Ms. C and I had quickly become naked.

> *"-and envy; drunkenness, orgies, and the like. I warn you, as I did before, that those who live like this will not inherit the kingdom of God" (Galatians 5:21 NIV)*

> *"So, put to death and deprive of power the evil longings of your earthly body [with its sensual, self-centered instincts] immorality, impurity, sinful passion, evil desire, and greed, which is [a kind of] idolatry [because it replaces your devotion to God]. [6] Because of these [sinful] things the [divine] wrath of God is coming [a] on the sons of disobedience [those who fail to listen and who routinely and obstinately disregard God's precepts]." (Colossians 3:3-5 AMP)*

After the poker game, Shaun went in his room to get something, and I followed behind him. I closed his door behind me and cornered him. I told him that I had been waiting for this moment ands tried to kiss him as I pushed him backwards onto his bed. He tried to release from me, but I wouldn't let up.

"Pat, you know I have a girlfriend," he told me. I knew this, but I didn't care; I wanted what I wanted, but nothing happened because his mom came home from work early.

"What is it about her?" I asked him in a frustrated tone.

"She was already my girlfriend when I met you," he exclaimed.

"I just want to be faithful to her. You are going to meet someone one day, and he is going to treat you like you should be treated," he sighed while looking everywhere else but at me. I just stood there and for the first time, I listened to him.

"I already told you, I couldn't have you as a girlfriend, I would have to hurt somebody. I want to always be your friend," he said kindly.

"Okay," I said.

Deep down on the inside, I still had love for him that I couldn't shake, but I wanted to respect his wishes. Thereafter, Ms. C and I left, and I decided to move on from Shaun. Although I had moved on, I would randomly see him riding his motor pad from afar. We would always wave at each other, but this day, he stopped to greet me and see how I was doing. As we spoke, I complimented his ride.

"Would you like to ride?" he offered.

"Hmmm, I don't know," I said cautiously.

"Don't be afraid. I got you" he assured me.

"Okay, let's ride," I agreed.

"Hop on the back, put on my helmet, and hold on tight" he told me. Once I got on, I held onto him tightly, like he said, and laid my head on his shoulders. He started laughing at me.

"Pattttt," he said while chuckling, "I can't breathe."

I laughed and loosened my hold on him a bit. We took off, and he took me a few blocks up and then back to my destination. He made me feel so special that day, unexpectedly. I appreciated him for that. When I thanked him, he gave a beautiful smile showcasing his pretty white teeth.

"There's someone I want you to meet," he said briskly. "He's my best friend, but we're more like brothers."

"Okay, let me know when and where," I said openly. I walked away with a smile and a new interest in meeting his best friend.

Chapter 21
High School Dropout

The next day, I met Shaun at school, and he gave me the address to his house. His house was on the way to my house, so I got off the bus a few stops early.

Shaun and his best friend were standing outside waiting when I made it to his house. His best friend was slightly taller than me and brown skinned with naturally wavy, curly hair on top of his head. Shaun introduced us, and I learned that his name was Jazz. Jazz sounded like he was from the Islands. This was because his mother was Trinidadian, and his father was African American and Irish.

Jazz was strictly hood, which is exactly what I preferred. I was more interested in hood guys because of their demeanor, strength, street smarts, and as well as the challenge that came with them. He was nineteen years old, which was three years older than me, and I liked it that way. Jazz and I talked for about three weeks or so, before he asked me if I would be his girl. Most importantly, he was a sweetheart.

I told him that I needed to think about it because I wanted to get to know him a bit more before I said yes. I would visit Jazz on school days, as we were becoming more acquainted with each other. This also meant that I barely went to school, but I just didn't care anymore. When his mom went to work, we hung out at his house and talked about different things. I had asked him what happened in his last relationship and he told me that he and his ex-girlfriend had a *very* short-termed relationship. He said, "I mean very short."

One day, I had the *pleasure* of coming across her. Ebony appeared to be very tomboyish and her demeanor was strong. When I first saw her, she was walking with one of her sisters behind me as I was entering into the store, and they were talking loud enough for me to be able to hear what they were saying. Evidently, she knew who I was and went through extreme, unnecessary trouble to tell her sister that she used to be Jazz's girlfriend.

"Jazz is still diggin' me," she told her sister.

I believe she was looking for a response, but I didn't say anything. I continued to walk, while shaking my head and smiling. The next time I saw Jazz, I told him all the things that she had said.

"It wasn't nothing. I dated her for one day because it wasn't working out. I'm not thinking about that girl; I never even kissed her. That mess she's talking is all in her head. She is mad crazzzzyyy," he stressed.

"I'll tell you what: come with me," he spoke, and we began walking down the street to where Ebony hung out.

"Ebony, as you can see, I've moved on. Stop telling lies to my girl. I don't want you bothering her, so leave her alone about it," he spat.

"You better get out my face before I tell my brothers," she warned.

"Get your brothers; I'm not scared of them. You just stay out of my girl's face," Jazz said while walking away.

"Now Pat, will you be my girl?" he asked me.

"Yes," I replied with a big smile on my face.

He knew that he had to prove to me that there wasn't anything going on between them. Later, Jazz said that Ebony apologized to him and wanted to be formally introduced to me. I thought it was unusual that she wanted to befriend me, even though I was the girlfriend of her ex. Oh, I had both eyes open with this and so did Jazz.

"Be careful, Pat. I don't trust her," he warned.

Ebony and I had gone somewhere together, and I had gotten an epiphany that she wanted to get close to me, so she could get close with Jazz. She had begun plotting and starting a lot of confusion with me to get him back. She wanted to fight me over *my* boyfriend. She was so belligerent towards me for someone that didn't even want her. Ultimately, I thought we would both look like fools for fighting over a boy. Her stupidity, in wanting to fight me over a guy, a guy that was my boyfriend, irritated me. It was clear that I didn't believe in fighting over a guy, but she didn't care.

"You know what... fight her Pat and get it over with. If you don't, she will continue to bother you!" Jazz's mom yelled from her window, having watched the whole scene.

Mrs. Smith, Jazz's mom, came rushing downstairs to intervene. She refereed and made sure it was a fair fight. Ebony and I fought like cats (if you get my drift), until Jazz came around the corner to break it up, and he told Ebony to go home.

"Now, I have to say this in front of everybody: I don't want you, Ebony," he announced loudly with anger while pointing his finger to her head.

"You wanna fight somebody, fight me. She hasn't done anything to you," he told her while getting in her face.

"For the LORD will vindicate His people, And will have compassion on His servants, When he sees that their strength is gone, And there is none remaining bond or free." (Deuteronomy 32:36 NASB)

"I really didn't want to fight her. I got to know her, and she's nice. I was pushed into it, and I was a little jealous," she confessed.

She, then, sincerely apologized to me for the trouble she had caused.

"No hard feelings?" she asked.

"No hard feelings," I agreed.

"Let's go get us some beer and a smoke," she said as she put her arm around my shoulders, and we preceded to walk.

"The Lord will cause your enemies who rise against you to be defeated before you. They shall come out against you one way flee before you seven ways." (Exodus 28:7 NKJV)

After a while, Ebony moved on from us, and we found out later she was pregnant, but not by Jazz. She invited me to her baby shower, and we remained friends, but in passing.

"Walk with the wise and become wise, for a companion of fools suffers harm" (Proverbs 13:20 NIV)

It was back to just being Jazz, and I with no interruptions from ex-girlfriends. I was still leaving home every day as if I were going to school, and this was eventually noticed. Nearing the end of tenth grade, my mother had to come to the school because I wasn't promoted to the 11th grade. I had no credits because I wasn't attending class or going to school at all. Once we got to the school and talked to my guidance counselor, my mother was furious with me; her eyes were bloodshot red. When we reached the inner hall of the school's front door to leave, she began to question me.

"Why wasn't you going to class?" she questioned angrily with her hands on her hips.

"I just stopped going to class," I told her nonchalantly.

Right then, she grabbed me by my neck, preparing to punch me. The next thing I knew, I had blocked her fist from bashing my face.

"Let go of me! If you don't, I will leave you out here-stranded" I yelled as I cried hysterically. "I am sick and tired of yawl putting your hands on me! Why should you care, anyway? Nothing I do satisfies you."

I knew I had one over on her in this situation because she didn't know how to read; therefore, I knew that I could leave her stranded. She would not be able to read the street signs. I had found this out when I was filling out the Social Services forms for her. I asked her about something that was on the paper.

"Oh so, you're trying to make fun of me," she asked.

"Make fun of you. What do you mean?" I asked with confusion

"You know I can't read," she said.

She didn't allow me to defend my reason for asking her the question; God is my witness. Until that day when she told me, I didn't know anything about her illiteracy. It became very clear that her excuse of her eyes hurting for so many years, was a lie.

> *"A false witness will not go unpunished, And he who breathes lies will perish." (Proverbs 19:9 AMP)*

As I said, I knew she couldn't read the street signs because she wasn't familiar with the area; she would not have any recognition of the words. Once, I told her that I would leave her, she became very humble, and I began to call the shots- per say.

"Mommy, you have to promise me you won't beat me over this- neither you or Daddy. I'll get a job," I told her.

"I promise," she said calmly.

I knew that she could persuade my dad to not be upset; therefore, I wasn't worried about that. When we returned home, my mom told my dad about the meeting we had with the guidance counselor.

"We had high hopes for you. You are messing up your life just like your mother said. Now, I'm just waiting for the babies to come along. Now, you're going to go out there, and get your a-- pregnant," he spat in a disappointing tone.

I just stood there numb with tears flowing down my face and boiling mad on the inside. To myself I said, *"That's what you all think, but I beg to differ. I have too many dreams for my future on the inside of me. So, what they both think doesn't matter to me anymore."*

> *"Eye has not seen, nor ear heard, nor have entered into the heart of man The things which God has prepared for those who love him" (1 Corinthians 2:9 NKJV)*

I was officially a high school dropout, and he was so disappointed in me. Did I like it? No, I was disgusted about it and blamed my parents? Yes. Despite how I felt, I had enrolled into the summer program to receive credits. This same program had offered to find a summer job for me. The Guidance Counselor told my mom that I could attend an alternative school to receive my G.E.D, if I passed the test, or I could take the summer classes to gain credits.

After a while, I lost interest in the school, and I wasn't ready to take the G.E.D. I feared that I would fail it, so I forfeited the test. I felt that waiting to get my G.E.D was the best option for me because I didn't feel confident nor knowledgeable in academics at the time.

I decided to fill out an application as a part-time messenger in Manhattan. After filling out the application, they called me for an interview and not long after, they hired me. I loved this job; they gave me tokens for the train. Because I was so hungry when I got there, I traded the tokens for money to buy a chili dog. When delivering messages, I would either jump the train's turn-stop or walk to my destination if it wasn't too far. Sometimes, I would get home around 7:30p.m. or 8:00p.m. I didn't mind getting home at that time during the summer; however, during fall and winter months I didn't like it because of the cold. I would have to be out there by myself: thank God for my boyfriend.

> *"For God did not give us a spirit of fear, but of power and of love and of a sound mind." (2 Timothy 1:7 KJV)*

Jazz would meet up with me and help me deliver the remainder of my packages when it was cold. Unfortunately, during the winter, I didn't have a coat nor gloves since my mother bought everyone a coat, except me. Jazz had taken notice of this as well and the fact that Christmas was close.

"I'm going to make some money and buy you a coat," he told me.

Every night, he took off his coat and placed it around me, leaving me in awe. He would tell me how much he loved me and that he cared about me a lot. By his words of affirmation and actions, he made me feel so special. In my own heart, I was planning to do something special for him also; he deserved it.

Chapter 22
MY WAY OUT!

Despite the cold, I was glad to be working up until the holidays because I had plans for my last check. I gave my mother most the money that I previously made, since I made good money with a little overtime. I had already prepared my mother by telling her that I was going to keep my last check. This would be my last one because it was too cold for me to continue working. Some of the places where I was sent were very far away, and it wasn't worth me getting sick or frost bitten.

While Jazz was planning to buy me a coat, I was planning to get him something for Christmas as well. With my last check, I had bought him a suede sweater- jacket, a pair of Lee jeans, and a nice shirt. Though he tried to persuade me not to get him anything, I did anyhow. Although I wasn't his responsibility, he made it his business to ensure that I had a coat. One thing about Jazz was that he was very selfless, thoughtful, and generous in caring about my well- being.

The day that I came home with Jazz's gift, my mother was furious because I didn't give her anything.

"Mommy, he is buying me a coat because all I had was these two little jackets and no gloves," I whined.

"Who told you to spend that check?" she said belligerently.

"Mommy, you didn't care enough about me to buy me a coat. I had been giving you all the money, and you haven't bought me anything since I been working." I said sadly.

> *"Then He said to them, 'Watch out and guard yourselves against every form of greed; for not even when one has an overflowing abundance does his life consist of nor is it derived from his possessions.'" (Luke 12:15 AMP)*

"Who do you think you are talking to?" my stepfather intervened as he began to raise his hand at me.

I stepped back with the phone in my hand and yelled, "Don't you touch me because if you do, I will call the police. Don't you take another step! If you do, I will bash you with this phone. You're not my daddy."

> *"Fathers, do not provoke your children to anger [do not exasperate them to the point of resentment with demands that are trivial or unreasonable or humiliating or abusive; nor by showing favoritism or indifference to any of them], but bring them up [tenderly, with lovingkindness] in the discipline and instruction of the Lord." (Ephesians 6:4 AMP)*

"You handle it," he slurred to my mother. He stumbled over his feet as he walked away due to his intoxication.

"You got a nerve. You don't even work nowhere. Mommy is taking care of you. You can't say nothing to me. I'm working: something you should be doing," I told him in a disgusted tone. I had reached my limit; I was tired of them both.

"GET OUT!" my mother yelled at me while pointing towards the front door.

"Oh, get out? No problem," I said while shrugging and turning towards my room. This was the best thing she had ever said to me.

"I will get my clothes," I told her.

"NO! Don't take nothing I bought you!" she shouted.

"Well, that wasn't much. I will take what I bought." I said sarcastically.

I was so happy to get out of there that I didn't know what to do. Her telling me to **LEAVE** was my way out.

"Please don't go," my sister cried.

"She wanted *me* to leave," I told Denise as I walked past her with my belongings.

My mother had opened the door, but suddenly, she came to her senses.

"Don't go. I didn't mean it," she pleaded.

"Yes, you did. Bye!" I said while walking out the door quickly.

I couldn't have gotten down the stairs any faster; I ran so fast. It was like I knew it was time for me to go, and she was my confirmation. If I would have stayed, I don't know what would have happened, and I didn't want to find out. The conflict had already been escalated, and I didn't want to add fuel to the fire. Too many harsh words were shared, especially on my part, so it was best that I left.

> *"No temptation but God is overtaken you except such as is common to man; faithful, who will not allow you to be tempted beyond what you are able, but with the temptation will also make the way of escape, that you may be able to bear it" (1 Corinthians 10:13 NKJV)*

On my way to call Jazz, he turned the corner on the block I lived on. I literally bumped into him.

"Oh my God! You're right on time," I expressed. "I was just getting ready to call you to meet up with me." Then, I told him everything that had occurred back at home.

"Everything is going to be okay," he said comforting me.

He helped me with the things I had in my hands, along with his gift. When we arrived at his home, his family welcomed me with open arms, empathy, and love; they were extremely wonderful to me. Moreover, Jazz was the oldest of his four brothers that he lived with but was the youngest of his older brother and five older sisters that didn't live in the house.

I believe that he couldn't wait until Christmas to give me my gift because he was convinced that I needed it now. He gave me my first gift: a three-quarter dark, lavender coat. After thanking him, I put it on, and it fitted perfectly.

"You should go ahead and give her everything else because she's going to need them," his mom told him.

He went into the living room, came back into the kitchen, and handed me the box. Once I opened it up, I started to cry because he didn't just get me one coat, but two long, warm coats, a pair suede boots, a pair of pants, a hat, and a pair of gloves. I cried like a baby because I was so grateful. I grabbed him and embraced him tightly with overwhelming joy and gratefulness.

"My mom helped; I asked her for her opinion on size and color," he spoke as he hugged me. I walked over to her and hugged her as well.

"I will give thanks to you Lord, with all my heart; I will tell of all Your wonderful deeds." (Psalms 9:1 NIV)

When I gave Jazz his gift, he was a little upset that I had gotten him something which was strange to me.

"It's his pride. He is the giver and never the receiver unless I give it to him. Outside of that, he's not used to it," his mom explained to me. I just nodded in understanding.

Later, he hugged me and said, "Thanks Pat. You didn't have to get me a gift. I love you."

"Yes, I did. You were kind and generous towards me. I love you too," I said while giving him a smile and a kiss.

"A generous person will prosper, whoever refreshes others will be refreshed." (Proverbs 11:25 NIV)

I ended up spending the night there until we figured out what we were going to do. Earlier in the relationship, I asked Jazz if he had ever had sex before. He told me that he almost did but not really. He suggested that we didn't discuss it because it was embarrassing.

"Have you had sex before?" he asked me.

"Yes," I told him.

"I guess you will be teaching me then, hmm?" I smiled at him.

"I guess so," I spoke.

The first night I stayed was the first time that he and I had sex after two months of being a couple. It was quite interesting since Jazz was a virgin, and I was his first. Having sex was no issue; we already had fallen in love with each other so why not? I was his, and he was mine.

*"Now concerning the matters about which you wrote: "It is
good for a man not to have sexual relations with a woman."
(1 Corinthians 7:1 ESV)*

Chapter 23
I Got Just What I Wanted

The next morning, my sister had delivered a message to me from my mom saying that I needed to call her. Afterwards, I made my way to the pay phone to do so.

"You need to call this social worker because I told them I didn't want you here, and you are not in school," my mom said harshly through the pay phone. "I also told them that I want you to be put in a group home. See how you like it in there, so they can beat your a--."

"Mommy you always threaten me with that but that's not going to happen. I am going into a foster home," I explained.

"No, you're not. Over my dead body!" she yelled angrily.

"Well, we will see," I said as I hung up the phone.

Because of that phone call, I went to see the social worker. She began to speak about my transition.

"Is it possible that I could become a foster child?" I inquired.

"You passed the age that most households would accept which is fifteen years old. You're sixteen now."

"Ma'am, could you please try?" I asked kindly.

"I will see what I can do. Give me a couple of days, and I want you to call me," she told me.

I hugged her and said, "Okay, I will. Thank you."

"*Yes,*" I said to myself. I had already discerned that everything would work out. My mother was something else with her antics; she was absurd. I couldn't believe that she wanted me to reside in a group home, just, so they could hurt me. There were a lot of unscrupulous things happening in group homes that she had heard about, and she did not care about me being subject to those things.

> *"As for you, you meant evil against me, but God meant it for my good in order to bring about this preset outcome, that many people would be kept alive (as they are this day)"* (Genesis 50:20 AMP)

> *"Ask, and it shall be given you; seek, and ye shall find; knock, and it shall be opened unto you:* [8] *For every one that asketh receiveth; and he that seeketh findeth; and to him that knocketh it shall be opened."* (Matthew 7:7-8 KJV)

I continued to stay with Jazz and his family for a few days until I called the social worker.

"I have good news: **I found a foster home** that would accept you, but it is in Laurelton, Queens. I'll be the one transporting you there," she informed.

"Great! What about my mother?" I asked

"Don't worry. I will talk to your mother," she assured me.

"**Thank you, Lord**," I said while looking to the sky.

I had gotten exactly what I wanted. Although my mother didn't see her wrong in all this, I knew one thing for sure: she was going to miss me because I did everything around the house. Regardless, she was downright hateful towards me. Tell me, who in the world would wish bad on their child? I prayed hard that I wouldn't ever treat my children the way that my mom treated me.

> *"The Lord bless you and keep you; The Lord make His face to shine upon you, and be gracious to you; The lord lifts up His countenance upon and give you peace" (Numbers 6:24-26 NRSV)*

The only thing that I was concerned about was not being able to see Jazz because of the distance, but he promised me that he would visit and call every day, thus he carried around a beeper. We kept in touch by either use of his beeper or by me calling his mom's house. When the social worker arrived, Jazz and I said our goodbyes, and I got into the car heading to my new residence.

As the social worker drove, I admired the scenery as we rode through Queens. Laurelton, Queens looked like the countryside with its beautiful houses and tall trees. The drive was long but, eventually, we arrived there. When we rang the doorbell, a woman by the name of Ms. Louise answered the door. She was a short, dark-skinned, older-looking lady. She invited us in, and the inside of her home was beautiful; I was excited. After Ms. Louise had signed papers for me to be released to her, she showed me my room; in which, I would be sharing with another foster child, who was a year older than me.

"There are two other boys that are younger than you. They'll be back later from visiting their parents," she informed me.

The social worker finally left, and I had the opportunity to get acquainted with Ms. Louise. She told me her rules and regulations of her home, as well as the usual time for dinner. Ms. Louise informed me that the social worker would be sending money for me to spend on clothes and other essentials; I was glad to hear this. That evening, all of us came together to greet and meet one another. I met Niecy and her younger brother, Henry, as well as Richard, whom was the youngest of us all. They were cool, except for Niecy who acted like she had a chip on her shoulder. She had a nasty attitude all the time.

I just wanted to get along with everyone, but I found out that she had some issues going on internally that may have caused her attitude. Apparently, there was some animosity she had towards her father that she needed help letting go. I told her that she would feel better if she talked about it. She kept having pains in her chest, and once she decided to let go of the animosity, the pains stopped. I allowed her to cry into my arms, as I comforted and encouraged her. Her cries became laughter, and I began to laugh with her. I believe her brother said something stupid that made her laugh. Moreover, the most amazing thing happened: her whole attitude changed for the better. Her expression was no longer dreary, but she had such a glow. Everyone was glad about her turn around. We all became good friends and looked out for one another. She stopped harshly cursing her brother out as well. Also, she started reading the Bible more.

"For his anger endureth but a moment; in his favour is life: weeping may endure for a night, but joy cometh in the morning" (Psalm 30:5 KJV)

"He heals the brokenhearted, and bandages their wounds." (Psalms 147:3 NLT)

"Stand fast therefore in the liberty wherewith Christ hath made us free, and be not entangled again with the yoke of bondage." (Galatians 5:1 KJV)

Being around Ms. Louise was okay when she wasn't drinking. Once when she was drunk, she tried to beat me because I came home past my curfew after seeing Jazz. He would come on the weekends to visit, or I would go visit with him and his family. It was funny because while she was drunk, she would miss me with her belt, and I kept running around the house. Constantly, we told her to go to bed and sleep it off, after I had apologized to her. She'd finally took our advice and told me she would talk to me in the morning. Niecy and I laughed at Ms. Louise so hard before we went to bed that night.

The next morning, she repeated the rules with me again, and a consequence was established; I was punished. I couldn't have any company the next weekend, but she did allow me to call Jazz to let him know I was punished. When I was free from my punishment, he would be able to pick me up.

Being so far from each other, Jazz and I began to miss each other, and we communicated every day. I hadn't seen him in about a month because he had been busy working and couldn't visit me right away. Ms. Louise told me that he had to wait to see me. When we talked on the phone, the eagerness of seeing one another was there, but there was a rule for visitors: weekends only.

It was hard because I loved me some Jazz, and he loved the ground I walked on. I was his Pat, and he was my Jazz. As young as we were, he wanted to take care of me. He would say, "I'm the man, and you're the woman. I'm supposed to take care of you, Pat," with his West-Indian accent. Every time he came to visit, he would bring me something to eat and leave money with me. He just wanted to make sure I didn't need anything.

> "The LORD is my Shepherd [to feed, to guide and to shield me], I shall not want." (Psalms 23:1 AMP)

Chapter 24
Crossing the Line

One evening when Jazz came to visit me, things didn't end so well. We were standing near a train station when we saw a guy that my foster sister, brothers and I met some time ago at a store where we always hung out to play arcade games like Pac- Man. His name was David. He was an older young man about twenty-three years old. He had his own home, and I remember him inviting Niecy, my foster brother, and me. We agreed to go with him, since he only lived around the corner from the store.

We walked along with him into his beautiful, extravagant home with shiny floors. He offered us liquor, soda, or beer, and of course I wanted beer. I believe that he was interested in me more than anything. David asked if I had a boyfriend, and I told him that I did and was very much in love with him. We stayed for a while until Niecy and our foster brother were ready to leave, but they didn't want to leave me there.

"Yawl know where I am. I'll be fine. I'm fine," I assured them.

> *"For such people do not serve our Lord Christ, but their own appetites and base desires. By smooth and flattering speech they deceive the hearts of the unsuspecting [the innocent and the naive]." (Romans 16:1 AMP)*

I stayed to talk with David a little more. I guess I liked the idea that he was interested in me. I had drunk a little too much and ended up taking a nap on his sofa. He was a perfect gentleman and didn't try anything. As a matter of fact, he went upstairs and went to sleep, leaving me be.

The next thing I knew, it was morning, and I panicked because I didn't mean to spend the night. I called out and let him know that I was leaving. He came downstairs and walked me to the door. Even though he wanted me to stay for breakfast, I told him that I had to leave.

"The least you could do is kiss me on the cheek. I mean, we are friends," he said.

I waited and pondered the thought of it. "It's harmless," I thought to myself, but when I leaned over to kiss him on the cheek, he turned his head and kissed me on my lips.

"I have a boyfriend," I gritted while pushing him.

"You're right. I shouldn't have done that," he said. After he said that, I turned around and left.

When I arrived home, Niecy said that Jazz had been calling me. I was glad she told me this; we always had each other's back.

"I told him you went to the store," she told me.

"Okay, we have to stick with the story," I told her. Everyone agreed, and when I spoke to Jazz, everything was cool.

Getting back to when Jazz, and I were standing at the subway station. David came down the stairs, off the subway, and introduced himself to Jazz.

"I heard a lot about you. All good, may I add. Can I talk to you for a moment?" David said.

"Sure," Jazz said suspiciously.

They went a little way up the subway where I couldn't hear what was being said. Here I am thinking everything is cool with my naive self. As they were coming downstairs, I saw the unreadable look on Jazz's face.

"Pat did you spend the night at this man's house?" he asked me.

"Yes, but nothing happened. Did you tell him that, David?" I asked while facing David.

"Tell him the truth," he said.

"I am telling him the truth," I exclaimed in a frustrated tone.

Jazz got quiet, and I thought that Jazz believed me over David, but I was wrong. We kept arguing back and forth as I tried to convince him that nothing happened. Uncontrollably, he kept hitting the walls in frustration.

"You had no business at his house anyway," he told me.

"The only thing that happened was I went to kiss him on his cheek, but he turned his head and kissed me on the lips; I pushed him away," I explained.

After lying and blowing everything out of proportion, David left, and it was just Jazz and I. He was so angry and vindictive towards me, then his hand went flying across my face; he smacked the daylights out of me. I couldn't believe that he had hit me. No matter how much I apologized, it didn't soothe the hurt and anger he felt. I was so scared because I had never seen him like this before, and at that moment, I knew things were never going to be the same between us. The love that we had was tainted with distrust; therefore, the validity of our relationship took a shift. However, we still wanted to be together because we still loved each other, but I learned a lesson from this.

> *"Abstain from all appearance of evil."*
> *(1 Thessalonians 5:22 KJV)*

I saw David again in passing, and I decided to confront him.

"You thought that a lie would have interrupted Jazz and I's relationship, but it didn't. You look lost and stupid. I don't want you, and I never will," I spoke harshly. I was so hurt and disgusted at what he did. Niecy and I cussed him out and told him off.

> *"Thus saith the LORD; Cursed be the man that trusteth in man, and maketh flesh his arm, and whose heart departeth from the LORD." (Jeremiah 17:5 King James Version)*

When I'd speak to Jazz over the phone, I could still hear the devastation in his voice from what had occurred. I kept apologizing and expressing to him that it will never happened again. I guess he believed me since he never brought it up again.

Chapter 25
Homelessness

We celebrated my seventeenth birthday at his mom's, Mrs. Smith house since she loved throwing parties on the weekend. Mr. Smith and I's birthday were in the same month, so we celebrated it together. Jazz was the DJ, and we had such a good time. Mrs. Smith invited some of her older friends, and some people Jazz and I knew as well.

I stayed on the dance floor, and after a couple of drinks, the shyness of dancing went away. I danced and drank until I couldn't dance or drank anymore. Take it from me: b*eer, Bacardi, and Coke* don't mix at all. This was the third time that I had overindulged in drinking alcoholic beverages. The intoxication consumed me in the forms of dizziness and vomiting. After everyone had gone home, I was a complete wreck.

I had such a terrible hangover that Jazz's brothers had to help take care of me. One of them wanted to fix me breakfast while the others wanted to find a remedy to help my stomachache and headache. They were benevolent boys, and they treated me like I was their sister. Also, they would lecture Jazz about how he shouldn't allow me to drink so much. I thought that this was very thoughtful of them to do that.

Jazz, as the older brother had his brothers well trained. They always cooperated with what Jazz asked of them. I was very impressed by his leadership over them. Being the observant person that I was, I noticed that he only had to say things once, and they were obedient.

Furthermore, they all loved to smoke weed except me, as I mentioned before. I had tried it with Jazz, but it wasn't my forte. Smoking weed had made me feel unhappy and sleepy, whereas alcohol allowed me to be joyous and bold. I drank beer and smoked cigarettes because I felt mature, and it eased my mind and calmed my nerves. I drank beer every day, but when I returned home to Queens, I didn't drink as often.

Nevertheless, I looked forward to the next party which was on Jazz's birthday in March. He was turning twenty, so we celebrated him just as we celebrated me. Again, I had such a great time; I was the life of the party. No one could touch me on the dance floor, even the times when I was on the dance floor alone; I didn't care. **I felt free by myself, and everyone else got a kick** [laugh] **out of it**.

Jazz did do me the pleasure of joining me on the dance floor from time to time. "Take it easy, Pat. I'm not that good of a dancer," he would say, and I would laugh at him. I joked with him while we danced which made him blush a lot. When it came to dancing fast, he was absolutely right about his dancing skills, but he was a wonderful slow dancer. Dancing to music like Reggae was more of his thing and not American music. He was never bothered by my way of dancing nor was he bothered with me dancing with someone else. He kept his eye on me and my dance partner since he wasn't one to easily trust others. I never wanted the night to end knowing that I had to go back to Queens the next day. I really didn't want to leave, and Jazz didn't want me to leave either.

Jazz took me back home, and it was hard to depart from him after spending time together. Nevertheless, we talked every day, and once he asked me if I had spoken to my family.

"Try calling them," he suggested.

"My mom doesn't want to speak to me. The last time I called, she hung up on me," I explained to him.

"Pat, it has been awhile. Try it again," he said.

"I do miss talking to my sister and brothers. I'll try, and I'll see what happens," I said agreeably.

I talked to Niecy about it, and she also felt that I should call. Finally, I felt compelled to call and nervous at the same time. I prepared myself just in case she didn't answer the phone, but to my surprise, she answered.

"Hello, Mommy, how are you?" I greeted.

"Hi, how are you?" she asked happy to hear from me.

"I'm doing fine," I told her.

She asked, "Are you able to visit?"

"Yes," I answered.

"Next time you come, pay us a visit," she said.

"Sure," I told her.

Afterwards, she allowed me to speak to everyone else, and when we ended the call, I was stunned that it went well. *"This may be a start of a better relationship"*, I thought to myself. Aside from small talk, she said that she didn't mean for things to turn out the way they did and apologized to me. I accepted her apology and asked her to forgive me as well. Once she forgave me, I told her that I missed her. She responded the same. It was nice to hear my mother's voice. I had enjoyed speaking to my sister and brothers as well, and I told them that I was going to visit them; they were excited about that.

> *"Get rid of all bitterness, rage and anger, brawling and slander, along with every form of malice. be kind and compassionate to one another, forgiving each other, just as in Christ God forgave you." (Ephesians 4:31-32 NIV)*

Meanwhile, I was anxiously waiting for the weekend to arrive, so I could visit my family. Niecy and my foster brothers were also preparing to leave for the weekend to see their families, as well. We started packing on Thursday and were ready to go the next day. I arrived home in Brooklyn, on Friday morning. Jazz met me at the train station, and we were very excited to see one another.

"Jazz, do you want to go visit my mom with me?" I asked him.

"Yeah, sure," he nodded while carrying my luggage.

After, we dropped my luggage by his mom's house, we decided to walk to my family's apartment since they didn't live too far. Before going on, I called my mom to ask if it was okay for us to come now, and she said that it was okay. When we reached the apartment, I formally introduced Jazz to my family, and it surprised me that my mother liked him.

"You're a handsome young man," she complimented him while smiling which caused Jazz to blush; he was flattered by the compliments.

"Thank you, Mrs. Crawford. I try to keep myself up," he spoke while smiling uncontrollably. We all laughed at his response.

Also, my siblings showed me much love through their great, big hugs and kisses. It was such a great joy to see them, but little did I know I was going to see them more often.

Jazz's mom had a small gathering on Sunday, and I didn't want to miss it; so instead of returning to Queens, I stayed for the party. I called Ms. Louise and told her that I was going to stay in Brooklyn for an extra day. However, my one extra stay turned into weeks and then months. Mrs. Smith said that I couldn't stay with them any longer, but Jazz would still sneak me in at night. Jazz's brothers helped hide me in between the bed and the wall. I was so skinny that no one would have ever known I was there. They stuffed many blankets near that side of the bed to hide me. When Jazz's parents went to work, I would come out from behind the bed, take a shower, and change clothes. I didn't have many clothes at all, but there was no doubt in my mind that Jazz was going to make sure I had clothing. He was excited that I was never going back to Queens, and he assured me that we were going to get through this together.

"I'm never going to leave you alone in these streets by yourself. I love you, Pat." We then embraced and kissed each other.

Jazz sold nickel and dime bags (bags of marijuana) to bring in money. Also, his brother stole cologne and perfume from the drugstore he worked at, so that Jazz could solicit them in the streets. Unfortunately, he wasn't doing a very good job in selling the product.

"Let me to take over," I told him.

"Oh, you think you could do better?" he challenged.

"I know I can. Look, you take a couple, and I will sell the rest," I said with confidence.

I had seven or eight bottles to sell, but I only needed a few minutes. I went to people I knew and sold on the streets to complete strangers that took a liking to me. I came back empty handed: I had sold out.

"That was quick. I got to give you your props. You're good at this," Jazz admitted.

"Do you want me to finish selling yours?" I asked him which caused us to laugh.

"Pat, you're trying to be smart now," he said with a smirk.

"No, I just know what I can do, and what I can't," I shrugged.

"You're a good salesperson," he complimented.

While we were trying to sell the rest of his share, I told him I used to dream of working at a clothing store. I would play with my siblings and pretend that I was the store manager, cashier, and salesclerk while they were the customers. I had plenty of practice at this. Jazz split the money that we obtained from the sales between me, himself, and his brother. We bought food and used the money for the necessities that I needed. Regardless of the success with the cologne and perfume, I was always afraid that Jazz would get caught selling weed, but Jazz reassured me that he had a strategy if the police ever ran up on him. They patrolled heavily around where he lived because of the heavy drug distribution.

"Pat, I never want you to be involved or to go to jail," he said, and I understood that.

Once, when we were walking together along the sidewalk, he'd spotted the police driving slowing behind watching us closely.

"Walk up ahead of me," he whispered.

I walked speedily far as I could. When I turned around, the police were searching Jazz. Not long after, they read him his rights and placed handcuffs on him. I was devastated as tears streamed down my face.

"Pat, don't worry. They didn't find anything; they're gonna have to release me!" he yelled as they placed him in the car.

He smiled the whole time, with no worries because they didn't confiscate or find anything on him. He never wanted me to tag along when he was selling weed because of this very reason. He was right they released him. The downfall of Jazz's demise is himself. His stubbornness contributed to his failure to follow instructions from authoritative figures. He couldn't keep a nine to five because he didn't want anyone telling him what to do, yet he's gifted in many things.

In addition, I called my mother to let her know that I never returned to Queens, and I was still here in Brooklyn, at Jazz's parents' home.

"Why didn't you go back?" she asked curiously.

"I just didn't want to stay there anymore," I told her.

"What are you doing tomorrow?" she asked.

"Nothing," I said plainly.

She said, "Why don't you come and go with me? I have to go pay on a layaway bill."

"Sure, I would love to go," I said. I let Jazz know that I was going to spend some time with my mother.

He said, "Okay, I will see you when you get back."

I visited her the next day, and when I arrived, she was ready to go. We took a bus up Flatbush Avenue, got off, and walked into the clothing store to pay the bill. My mother knew the manager, a white, Jewish man, and he told me that she was one of his finest customers.

"Are you hiring?" I said in a joking manner.

"You really want a job?" my mom asked when she overheard me.

"Yes," I told her. I noticed that he only had one salesclerk.

"Are you hiring?" she asked the manager on my behalf.

"No, but she could fill out an application," he offered.

I filled out an application before I left out of the store. My mom and I were excited that I was able to; this was a plus in our book. Once we left and I returned to Jazz, I didn't think anything else about it.

> *"But do you want to know what O foolish man, that faith without works is dead?" (James 2:20 NKJV)*

Jazz and I were still trying to figure out where I was going to lay my head but that night we slept on the roof of his building. His brothers helped us out by sneaking pillows and blankets up there so that we would sleep comfortably. I was grateful that Jazz became **homeless** along with me, and I understood that he wanted to protect me. I realize that he didn't *have* to sacrifice his well-being to be out there with me. He wasn't **homeless;** I was.

Wondering where your next meal or where we were going to sleep it wasn't fun, but I must say that I never missed a meal. Jazz made sure I ate even if he had to sacrifice and starve. His determination in wanting to take care of me was amazingly captivating.

> *"Therefore, I say to you, do not worry about your life, what you will eat or what you will drink; nor about your body, what you will put on, Is not life more than food and the body more than clothing." (Matthew 6:25 NKJV)*

Beforehand, Mrs. Smith made it clear in subtle remarks throughout our conversation that I couldn't reside in their home because she had all boys. She had *concerns* which were understandable. I loved that she and I had a wonderful relationship. We communicated numerous times not just on the occasions of her gathering, but she thought of me as one of her daughters.

> *"Greater love hath no man than this, that a man lay down his life for his friends." (John 15:13 KJV)*

Out of the blue, Mrs. Smith was compelled to share some things about Jazz.

"Jazz has a bad temper. The only reason I never kicked him out was because he kept the house clean and his brothers in line," she confessed with a small dry chuckle shaking her head.

I listened very closely to this advice and kept it at the back of my mind.

"A quick-tempered man acts foolishly and without self-control, and a man of wicked schemes is hated." (Proverbs 14:17 AMP)

The next morning after sleeping on the roof, we got up as usual and waited for his parents to leave for work, so we could do what we usually do: take a shower, change clothes etc. Unexpectedly, there was a knock at the door, and it was my sister.

"Trisha, mommy wants you to call her," Denise told me. I went to a pay phone to do so after I got myself together.

"I have some good news- you got the job!" she happily told me over the phone.

"Really? Oh my God, I can't believe it!" I said in disbelief.

"Let's just say I had a talk with him," she said.

"Wow. Thank you, Mommy. I appreciate that," I said thankfully.

"Take the number down and call right away!" she told me.

After she read the number to me, I called it right after we hung up.

"Hello?" the manager answered.

"This is Patricia. My mother told me to call you. She stated that I got the job that I had inquired about," I explained.

"When can you start?" he asked.

"Monday," I told him since it was now the weekend.

"I will see you then," he told me, and we ended the call.

I told Jazz about everything although he claimed to be happy about it, his body language and facial expression said otherwise. I believe that he was accustomed to my constant presence, and now it was going to be awkward and lonesome without me around him 24/7. As I expressed earlier, we were like two peas in the pod, Bonnie and Clyde, or Sonny and Cher.

> *"For His anger is but for a moment, His favor is for life; Weeping may endure for a night but joy comes in the morning." (Psalms 30:5 NKJV)*

> *"So that you may (show yourselves to) be children of your Father who is in heaven; for He makes His sun rise on those who are evil and on those who are good, and makes the rain fall on the righteous (those who are morally upright)and the unrighteous (the unrepentant, those who oppose Him)." (Matthew 5:45 AMP)*

Meanwhile, we still had to figure out where we were going to stay and sleep. We kept staring at this abandoned building that was diagonally across from where his parents lived. Jazz stated that he would scope out the area at night. He and his brother went inside the building late at night with a flashlight, making sure that no one saw them entering the building. I stayed put and waited inside his parent's apartment building. When they came back, they told me the most unimaginable thing that one of the abandoned apartments had: **electricity.**

The electricity was only in one bedroom, but Jazz had plans; we could see the imaginary light bulb above his head. The next evening, they moved a mattress and television set in the apartment. There were plenty of tall white buckets in there as well; in which, we added water and disinfectant to fumigate the apartment if we had to use the bathroom.

It was the summer, but it stayed cool during the night, and we used a fan for those hot days.

"But my God shall supply all of your needs according to his riches in glory by Christ Jesus." (Philippians 4:19 KJV)

We were careful sneaking out in the mornings, so that no one would see us; this was the difficult part. Amazingly, no one would have ever thought I was **homeless** because I didn't look like it. My hair was always done, and Jazz made sure of this every two-weeks. Since my hairdresser, a friend of the family, lived right around the corner, this was not an issue. Her family was also very generous in opening their home to me for a shower, a meal, and to change my clothes. Jazz and I would go to the laundromat and wash our clothes just like anyone else. He would press my clothes, and his ironing expertise was phenomenal. Ironing wasn't the only thing he did in excellence: he worked construction jobs, painted, and put up sheetrock; it was interesting watching him work. Also, he did wonderful designs on ceilings. He was a jack of all trades, but a master of none. Anything he dealt with his hands was of excellence, and he could clean a home to an unrecognizable degree. The disappointment came into play when people didn't want to pay him for the work he'd done. He'd make excuses for their lack of integrity, but I was different. I pushed him into demanding his money, and when he didn't question the people about his money, I did. When I spoke up for him, he always got his money. I made sure that no one took advantage of him.

"That the God of our Lord Jesus Christ, the Father of glory, may give unto you the spirit of wisdom and revelation in the knowledge of him..." (Ephesians 1:17 KJV)

"Pat you always know what to say to get my money," he told me.

More so, it became *our* money because he always shared it with me. If he didn't trust me with anything else, he trusted me with his money.

Now, I had a place to sleep, and a job to go to. Monday was my first day of employment, and when I arrived, it was quiet and slow in the store. That day, I was trained by the one salesclerk. She was genuinely nice, and she was old enough to be my mother. Because of her accent, I knew she was a native of the Islands. She shared with me that she'd been working there for years, while I sat quietly, observing, and listening to her closely.

The next day, Tuesday, was a little different because I had drunk some beer before I came to work. I wanted to become more confident in communicating with others since I didn't talk as much when I was sober; so, I needed a little "boost". Boy, when I worked that day, they couldn't stop me from talking. Customers came in with intentions of window shopping but left with bags of merchandise in their hands.

"Patricia, you have a gift so keep on talking. When the coats come in, I need you to make sales because the customers love you," the manager told me.

"You got it!" I said enthusiastically.

"If you sell a certain number of coats, I'll buy you lunch," he told me.

"How about a bonus? - a little more money added to my check," I inquired kindly.

"You can forget that. He is cheap and stingy," the salesclerk added.

"We'll see," he said while side eyeing the salesclerk.

Fortunately, this came to pass. I came in a little intoxicated to help me because I was a little shy, but I had become even more confident in myself by praying, "***LORD HELP ME TO SELL THESE COATS ON TODAY.***" I was laughing and clowning around with the customers. When the customers asked me how the coat looked on them, I told them the truth; they truly respected my honesty. If the coat didn't fit right or suit them, I would find them something that did. As he promised, the manager did treat me to lunch, but the salesclerk was right. He wouldn't give up any extra money. Regardless, he was so happy about the many coats I sold, and I was happy as well. Also, this job caused me to learn that I was a people person due to all the interactions that I had with different people.

There were other days when I came to work intoxicated and ready to talk but business was awfully slow. Suddenly, I would become sleepy, and I just wanted to lay down because my high was subsiding. I felt terrible and a little dizzy; instead of, energized and enthused. It became so bad that I needed my bed. It was a temporary high for a long-term pain. Once the high was gone, it was **back to reality**.

> *"He heals the brokenhearted and binds up their wounds [healing their pain and comforting their sorrow]." (Psalm 147:3 AMP)*

Everyone noticed my intoxication various times, including my boss, but he never said anything because he just cared that a lot of money was being made.

> *"A merry heart doeth good like a medicine: but a broken spirit drieth the bones." (Proverbs 17:22 KJV)*

Chapter 26
Rescued

Mrs. Smith had another one of her infamous gatherings, and I didn't want to go to work. She had liquor, beer, food, and music, and I wanted to have some fun and dance, dance and dance all night. Remembering, I wouldn't have been able to move so well without a dear friend of mine, Sharon, who hid me in her home when I ran away. She taught me how to dance, telling me "Your hips are too stiff... move them hips, girl. Shake what ya' mama gave you," with laughter. I practiced the moves until I made them my own. While dancing, I felt like I was in my own world away from everything, away from the pain. I downed drinks continuously though I knew I had to go to work. I began skipping work and calling out sick, so I could stay at the parties.

As the months passed, Jazz became *extremely protective* over me. Anytime that a person is ready to stand around your job until you get off, there is a problem. I told him that he didn't need to do that, but he insisted.

"What is it? You don't trust me?" I asked angrily.

"No, it's not that, Pat. I don't trust others," he stressed.

He knew I worked overtime, so why the sudden change? I honestly believe that he thought I wouldn't need him any longer, and I would terminate our relationship. If he thought this, he was wrong; it never crossed my mind. However, the way he was going about things and his behavior could have very well changed that. His aggressive, possessive behavior was affecting me especially when he drank. I didn't like that I was walking on pins and needles with him, or the intimidation I felt.

One morning, Jazz's erratic behavior almost cost me my job. We had a heated argument over an accusation from someone that claimed they saw me talking to another guy. This was a blatant, flat out lie, but Jazz believed it, and I was furious with him.

"Well, since you want to believe what someone else said about me, you can be with them then," I told him

"I didn't say that I believed them, Pat," he responded.

"So why are you bringing this up in my face and acting crazy?" I exclaimed.

I could tell that he had been drinking. When we arrived at my job, he started pulling on my arm and pushing me against the window and saying crazy stuff like, "If I can't have you, nobody else can't."

"Why don't you just go home?" I asked him in a frustrated tone.

"Do you want me to call the police?" The salesclerk inside the store shouted.

"No," I told her.

"I'm not going anywhere. I'm going to stay right here until you get off." Jazz said as I walked into the store.

"Oh no you are not. Get from in front of my store before I call the police," the manager demanded.

"Pat, I'll be back," Jazz said in an abrupt tone while turning to walk away.

When my shift was over, there were crowds of people walking in each direction, and I thought I was in the clear because I didn't see Jazz. However, as soon as I walked a couple of doors down, there was Jazz, and he startled me.

"Jazz, it's over. Leave me alone." I told him.

"What, Pat, it's over? What do you mean it's over?" he spoke in an intimidating tone while stepping closer.

First, he blocked me from getting pass him and pushed me near another store until a friend of my family, Inez, suddenly intervened. She was irate at the sight of Jazz harassing me. She consoled me, asking if I was okay, but I was too scared; Inez saw the fright in my eyes.

"She's coming with me!" she told Jazz sternly.

"Would you like to come with me?" she asked me in a soft tone.

I answered with a quick yes; I was scared out of my wits.

"If you don't leave, I will scream to attract attention," she threatened while facing Jazz.

This would have been no hard task because Flatbush Avenue was always crowded; you would've thought we were in Manhattan or Times Square. She would have attracted plenty of attention to my situation.

"Alright, alright, you don't have to do that. Pat is this what you want?" he said while facing me.

"Yes," I replied.

This was not the only time that Jazz had been physically violent with me. When he was drinking, he dragged me in the hallway and beat me as I tried to get away from him in his parents' apartment building. I don't remember what we were arguing about, but I do know that I was tired of fighting with him. I needed a break. Moving forward, Inez and I made sure that Jazz was nowhere in sight before we started walking.

"Rescue me, O Lord, from evil men; Preserve me from violent men." (Psalms 140:1 NASB)

Also, this was not the first time that I had to be rescued from Jazz. Jazz's brother hated to see Jazz overindulge in alcohol because Jazz wanted to fight me for no reason. His brother had to pull, restrain him, and he told me to run. Jazz would be furious with him, but he didn't care.

"I'm not going to let you hit her; she is a young lady. You need to go somewhere and sober up, so let me help you," he told Jazz.

After Jazz saw that his resistance wasn't getting him anywhere, he finally settled down. When I left, I would go visit with some friends, call to check on him, and see if it were okay to return. His brother had asked me multiple times, "Why do you put up with this?"

"I love, Jazz. He's always there for me. I know he only gets like this because of the drinking," I expressed to him.

Jazz was a sweetheart, but alcohol made him a totally different person. When smoking weed; he was totally different as well. He would have the munchies (strong craving for food), constant laughter, and sleep; there would be no violence.

Anyhow, Inez's residence wasn't far from where we were; she lived right down the street. In case we were being followed, we took a cab down the street to outsmart Jazz. Inez's apartment building was big, nice, and had a doorman. She lived alone; it was spacious. She started asking me questions about Jazz and what had happened.

"Well, we're over now," I told her.

There I was thinking to myself, "*What am I going to do?*" Jazz wore me out; I was so exhausted and discombobulated from arguing with him.

"You're welcome to stay here tonight. We will figure out something in the morning." Inez said.

I thanked her for her hospitality and told her how much I appreciated her. In addition, I was glad that Inez was a beer drinker, and when she offered me one, of course, I accepted and drank it before I went to sleep. Then, the next morning, there was a knock at the door. Inez answered it and entering in was a fine, light skinned gentleman with a beard and delightfully intoxicating cologne-the kind that caught my attention. We shook hands and introduced ourselves, and I learned that he was Inez's brother.

"You don't remember me, do you? My name is Harley," he said with a deep southern accent.

"I believe I do. Back then I was about fifteen years old. Now, I'm seventeen, but I will be eighteen years old in a couple of days," I informed him.

"Oh really. I guess we were introduced at the right time," he spoke with a slight grin.

"I guess so," I blushed.

"Would yawl like anything from the store?" he asked.

"Yes, breakfast," we replied.

He went to McDonalds to get us some food, and when he returned, we got better acquainted. Harley was from Syracuse, New York, by way of the south. He told me about his wife whom he'd been separated from for almost a year. His honesty was impressive; most people would lie or omit this information. However, I didn't care that they weren't fully divorced; I just wanted to have fun. He called me every day in a mission to become more acquainted with me. I was really flattered by the consistent chase. Harley would even visit me after he got off work.

"-but whoever commits adultery with a woman lacks common sense and sound judgment and an understanding [of moral principles]: he who would destroy his soul does it." (Proverbs 6:32 AMP)

He wondered why I was here, at his sister's house, so I told him what happened with Jazz. This led to his questions about Jazz and me, and if we were still together.

"No, not after that last fight. I told him it was over," I said.

"You know I'm much older right?" he inquired while tilting his head.

I nodded and said, "Yes. How much older?"

"I'm thirty-six," he spoke waiting for my response.

"Well you don't look that old. I'm fine with it," I shrugged.

"Can I take you out for your birthday?" he asked when I told him the date.

"Sure," I told him with a smile.

"Where do you want to go?" he asked me.

"I would like to go to a club because I love to dance"

"Okay. I can make that happen, but I must warn you: I'm not a good fast dancer, but I'm more of a slow dancer."

"That's fine. Well, I have one problem," I said.

"What's that?" he asked.

I told him that I didn't have anything to wear and that my hair needed to be done.

Inez came to my rescue and said, "I'll do your hair."

"Don't worry about clothes," Harley said while shaking his head and digging into his wallet to hand me a crispy hundred-dollar bill.

"Go get what you want," he said.

"*Wow,*" I said to myself.

"Thank you so much," I said.

Later, Mr. H told me that he shared a family-owned garage business. This is the family business that ruthless Tory was a part of. In fact, Tory was Harley's nephew. When I disclosed that I knew Tory and what he did to me, Inez and Harley weren't surprised to hear this. Apparently, Tory was now in jail on domestic abuse charges. "*That's good for him,*" I said to myself.

> "*But whoever commits adultery with a woman lacks common sense and sound judgment and an understanding [of moral principles]; he who would destroy his soul does it.*" (Proverbs 6:32 AMP)

I hadn't worked since the incident with Jazz and returning wasn't an option right now because we suspected that Jazz would show up. However, on numerous occasions, I would call to see if they needed me though around this time, business was slow. They, too, thought it would be best for me to not return just yet. Amid my drama, Inez didn't mind me staying with her for a few more days until we figured something out. During the day, Inez would go to work, and I would stay in the apartment until she returned.

When she returned home, I took the hundred dollars and bought a new outfit, shoes, as well as accessories to compliment my apparel. Oh, I just couldn't wait for Friday night; I was so anxious and excited about going to a club.

Did I think about Jazz any? No. I was so distraught by his abusive ways towards me. Now, there were memorable times we shared together like when he picked me up from work. We rerouted because I wanted to visit my mother. We were at the corner waiting to cross the street when I looked up and saw that my mom's apartment had caught on fire. I couldn't believe that my dream, a reoccurring dream had manifested before my very eyes. When I had this dream I would wake up, shaking it off and not telling anyone. Looking back, I wonder if it could have been prevented if I told someone. I found out that my brother was playing with matches in the kitchen near the trash can which caught on fire and spread. Fortunately, no one was hurt.

> *"And He said, "Hear now My words: If there is a prophet among you, I the LORD will make Myself known to him in a vision And I will speak to him in a dream." (Numbers 12:6 AMP)*

Because of the damage from the fire, my family had to move. I found this out when Jazz and I knocked on the door. It cracked open, so we were able to enter and look around. My mom was packed and ready to go. After we looked around, we left and made sure the door was locked making our way to Jazz's house. My mother failed in finding a place to live, so social services helped by putting them in a hotel in Manhattan, New York. Denise, Willie, and Daniel had to sleep on the floor, but it was a pretty big room, so they had space. My little nephew, Tory, Denise's son, lived with them as well. He was such a sweet adorable baby.

Subsequently, my mom was upset with me because Jazz had told her that I stole something the day we visited the apartment when no one was there. He had only lied to her because I left him. She believed Jazz over me. I was devastated with her, and I begged her to believe me, but it was no use. I just left. I couldn't believe my ears; she believed Jazz over me. It was nothing I could say to change her mind. *"He probably came back and took her jewelry,"* I thought to myself.

Jazz was a true thief; he'd rob your house in a quick minute. Also, all his brothers were thieves except Nate. One time, I was on the lookout making sure no one showed up while he and his younger brother were robbing the apartment of his mother's neighbor. He climbed on the fire escape and went through the window. I was in fear that we would get caught. Boy, I tell you; he had the wrong one watching out. I forgot what Jazz and his baby brother took, but whatever they took, they sold it. I told Jazz that we could never do this again, and he promised me he wouldn't.

Then, there was an incident where Jazz's mom and father were looking for us. When they spotted us, they started running towards Jazz and me. We didn't know what was going on. They jumped Jazz, beating him in the street, and then his mom came after me and tried to smack me, but I pulled away from her and ran. It was crazy. We tried to tell them that we didn't know what they were talking about. It was evident that allegedly Jazz had stolen from his mom. I didn't know if Jazz did it or not, but Mr. and Mrs. Smith knew Jazz a whole lot longer than I had; he was their son. They tried to attack me because they believed I was with him, but I certainly wasn't when he did the crime this time.

> [1] *"You shall not steal, nor deal deceptively, nor lie to one another." (Leviticus 19:11 AMP)*

This incident with his parents hindered us from going back to the abandoned building because they threatened to call the police if we were in the area. Therefore, we had to find somewhere to spend the night. We went to downtown Manhattan to seek shelter, but the shelters were full, but we didn't give up and continued our search. Finally, we found a shelter, and they took us in. Living in a shelter was the worst experience ever.

> *"[a]Ask and keep on asking and it will be given to you; seek and keep on seeking and you will find; knock and keep on knocking and the door will be opened to you. [8]For everyone who keeps on asking receives, and he who keeps on seeking finds, and to him who keeps on knocking, it will be opened." (Matthew 7:7-8 AMP)*

We had to keep a close eye on our belongings so that they wouldn't get stolen. Jazz, also had to keep his eyes on me and make sure that no one touched me, so he kept me close to him while we slept. The next morning, after our first night, we got up and left. In our travels, we bumped into Ms. C, who was staying with her boyfriend, and I told her our situation.

"You both could come and stay with us until you both figure out something," she said.

Our stay with her didn't last because Jazz was feeling a little uncomfortable, so after a week or two, we left.

I remember while we were staying in an abandoned building, Jazz wanted me try pure cocaine in a joint. It smelled worse than marijuana. After experiencing that, I told him that he would never talk me into smoking that again. I didn't like the idea that I couldn't sleep after I smoked it; I cried. This cocaine joint had full control over my body, and there was nothing I could do about it. A drug that powerful amazed me; it was scary.

> *"Do you not know that your body is the temple of the Holy Spirit who is within you, whom you have (received as a gift) from God, and that you are not your own (property)?" (1 Corinthians 16:19-20 AMP)*

I was truly angry because nothing should have this much control over me. I began to wonder if this was the same experience that others had when they snorted cocaine. If so, oh my God, and then I wondered about the power of smoking crack. I just shook my head. I won't ever know because I would never indulged in that type of substance.

Crack was new on the block. After I had seen the results of the manipulative and controlling attributes of this drug, I wanted to stay far away from it. I was addicted to alcohol substances, and I wouldn't go any further than that. I couldn't let a day go by without drinking beer. It helped me cope with the pain I felt within, and it allowed me to be someone else other than myself. Truthfully speaking, I wasn't happy without it. It made me believe that I had to have it and couldn't function unless I was intoxicated. Not only that, it helped me to communicate strongly and boldly. At times, I couldn't believe it myself.

My drinking options had increased intensely and strength. Aside from beer, I would occasionally overindulge in stronger alcohol such as *Bacardi (rum) with coke, Gin with grapefruit juice*, and sometimes *Old English* which was the nastiest beer I had ever tasted, but it was potent. I would drink two full cups from a 40-ounce bottle, and after that I was toasted.

> *"At the last bites like a serpent and stings like a viper. Your (drunken) eyes will see strange things and your mind will utter perverse things (untrue things, twisted things)."* (Proverbs 20:32-33 AMP)

My drinking habits may have been passed down to me since my mother told me that my biological father drank a lot. Also, I watched my stepfather drank until he couldn't drink anymore. My mother drank but very discreetly, and she never overindulged. She knew her limit, but at age 17, I didn't know mine.

Chapter 27
Searching for Love 18yrs. Old

The day had come: my eighteenth birthday. Inez did my hair as she promised in an updo with Shirley Temple curls. I wore a long sleeve blouse with black and gray ruffles in the front, a black mermaid pencil skirt with ruffles at the bottom that came over my knee, gray patent leather shoes with a ruffle flower on top, paired with black earrings, and let's not forget the finishing touch: my brown lip gloss. Harley arrived at Inez's apartment about 9:00 p.m. and brought along his cousin who knew more about New York clubs than he did. When Harley saw me, he couldn't keep his eyes off me. I knew I looked completely different from what he had seen earlier through the week. In his eyes, I may have looked like a sophisticated schoolteacher or businesswoman.

"You look beautiful!" he said.

"D---- You look good with those pretty white teeth and those soft pretty lips grinning at me." I thought to myself. I hadn't kissed him yet, but my imagination sure could wonder.

"You look very handsome yourself." I said blushing overwhelmingly.

We arrived at the club where they had a bar and booth where we could order drinks. They also had a dance floor, so we decided to sit at the booth and order our drinks first. We talked a little bit, but after a few drinks, I was ready to dance. I pulled Harley by the hand, and we danced until the slow music came on. He was a wonderful slow dancer, just like he said. We had such a wonderful time; we talked and laughed until it was time for us to leave.

After we dropped his cousin off, he asked me if I would like to go somewhere we could be alone; instead of, going to his sister's house. I agreed to this, and we went to an extravagant hotel. I had never spent a night in a hotel, so I was more than excited. The hotel and the room were beautiful. In the pleasantry of the moment, we seated ourselves on the bed, talked for a while, looked into each other's eyes, and then we kissed. We attempted to have sex, but nothing happened; so, we just laid there as I reassured him that it was okay.

Unfortunately, we didn't stay long because we didn't want to worry Inez. I believed he either had a little too much to drink and was a little bothered by what didn't occur. We stayed at the hotel for half of the night, so it was still dark when we arrived at Inez's house. Harley stayed with me at Inez's house until morning; then he left to go to work.

"We are going to figure out where you are going to stay," he said before he left.

"Okay," I replied, and he placed a kiss on my lips.

Later, arrangements were made for me to stay with Harley's brother James, and his wife, Rose. I knew Mr. James and Ms. Rose through my parents who had known them for years. They were old enough to be my grandparents. I really didn't have any money, and I couldn't go back to my job because of Jazz. They understood this and were open to me staying with them for a while. In residing there, I took notice that Mr. James having an eye for me when he was intoxicated; therefore, I knew, sooner than later, I had to vacate before something happened. I had to sleep with one eye open. Ms. Rose knew this as well and she confirmed it. I was in awe that she knew this.

"You're going to have to leave because he's gonna come after you. Don't worry; I don't blame you. He's like that when he's drunk," she told me.

"Yes ma'am," I said in awe.

"Through pride and presumption come nothing but strife, but [skillful and godly] wisdom is with those who welcome [well-advised] counsel." (Proverbs 13;10 AMP)

Amid, I had to call Jazz so that I could get my clothes from his mother's house because I didn't have any.

"Jazz, I need to get my clothes," I told him.

"Okay. Where are you staying?" he asked.

"I'm not telling you, Jazz," I said plainly.

He seemed to be in a good mood, but I wasn't taking any chances.

"Well, I'm sorry for everything, Pat," he apologized with sorrow.

"I accept your apology," I told him.

"You could come tomorrow and get your things," he told me.

"Okay," I replied before we ended the call.

Meanwhile, Harley had been visiting me, and we were spending a lot of time together after he got off from work. I must say that he was very thoughtful towards me.

For example, once, he took the time to ask me, "Do you need anything?"

"Yes, you could bring me some beer and some cigarettes," I said nicely.

When he arrived, we talked about various things. I asked him about his wife, even though they were separated.

"I'm not going back," he told me.

"Maybe that will change," I said.

He would ask me about my dreams, and how I envisioned myself in the future.

"Where do you see yourself in the near future?" he asked while folding his arms.

"The first thing I want to do is go back to school to get my G.E.D. and continue my education to be a teacher or businesswoman," I answered.

It seems as though he was very impressed with my answers.

Harley was becoming more engrossed and involved in me than I was with him, but I just wanted to have fun. I knew I had to relinquish this relationship for sure. Don't get me wrong, he was a nice man, but I didn't want to take advantage of his feelings for me and lead him on.

The next day, the time came for me to go to Jazz's house, after Ms. Rose and I returned some cans for money to buy some beer. Thereafter, I walked to Mrs. Smith's house, and when I arrived there, Jazz answered the door. His disposition was very cordial.

"I wanna talk to you, Pat," he said quickly. "I mean...Pat, can I talk to you for a minute?"

"Jazz, what about?" I asked irritably.

"So, Pat you're telling me that there's no more me and you?" he asked with this look: one eye opened and one eye half closed he did this look when he wanted clarity on something).

"Yes, there is no more 'me and you'. I'm tired of the fighting," I told him.

"Well, I told you I'm sorry," he exclaimed.

"You told me that the last time, and the last time, and so on," I said.

"You know I love you, Pat," he said softly.

"It's time for me to go," I said while getting ready to leave.

"Well, I'll walk with you- I insist," he spoke.

"Okay," I said

Though I allowed him to walk with me, I didn't want him to walk with me the entire way to Ms. Rose's house. While we walked, he was still trying to talk me into being his girlfriend, and I told him no.

We halted at the street corner, and I said, "You can go ahead and leave. I can walk the rest of the way by myself," in a dismissive tone.

He started looking over his shoulder ensuring that no one was around in the broad daylight. Seeing that no one was around, he yanked me by my arm and pulled out a knife pointing it at my side, so I could feel it. Frantically, I became aware of myself and what was going on. I knew I had to think fast.

"I want you to come back with me, and if you scream, I'm going to kill you," he threatened while gritting his teeth.

"J-Jazz...the-there is no need for all of that," I stuttered in fear. "I tell you what let me get my pocketbook that I left there. I need my I.D., social security card, and my birth certificate."

"Pat, you're pulling my leg. You think I'm stupid?" he spat while raising is eyebrow.

"No, I don't. Let me prove it to you," I told him.

I leaned over and kissed him passionately. Those old feelings were starting to come back, but this was the only way I could outsmart him.

"Now, tell me. Does that seem like I am lying about coming back?" I asked him. I began to tell him I missed him like he had missed me. "Just wait here. I promise I will be back."

"Okay," he said trusting me to walk the rest of the way to Ms. Rose's and to return.

When I left, I went on to Mr. James and Ms. Rose's home, and I didn't return to Jazz. However, I knew that I was going to be calling him sooner than later because the love I had for him was still there. This whole situation was complicated, and I didn't want to hurt anyone. I thought about how Harley was becoming more attached to me; I didn't want that to happen. I felt he needed to reconcile with his wife and revive their marriage.

"Thou shalt not commit adultery." (Exodus 20:14 KJV)

"Whoever commits adultery with a woman lacks understanding; He who destroys his own soul." (Proverbs 6:32 NKJV)

One night, Mr. James was sitting in the living room staring at me while I was asleep. He came near me as if he were going to kiss me, and the next thing I knew my quick reflexes kicked him. I nearly pushed his drunk tail on the floor. That was my cue; I knew it was time for me to vacate. The next day, I called Jazz and told him the reason that I didn't come straight back to him was because things were complicated.

"Pat, I know where you are. I been watching you. If you don't come home, I'm going to start some trouble," he threatened.

I got nervous because I didn't intend to bring trouble to Mr. James and Ms. Rose's way. When I told them about my departure, they tried to convince me to stay. They weren't afraid of Jazz, but I told them that it was best for me to leave. I didn't want any dealings with police or anyone getting hurt. That evening, Jazz was waiting outside across the street for me. I had already apologized to Harley and told him that I had to go. I thanked them all for opening their home to me, and it was very much appreciated. I ran downstairs in hopes that no one would follow me leaving with Jazz.

He told me that he had found a place for us to stay. I told him that since we were back together, he needed to change.

"I am. I started going to church and reading the Bible," he told me.

Later, he introduced me to some people from the church that were apostolic. Jazz had been residing with someone from the church, and he told them about me; therefore, they had a separate place for me to stay as well because we weren't married. We went to church that Sunday, so Jazz and I were able to see each other then. We weren't exposed to television- only radio, and had to be in bed at a certain time.

"Pat, I don't know how much more of this I can stand. It is hard not being able to touch you or kiss you," he said while gritting his teeth and forcing a smile.

"I know the feeling," I responded.

"Pat, are you ready to ditch this place? I feel like we're in a cult," he said irritably.

"I feel the same way. Let's go," I told him.

After church, we left and never looked back. Now, I understood my mother's disdain concerning the holiness church. You couldn't wear pants or make up, and they were strict in a lot of ways. They did everything that their Pastor told them to. The atmosphere was strange to us; the people in the church were tightly knitted together.

When we left the church, we went to his mother's home. Upon our arrival, Jazz's sister, Linda, who lived in Bronx, N.Y. had called and said we could come and live with her. I had already met Linda at one of the gatherings their mom had. She was genuinely nice and friendly. Moreover, we called Linda to let her know we were on our way that evening. We rode the train and walked five long blocks to reach the five- story apartment building where she lived on the first floor. Finally, I was incredibly happy to be in more stable environment, especially since fall and winter were on the way.

"**Thank you, Lord**," we said as we looked towards the sky.

Jazz read the Bible every now and then, even when he didn't understand it. I didn't read it at all.

"In everything give thanks; for this is the will of God in Christ Jesus for you." (1 Thess. 5:18 NKJV)

"Oh, give thanks to the Lord, for He is good! for His mercy endures forever." (Psalm 107:1 NKJV)

Linda was overwhelmed with joy that we decided to come live with her and her one-year-old son.

"I needed you all as much as you needed me," she told us.

She didn't like the idea of living alone; therefore, it worked out perfectly. While we were living there, we pulled our own weight. I received food stamps and a monthly check, but only because I signed up for school. Jazz also contributed by selling marijuana; of course, and doing any odd jobs he could obtain. Even if he had to go out to collect cans, he did it. Linda and I would collect cans as well. When Jazz did work actual jobs, he worked hard. There wasn't anything lazy about him.

Although Jazz and I moved to the Bronx, we still had our ups and downs. I had become bored and reluctant in staying home most of the time. There was nothing to do but sit in front of the building drinking and smoking on the weekends. I wanted to party, but Jazz didn't like going out because he didn't like to dance. At times, we did go out to the movies and hang out in Manhattan if we had extra money, but this wasn't enough for me. I wanted to explore and have a good time. My first experience was on my 18th birthday with Harley and I wanted the opportunity to experience it again; my opportunity came.

There was a young lady I met in the building; whose sister's boyfriend owned a club. Soon I became acquainted with the two sisters, Niecy and Sandra. They had invited Jazz and I to go out with them. At first Jazz said no, but he changed his mind because he didn't want me to go out by myself. We all got dressed up and went out in the pursuit of having fun. Jazz danced for a little while, but I stayed on the dance floor. I was dancing, drinking, and smoking my *Newport* cigarettes; I had a good time. The next weekend they were going out again, and I wanted to go, but Jazz didn't.

"We're going to have to convince Jazz to let me go," I told Niecy.

She didn't think it was going to be a problem in asking him since he went out with us the first time, and it wasn't. Jazz said that he trusted her with me; therefore, I was able to go. Because he went last time, he was secure in knowing where the place was located; he really surprised me.

I was preparing to get dressed as time drew near, and Jazz started drinking. He was being manipulative and getting upset with me for no reason, but I didn't pay him any attention. He was playing mind games, but my mind was made up: I was going.

At the club, I saw a friend that I knew from a couple of years ago who was eighteen when I was fifteen. I was so happy to see him, and we danced together all night. Mike was short, about my height, dark skinned and handsome with a beautiful smile, broad shoulders, and a six pack. I remember that he always dressed GQ style. The last time I saw Mike, I was in foster care in Queens. He had come to visit me on the same day that Jazz surprised me by showing up without notice. That day, we saw Jazz from afar as he approached us. My foster sister and I had to outwit him by portraying that Mike had come to see her. Mike caught on very quickly and played along. Boy, I was sweating bullets at the mere fact that Jazz popped up on me. Jazz kissed me and eyed Mike up and down suspiciously. Before my foster sister took Mike by his arm, she greeted Jazz, and swiftly walked off.

Did he ever find out who Mike was to me? Of course not. Mike was just a friend that I hadn't seen in a while, but Jazz would have never understood this. I would have had a fight on my hands especially after that incident with lying David at the train station.

While we were on the dance floor together, I noticed that Mike was still a wonderful dancer. That night, I didn't have to buy any drinks; it was all on him. Boy, I had myself a ball, and my friends loved him. He was such a gentleman. I hated for the night to end. He wanted me to go with him, but I told him maybe next time. The girls were trying to talk me into going since they knew that Jazz was abusive towards me. Anyone who could put a fresh smile on my face without any stress, they were okay with them. It felt good to be pampered by a young man that I liked and was attracted to.

For that one night, I felt beautiful and special, and we just had to see each other again. Before we left, we discussed our plans for our next date at the club, but Mike wanted to spend some time with me at a bed and breakfast. "*This sounds interesting,*" I said while smiling to myself. It was set to take place in two weeks because Jazz would not permit me to go out every weekend; it would be too obvious. Therefore, we agreed, and our plans were set. I had to think of a lie to tell Jazz.

> *"For the lips of an immoral woman drip honey (like a honeycomb) And her speech is smoother than oil. But in the end she is bitter like (the extract of) wormwood. Sharp as a two edged-sword. Her feet go down to death; Her steps take hold of Sheol (the nether world, the place of the dead), "So that she does not think (seriously)about her path of life; Her ways are aimless and unstable; you cannot know where her path leads." (Proverbs 5:3-6 AMP)*

Through the week, Jazz and I did our share of cooking and cleaning around the house. When I cooked, Jazz and Linda enjoyed my cooking, and I could tell by the overwhelming number of compliments I received. Jazz told me that he only wanted to eat my cooking because he didn't like his sister's, and I didn't eat it either. Jazz, himself, was also a great cook, and his favorite dish was chili.

Jazz also enjoyed cleaning around the house. He would move furniture around to deep clean. He cleaned like this because the Bronx had rats like crazy, and they used no discretion at all. They would walk right beside you in broad day light (over exaggeration). Rat infestations were so common. Once he caught a rat in a cage in the apartment; you know that was scary. A decision had to be made between the rat staying or us fleeing the apartment; of course, we chose to stay. Jazz clogged up the hole that the rat was entering, and we had no more problems after that. Though they weren't inside, we would hear them in the alley fighting the cats during the night; these rats were just as big as cats. Well, enough about the Rat infestation; just thinking about it is creepy.

The second weekend had arrived, so my friends and I were excited. My friends and I had been secretly discussing it all week. The time came to ask Jazz if it was okay for me to go out.

"Yes," he nodded.

"Would you like to go with us?" I asked with my fingers crossed behind my back.

"No, I don't" he replied, "I just wanted to see what you were going to do."

"I guessed I passed the test," I responded.

After his approval, I told my friends that I could go. Later that evening, before I left, Jazz was high while drinking beer, and he was acting like a sour puss. Lately, Jazz and I had been quarreling; we just weren't getting along. I pondered on how once upon a time, I tried and wanted to get pregnant by him. We tried and tried, but nothing happened: it wasn't meant to be. I wanted someone to love me in return because I was feeling unloved. I was tired of him and my life. I believed that a baby would've made a difference although I was afraid of mistreating the child because of how I was treated. **So, I cried out multiple times to the Lord, praying that he would not allow me to follow my mother's example.**

Anyway, I couldn't wait to get to the club to see Mike. When we arrived, about a half hour later, he entered the door *"With his fine-looking self,"* I thought to myself. We greeted each other. Then, Mike and I sat, talked, drank, and danced. We had an awesome time together. While the night was young, we left and went to the bed and breakfast that night as planned. We all know *what happened* that night at the bed and breakfast. The time with him was delightful, but after that night, I would never see him again. I couldn't take a chance of doing this again, but, for one night, I just wanted to be loved: no fussing, no fighting... just love. Thereafter, we met my friends back at the club before it closed. We did everything as planned, and I went home with only memories.

As I stated previously, Jazz and I weren't getting along, so I wanted to escape; therefore, I found a way. I told Jazz that I wanted to visit my girlfriend, Lisa, and her mother, who lived in the projects of Bedford-Stuyvesant, another part of Brooklyn. Lisa's mother and my mom were best friends, and we stayed with this family for a while after my mom decided that she didn't want to reside in California any longer; so, Lisa and I were close. I had already introduced Jazz and Lisa, so he knew who I was referring to. We discussed it for a few days, and he finally approved, saying that he didn't mind me going because Lisa was cool.

When I arrived there, Lisa's mom, Ms. Carolyn opened the door. They were a little happy to see me. I wondered what was going on with them and if everything was okay after Jazz left.

"Yes and no," they answered.

"What is it?" I asked with a puzzled look.

"The last time you were here you were bragging about your new boyfriend," Ms. Carolyn said.

"Bragging? I don't recall that happening, but I do remember being very excited. I thought yawl were happy for me too especially in knowing how my mom was," I explained to them with furrowed eyebrows.

When she responded, she barely made any eye contact with me. I became a little suspicious of that.

"I'm sorry that you both felt that way, and that was not my intentions at all. I apologize. Could you both please forgive me?" I asked.

"Yes," they replied. Then, we embraced each other.

Lisa always had plans for us to do something, and I loved hanging out with her. She wasn't much of a drinker, but she did smoke weed every now and then. She once knew plenty of Rastafarians that sold weed, and we would visit those houses and the smoke would hit as soon as you walked in. You could get high off the secondhand smoke alone. The houses were filled with big bags of weed and money. Until she told me, I was unaware that she didn't hang in those houses anymore. Apparently, those places were raided and busted by the police. This was the end of smoking for her.

Lisa took me to a bar where she knew people, so we hung out there, played pool, and listened to music while I drank my beer and smoked my cigarettes. She introduced me as her sister. We'd been calling each other this since we were six years old because our mothers were so close.

She introduced me to this one young man who was interested in me. He kept picking with me and complimenting me, and I was digging him a little too. He was a little older than I was, but that didn't matter; I liked the attention he was giving me. He resembled the singer, Rick James. He was tall, dark, handsome, and well-groomed, wearing very memorable, shiny shoes. Becoming more acquainted with one another, we laughed, talked, and the next thing I knew, I was going home with him. I had a careless attitude. Lisa attempted to persuade me to stay with her, but she couldn't: I had a made-up mind. I told her that I was safe, and if something were to happened, she knew where I was and had his address.

We left the bar and went to his home, a nice, big studio that was clean and well organized. It was a Wednesday night, and I didn't leave until Friday morning. On Thursday, I called Lisa to let her know I was okay. Mr. Tall, Dark and Handsome and I ate breakfast and went back to bed. We slept in and had sex, sex, and more sex. He was on vacation from his job and in an odd way, so was I. I had such a great time with him. When it was time for me to go, he wanted me to stay longer.

"No," I shook my head, "I can't. I have to go."

"Am I ever going to see you again?" he asked.

"You already know the answer to that," I responded honestly.

Friday morning, I called Lisa to let her know that I was on my way to her home. Mr. Tall, Dark, and Handsome put me in a cab, and I was on my way to Lisa's house. I didn't get out of the cab at Lisa's projects; instead, I got out and walked the rest of the way. I had an inkling that Jazz was lurking around; therefore, I couldn't take a chance in him seeing me getting out of a cab in front of Lisa's projects. As I continued to walk up the street, I saw two guys from a distance walking my way. The closer I got, I began to recognize who they were: Jazz and his tall, baby brother, K. I knew it; my instincts never fail me. I prepared my lie.

"Hey Pat, why are you out here? You are supposed to be with Lisa," he said.

"Well, I just came from another friend's house visiting with them for a little while," I said dishonestly.

"K and I thought that we would surprise you since you were coming home today, so you wouldn't have to ride on the train by yourself," he told me.

"Oh, that was nice," I said with a closed lip, fake smile.

"*Oh, h---l. I'm in trouble,*" I thought to myself. Jazz was being too nice. We stopped at Lisa's house to pick up my belongings, and then we walked to the train station. It was a long train ride to the Bronx which we spent laughing and joking. They also told me about how their week went, and Jazz asked me about mine.

"It was fine. Lisa and I just hung out and caught up with each other," I told him.

I knew something was fishy: I felt it in my gut. He was too calm, and I knew him like a book. When we got home, Jazz called me into Linda's back room.

"Come here. I need to show you something," he said plainly from the back room.

Before I knew it, his fists were connecting with my body, as he fussed at me saying that he didn't believe what I told him earlier. After Jazz finished and walked out the room, K walked up to me and punched me in my nose

"That's for my brother," he spat and walked out the room.

I was seeing stars; I thought he had broken my nose. I couldn't catch my breath or gather my thoughts. I cried and I cried. I knew, then, that I had to leave for good and never return.

"The name of the LORD is a strong tower; the righteous runs to it and is safe and set on high [far above evil]." (Proverbs 18:10 AMP)

Chapter 28
A Plan of Escape

After the physical abuse, their plan was to not leave me alone because they didn't know what I would try to do. Irate as I was, they had every reason to be concerned and suspicious. Jazz knew from experience that I was very clever and a good actress as well. I knew how to play the game and come out a winner; therefore, I acted as if everything was okay.

Fortunately, some of the tenants in Linda's building threw a cookout in front of the apartment building, and we were invited to the party. "*Perfect,*" I said to myself. Jazz and K were asked to go to the store, so they left me with a neighbor whom I was helping to organize things. Honey, I saw this as a way of escape. The opportunity had presented itself, and I took the chance to escape. When no one was looking, I ran so fast like my life depended on it. This time, I was *never* going back. All I could do was reflect on the fact that he allowed *his brother* to hit me. Any remaining love that I had for him was *gone*. I was so hurt on the inside, as I cried uncontrollably while I was waiting to catch a train. I knew exactly where I was going. I was heading towards my destination. Coney Island, where I had never brought Jazz to visit; therefore, he would never find me. Staying with my mom was out of the question because he knew where my mom stayed, so that would be his first place to search.

"For by these He has bestowed on us His precious and magnificent promises [of inexpressible value], so that by them you may escape from the immoral freedom that is in the world because of disreputable desire, and become sharers of the divine nature." (2 Peter 1:4 AMP)

Coney Island was also where Lisa's aunt and uncle lived. I got to a pay phone told Lisa where I was headed and what had happened.

She said, "Go ahead there. I'll call my aunt and let her know you're on your way."

Lisa knew it would be okay since her aunt and uncle loved me like family. When I arrived there, everyone recognized me and was excited to see me because they hadn't seen me in years. They had two sons: one that was two years older than me and one that was one year younger than me. I remembered a few years back that they both had a crush on me, and now that I've grown, I looked more appealing to them. I told Lisa's aunt about what happened with Jazz, and she said I could stay for a while until things quiet down. I offered to help her around the house during my stay, and she accepted. Because I left my things at Linda's, she gave me some clothes for me to wear in the meantime. I felt so happy and liberated to be out of the presence of someone that didn't love me but only wanted to beat and control me.

"You will show me the path of life; In Your presence is fullness of joy; In Your right hand there are pleasures forevermore." (Psalms 16:11 AMP)

I had a very interesting stay with Lisa's aunt and uncle. Things were going fine until the older son tried to play me, but quite frankly, I knew his game very well. Simultaneously, I kept a close eye on the younger son. He was shy and appeared to be hostile at times, but he wasn't mean, in fact, he was nice and liked me. He reminded me of Michael Jackson with his big afro, so I guess that's why I was attracted to him. He made sure that I received anything that I wanted. Meanwhile, the older one was too cocky when it came to me, so I had to burst his bubble. He thought he was going to slither his way into my panties, and let's just say I outsmarted him. On the other hand, the younger brother and me things almost escalated but his parents came home early interrupting us from kissing and that was all that happened. I knew soon it was time for me to leave because things were getting a little complicated. I stayed there for almost a month, and I didn't want to overstay my welcome nor did I want to cause conflict between two brothers. Therefore, I left.

Thereafter, I went to visit my mother. They were still staying in a hotel but not for long since they had found an apartment. I ended up staying there at the hotel, with my mom, stepfather, my brothers, Daniel and Willie, and my nephew, Tory. Denise stayed there too but was sometimes with her boyfriend, Speed. Speed and I didn't know each other well during this time; he was new to the family.

> *"Do not merely look out for your own personal interests, but also for the interests of others. (Philippians 2:4 AMP)"*

My mom did tell me that Jazz had stopped by several times looking for me, but they didn't have a clue to where I was before. I was cleared from Jazz.

While I stayed with my family, I met this young man who stayed at the hotel as well. Every time Greg spotted me, he would chase after me and talk to me. Valentine's Day was coming, so he asked me if he could take me out on a date, but I told him that I would think about it. A couple of weeks had passed, and he was still very determined to get to know me. Greg would catch me going to the store for my mother and would quickly walk up to me to converse. *"That was very thoughtful of him,"* I smiled to myself at his kindness.

However, one evening I saw him arguing with a pretty young lady who looked like she was on something (meaning she looked to be high or intoxicated). I continued to walk past them minding my business feeling his stare on me. A couple of days later, I bumped into him and told him that I saw him conversing with the woman.

"Was that your girlfriend?" I asked curiously.

"Once upon a time. She doesn't want us to break up, but I told her it was over," he replied.

Greg was *very smooth* with his words, and he had a beautiful smile that graced his brownskin. He was tall and very well groomed and flashy always wearing gold rings on just about every finger, a few gold chains, and I can't forget his single gold tooth.

> *"Smooth talk from an evil heart is like glaze on cracked pottery." (Proverbs 26:23 MB)*

"Could I take you out for Valentine's Day?" he asked me for the second time, and I finally answered with a yes.

For our date, I had to decide on what I was going to wear, so I called Niecy, my friend who lived in the same apartment building as Jazz and me in the Bronx. I knew that she still had some clothes of mine, and she told me that I could come and pick them up.

"Hey, have you seen Jazz around lately?" I asked with nervous curiosity.

"Not much, so it's safe for you to come around," she told me.

With that, I went and picked up what was left of my clothes. All of them were dressy apparel, so this was great for the date. I don't remember exactly what I wore on the date, but I was dressed up and my hair was done.

The night was young, but cold. Greg took me to a fancy Chinese restaurant where the food was a little costly, but that didn't matter to Greg. The credit card that he had wasn't his. A woman's name was on the card, so to pay for the meal, I had to portray the woman and sign for it. I was worried that we would get in trouble for this, but he assured me that won't happened.

> *"He who walks in integrity and with moral character walks securely, but he who takes a crooked way will be discovered and punished." (Proverbs 10:9 AMP)*

We talked and enjoyed our meal and the tasty Chinese tea. We were talking about me staying with him for a few days, and I told him that it beats staying with my mom. Then, he asked me a ridiculous question.

"Would you sell your body for money if I ask you too?" he blurted out.

"NO! And don't you ever ask me that again," I shouted. There wasn't that much love in the world for me to sell my body.

"Calm down. I just wanted to see how you would respond," he claimed as we got up from the table.

"Now you know..." I said while looking up to his tall stature.

As he stood and looked down at me, he responded, "You are a feisty little something, but I like it." We sat back down and realized we hadn't paid for the meal.

Finally, he asked for the check, and I handed the waiter the credit card. He went off and came back, so I could sign for it. Afterwards, we walked out of the restaurant and made plans for me to stay with him for a few days.

"He who walks in integrity and with moral character walks securely, but he who takes a crooked way will be discovered and punished." (Proverbs 10:9 AMP)

I told my mom that I was leaving for a few days, so she gave me her address and new telephone number. She didn't want me to leave, but I told her that it was too crowded and said my goodbyes. Greg and I got into a cab that took us where he lived, and I don't quite remember where it was, but it was a nice area. He shared a nice house with his cousin who was barely there. Greg lived in the basement which was fully furnished and had a bedroom. All we did was eat and have sex. I was very promiscuous every few hours; we were like jack rabbits. We couldn't keep our hands off each other. However, in the middle of the week, I began experiencing a pain, below my stomach, like none other. I was walking doubled over in pain when we heard a knock at the door.

"Hushh, don't say anything," Greg whispered. It was his ex-girlfriend.

Greg told her to leave, but she repeatedly pounded the door and screamed for him to let her in. He let her in, but I didn't mind; I was in so much pain. Even, she had noticed my sickness. She placed her hand over my forehead for a fever.

"Yeah, you have a fever. You need to go to the hospital. I don't blame you for anything-I blame him," she said.

They called 911, and the ambulance came to take me to the hospital. I was crying terribly. They took some tests which confirmed that I had VD (as gonorrhea or syphilis). Gonorrhea and syphilis were terrible to receive through sexual intercourse, but luckily it could be treated. The doctor stated that I had to stay in the hospital for a week. I had a severe case: my tubes were infected. Being in the hospital gave me time to think about my next move. Of course, I wasn't going back to Greg because he was the one who transmitted gonorrhea to me. "*Nasty*," was all I could think. I realized that he was messing around with his ex-girlfriend, and there wasn't any telling of what she was doing. I was glad that I had an alternative to go elsewhere.

> "*Therefore see that you walk carefully [living life with honor, purpose, and courage; shunning those who tolerate and enable evil], not as the unwise, but as wise [sensible, intelligent, discerning people],* [16] [a] *making the very most of your time [on earth, recognizing and taking advantage of each opportunity and using it with wisdom and diligence], because the days are [filled with] evil.*" (Ephesians 5:15-16 AMP)

Chapter 29
Pain, Forgiveness, and Closure

Once the doctor released me, I called my mom and asked her if I could come over, and she said yes. She now lived on Kosciosko Street in Brooklyn, New York. The hospital was nice enough to give me bus fare, thus I began my journey. When I arrived at my mother's building, the area wasn't all that great, but they had a place to live, and I was happy for them. They lived on the fourth floor of the apartment building. When I knocked on the door, my siblings answered, and they were happy to see me. My mom, especially, was happy to see me. She offered me the invitation to come back home since I didn't have anywhere to stay; plus, she missed me, and she knew I wasn't going back to Jazz.

"Trisha, you were the only one that I could talk to, and you made me laugh," she confessed.

After staying there for a few days, I asked my mother if I could cook a Sunday meal and bake a pineapple cake for them which I knew she loved. I told her she needed to see what I learned from being in the kitchen with her all those years.

"Okay. What would you like to cook for us?" she asked me.

"I want to prepare cabbage, barbecue ribs, baked macaroni and cheese, potato salad, cornbread, and pineapple cake," I said with confidence.

I was very excited that I would have an opportunity to show my cooking and baking skills. Meanwhile, I was spending time with my family. My brothers were going to school, and Denise and Speed stayed with us from time to time. My parents loved Speed. It was as if he was a part of the family, and he helped raise my sister's baby, Tory, as his own. I could see that he was a nice guy, but I noticed that he tried to steer clear of me when I came around as if I had done something to offend him. One day, I was curious to know what I did to offend him, so I asked him.

"You weren't popular around here, especially with your sister. They barely talked about you, so I'm just now finding out about you," he stated truthfully, "I don't know what happened. Your sister had said a lot of bad things about you after the first time I met you. I guess with hopes that I wouldn't like you, and I can see why: you're a pretty girl."

He continued to explain what my sister had told him about me. I never thought that she felt that way about me. She had never showed it.

"I love your sister, and I would never do that to her," he stated.

"That's my sister, and I wouldn't do that to her either. Speed, you're not even my type," I said and we started laughing.

I told him thank you and that I appreciated him for sharing that with me although I knew it was difficult for him to do so. From that day forward, Speed began to get to know me for himself and apologized for Denise's insecurities. He made me promise not to discuss this with my sister, and of course, I kept my promise, especially because of his honesty. Moving forward, we treated each other like family.

"To slander or abuse no one, to be kind and conciliatory and gentle, showing unqualified consideration and courtesy toward everyone." (Titus 3:2 AMP)

Early Sunday morning, I awakened to cook breakfast, getting that out of the way, so there should be no reason for disturbance while I was in the kitchen to prepare dinner. I preferred peace and quiet, especially while baking a cake which I made first to get it out of the way. I started on the rest of the food all at the same time. I was very time conscious when cooking. My gift in timing was immaculate especially in preparing food because I wanted everything to be hot. The aroma of the food permeated the apartment. I was so anxious for my family to taste what I prepared. I was finished in no time, and my mom couldn't believe it. She was so sure that I under cooked something because I finished everything. Everything I prepared was hot except for the potato salad; of course.

It was time for the moment of truth: the taste test. I served my mom her plate. Her face was a sight to see, and she was amazed. There was no ridicule, criticism, and no talking; just chewing. The meat was falling off the bone and the macaroni and cheese, one of her favorite dishes was outstanding. Even, my stepfather was surprised.

"You did a great job. You almost cooked just as good as me," she complimented.

Furthermore, she loved the pineapple cake which was so moist compared to hers. It was nice to see a smile on my mom's face. We were getting along much better.

Moreover, Denise told me that our mom had gotten saved and was baptized the year before. This explained why she called me into the bathroom, one morning, to speak to me privately. She sat on the side of the tub as I stood in front to face her.

"Patricia, there's something I want to say to you. Out of all my children, no matter how I treated you, you never talked back to me," She exclaimed. She carried on and said,

> "HONOR [*esteem, value as precious*] YOUR FATHER AND YOUR MOTHER [*and be respectful to them*]—*this is the first commandment with a promise*— [3] *SO THAT IT MAY BE WELL WITH YOU, AND THAT YOU MAY HAVE A LONG LIFE ON THE EARTH.*" (*Ephesians 6:2-3 AMP*)

"The reason why I treated you like I did was because you reminded me of your biological father, I was jealous that your father loved you more than he loved me. He wanted you and not me, so I took my anger and frustration out on you. Would you please forgive me? I am very sorry that I took you through this," she said, solemnly.

She embraced me and for the very first time...she said that she loved me. I was in disbelief because I didn't expect her to do any of this. I forgave her, but I was still hurt from all those years of torment. To hear her say that she loved me was quite interesting to me. Just maybe she meant it, but deep down inside, I didn't believe her.

> "For if you forgive [a]others their trespasses [their reckless and willful sins], your heavenly Father will also forgive you. 15 But if you do not forgive others [nurturing your hurt and

> *anger with the result that it interferes with your relationship*
> *with God], then your Father will not forgive your trespasses."*
> *(Matthew 6:14-15 AMP)*

Surprisingly, the next day, she was being generous; therefore, I was giddy and gave her the benefit of the doubt. I tried not to sulk in how I truly felt. She wanted me to pick something out of her closet; that was filled with many beautiful things that still had tags on them. It was like a department store; I was excited until I couldn't choose the dress that I desired.

"NO, that dress **would** look good on you," she said. This "no" followed every dress that I picked. She told me that the dresses looked **good** on me; therefore, I **couldn't** have any of them.

"Your body is shaped just like mine at one time," she said.

She ended up choosing the dress that she wanted to give me. Unfortunately, the dress she picked was "too good" for me as well; she didn't want to give me that dress either.

"Well, Mommy, you don't have to give me anything," I shrugged.

"Okay," she said.

Actions do speak way louder than words, and once again, I was hurt by what she said and by her actions. I was her daughter, and she treated me as if I weren't. She said that she'd rather give the dress to my sister because she didn't have a body like hers. I had to give my mom her props; she was truthful about how she felt whether it hurt me or not. More so, she proved my instinct to be correct from the very beginning. As always, I just had to bury it deep like it never happened. I drank every day to numb the pain, and when

I didn't the pain would return. Therefore, drinking was my antidote.

> *"But He was wounded for our transgressions, He was crushed for our wickedness [our sin, our injustice, our wrongdoing]; The punishment [required] for our well-being fell on Him, And by His stripes (wounds) we are healed." (Isaiah 53:5 AMP)*

Throughout, I'd been living with my family for a while now, and it had been great thus far, until one morning, there was a knock at the door. I looked through the peep-hole, and it was Jazz. I assumed that Jazz had forgotten all about me and went on with his life. I wondered how in the world he found me.

"Pat, can we talk?" he asked through the door.

I opened the door and went into the hall to talk. Because the conversation wasn't going his way, I was becoming a little paranoid at the confrontation we were about to engage in. He started getting in my face, and I tried to get away from him, but he kept blocking me. Suddenly, I heard footsteps coming up the hallway stairs: it was Denise and Speed. They came right before Jazz was about to hit me. She moved me out the way, pulled her hand back, hit him, and jumped on his back. Thereafter, she jumped off of him and pulled out a knife, and Speed tried to take the knife from her, but she wouldn't let go of the knife. Her hand ended up getting cut.

"Jazz, don't you ever put your hands on my sister again!" she yelled and threatened.

After we told him to leave, he did just that. Denise wasn't afraid of anyone; male nor female. She could take care of her own, and I was so grateful that she was there. Speed was there to just ensure that Jazz didn't lay a hand on her. Later, we discussed what happened and went to bed.

My mother told me that I was doing the right thing by not going back to Jazz because of the physical abuse. Being with my family, I felt very secure and protected. When I woke up the next morning, my stepfather called me to come look out the window where there was a lot filled with bricks. There was Jazz. I realized that he stayed out there all night. He had arranged the loose bricks to form the words, "*I LOVE YOU, PAT*" in large letters facing our window.

"Oh! My God," I said with my hands over my mouth. I wasn't flattered-not one bit. I thought he was CRAZY!

"What is it about you, Trisha? "You must have some gold *down there* or something!" my stepfather said while laughing and shaking his head.

This was completely embarrassing. A few minutes later, Jazz began shouting out "*PAT, I LOVE YOU,*" waking up the whole building. I felt so humiliated. Everyone else thought it was cute, funny, and they even had empathy for Jazz.

"Anyone who would stay out there all night and build letters must truly love you," my family members said.

"He doesn't love me," I spat. "He allowed his brother to physically hit me, and he is the main one who hits on me too. Then, another brother felt my butt while I was asleep. His brother's excuse was that he was drunk, and he didn't mean it. He did apologize, but enough is enough!" I expressed. I refused to go back.

"Go home or I will call the police for harassment," I angrily shouted out the window to Jazz. I didn't go outside until I was sure that he was gone.

Once he left, I was looking forward to meeting Speed's brothers since Speed and Denise talked to me about them. I told them that I would love to meet his brothers. A few days after the Jazz incident, I was finally introduced to Speed's brothers. They were both handsome, but there was one who was my age and stood out to me. He had such beautiful teeth and a pleasant smile, and he was well-dressed and muscular built with a six pack. He was about my height with beautiful hair that was kept in braids. His name was Pee.

Pee and I began to talk and during our conversation, he asked me out on a date to the movies.

"Sure. When?" I answered Pee.

"When is it convenient for you?" he asked

"How about Friday evening?" I suggested.

"Sure," he agreed.

Unfortunately, Friday, on our way to the train station while walking and laughing hysterically, Jazz approached us. I was truly caught by surprise because it had been a few weeks.

Pee quickly jumped in front of me, but I told him that it was okay and that Jazz wouldn't do anything

"My beef is not with you. I just want to talk and ask Pat something," he told him.

"I see that you have moved on," he said.

"Yes," I said plainly.

"Pat, I got the message. Just remember I will always love you. I wish you all the best," he told me.

"I wish you the same," I told him.

Jazz made PEACE and had closure. Then, he left. Pee and I continued our conversation as if nothing occurred.

"If possible, as far as it depends on you, live at peace with everyone." (Romans 12:18 AMP)

Chapter 30
Death

Pee and I, along with Speed and my sister would hang out as couples and get high. We all would drink, and they would smoke weed. We always kept money to do what we desired to do. But as time went by, I truly began to observe small issues in Pee and I relationship. Sometimes he stayed at his mothers who lived in the Fort Greene Project where I met rap artist, Doug E. Fresh, and he rapped for me. Speed introduce me to him.

Anyway, Pee stayed at this man's apartment, and they were roommates, well that's what Speed and Denise told me. I wouldn't have been suspicious of this if it weren't for the tension and awkwardness between them when they told me they were roommates. I could have asked questions, but I didn't push the issue. Maybe I was afraid of what I would have found out.

During our relationship, we did have good times together. When we stayed at the apartment, his roommate was never home because he was a chef at a classy restaurant. I asked Pee how he ended up staying there, and he told me that his roommate approached him while he was living on the street after getting kicked out by his mom. The man took him in, and he had been staying with him for a while.

I didn't think anything of it. I just thought that the man was very generous in giving him a place to stay.

"The words of his mouth were smoother than butter, but his heart was hostile; His words were softer than oil, yet they were drawn swords." (Psalms 55:21 AMP)

When I met his roommate, he looked like he was old enough to be Pee's father. I noticed his accent; he wasn't from the states. Every time Pee brought me there, he made me breakfast with what the man brought from the restaurant. The food was rich and delicious. Pee liked my cooking, but I loved his cooking as well.

I would stay overnight when his roommate was out of town, and we would have crazy sex. There were times when we would spend the night along with Denise and Speed, at his mom's house. Their mom was a nice, beautiful, and a down to earth young woman who loved her boys. She loved Denise and I just like we were her own daughters.

The frequent stays and visits to my mother's house began to cease as I got closer to Pee and as he began to hit me. I was starting to believe that he was doing more than smoking weed because of his shift in attitude and mood. It was something different about him, and I couldn't pinpoint it.

My stepfather had helped Speed get a job and, later, Pee as well. Pee's didn't last long because he wanted to keep up with me and control my every move. When we got into an argument over something stupid, he would say terrible things to tear me down. One time, he pushed me into the room, beat me with a belt like I was his child, and dared me to scream. I was always frightened of what he was going to do next. He would cry express that he was sorry, and he would never do it again but that was a lie. Especially, when the weekend came around, he'd forget about his apology to me.

> *"A lying tongue hates those it wounds and crushes, and a flattering mouth works ruin." (Proverbs 26:28 AMP)*

I noticed that he was losing weight, so I became more and more suspicious, and observed him closely. My instincts had never failed me. He was sneakily doing **Crack Cocaine**, and I was losing weight also because my nerves were so torn up from being around him. One day, I tried to sneak away before it was time for him to come home from work. I took the back streets in hopes of him not spotting me if he tried to search for me. I didn't have any money, so I had to walk and run, but I couldn't do neither fast enough because he found me. I looked up the next block or street; he was walking parallel with me from street to street. He called out my name, and I ran as fast as I could, but he ran faster than me. He caught up with me, grabbed me, and pushed me against a brick wall.

"Oh, you're trying to leave me?" he gritted through his teeth.

"I was going to my mother's house. I haven't seen her in a while," I told him.

"Oh really, without telling me?" he yelled.

He took his hand and smacked me so hard, I didn't see it coming. My mouth opened so wide; I couldn't catch my breath and there wasn't enough oxygen going to my brain. His smack was so powerful that it cracked the inside of my bottom tooth. I pushed him away and tried to stop him, but I couldn't. No one was around to see or observe what was happening. There weren't any cars going by, and it was broad daylight.

"You're not going anywhere! If I can't have you no one else can have you," he said. *Oh my God! I've met another crazy one,"* I said to myself.

Everyone could see a change in my persona; I was miserable. When I contacted my mother to see how she was doing, she curiously asked me if Pee was hitting me.

"You don't have to answer, but I know that's why you haven't come to visit me," she said.

"Mommy, I'm okay," I said lying.

I knew Denise had been telling my mom a little of what she knew, but my sister wasn't sure because it never happened in front of her.

With Pee, it was one incident after another. For instance, it was a struggle getting to my mother's birthday gathering because Pee picked a petty little argument right before. He thought manipulation would stop me from going, but it didn't stop me. Besides, she was expecting me to come, so I was going with or without him. Despite his antics, I was able to visit my mom on her birthday, September 9th.

My mom and I discussed her plans of what she wanted to prepare for Thanksgiving. She came up with a nice dinner spread, and she wanted me to help her. I agreed to help her and was so excited about the preparatory fixings for Thanksgiving Day. It was wonderful being with my family on my mom's birthday. We all had such a good time. I didn't want to leave, but I knew I had to go. My mom wanted me to stay because she knew what was going on. She knew I had a busted lip, though it healed before her birthday. I didn't want my mother to see my disposition, but she made it clear that I'm always welcome to come back home.

> *"For there is nothing hidden that will not become evident, nor anything secret that will not be known and come out into the open." (Luke 8:17 AMP)*

It became evident that Pee, and his baby brother, Tee, were in competition with one another, especially when it came to the ladies. I knew this because of the smack talk that they exchanged. I admit that they were both handsome. I've always been very observant and a good listener when I needed to be. They even talked about who was going to have me as their girlfriend. Tee had told me that I picked the wrong one, and it made me wonder why he would say that. He didn't take back what he said either.

As I previously stated, I really became more curious, and I watched more closely than usual. I found out Pee had children, and he had violently hit the mother of his children as well, so she had a restraining order against him. Unfortunately, Denise and Speed knew this, and they didn't tell me until later. I continued to notice Pee's steady weight loss. He swore to me that he wasn't smoking crack, but no matter what he said, I didn't believe him; all he did was lie. A good thing about him was that he wasn't stingy when it came to money. He always shared, and he made sure I ate. I never knew how he got the money, but he did take care of me and his habit- the habit he kept lying about.

> *"You are of your father the devil, and it is your will to practice the desires [which are characteristic] of your father. He was a murderer from the beginning, and does not stand in the truth because there is no truth in him. When he lies, he*

speaks what is natural to him, for he is a liar and the father of lies and half-truths." (John 8:44 AMP)

Unfortunately, it was the unnecessary arguments that I didn't like. I felt this way: if you want to go out and do what you want to do, just go ahead and do it. Don't make up stuff to create an argument to do what you had planned to do, anyway, without me. Why in the heck do guys do that? I thought to my myself. Epiphany, they do this because they think that they will never get caught. Then, they think they are getting over on us, but all along, we know what they are doing. It's just stupid. In addition, he had threatened me that if I tried to leave, he would kill me.

"Be sober [well balanced and self-disciplined], be alert and cautious at all times. That enemy of yours, the devil, prowls around like a roaring lion [fiercely hungry], seeking someone to devour." (1 Peter 5:8 AMP)

Moreover, he would bring up my sister to tear me down by stating how she wasn't scared of anyone, and she was strong. Oh, he was just comparing us, and the fool sounded like he liked Denise for himself. I was astonished at what was being said. Thinking to myself, *"Is he really serious? Tearing me down to build her up?"* I couldn't believe what I was hearing, but I knew sooner or later I had to find a way of escape from this crazy n----!

I realized that my nerves were getting worse. I looked down at my foot, and it seemed to be deformed. While I was walking, my shoe came off, and I couldn't put it back on my foot because it was twisted. It was the strangest thing that I had ever experience in my life. Pee's craziness had me so twisted-literally. My sister was walking with me, but she couldn't see what I saw happening to my foot. I relaxed and **I cried out, "Oh Jesus, please! help me to walk!"** and **suddenly, my feet straightened up.** In my inner being, I said, *"Thank you Lord."*

I told my sister while we were walking, "I believe Pee is cheating on me."

> *"I have seen his [willful] ways, but I will heal him ; I will lead him [also] and will restore comfort to him and to those who mourn for him,* [19] *As I create the* [a] *praise of his lips, Peace, peace, to him who is far away [both Jew and Gentile] and to him who is near!' says the LORD; "And I will heal him [making his lips blossom anew with thankful praise]."(Isaiah 57:18-19 AMP)*

"What's making you think that?" she asked.

"I just know, and I'm tired of his mind games. This is what guys do when they are cheating or doing something that they don't normally do. I'm not stupid, but he thinks I am." I said. Denise just looked at me not knowing what to say.

Due to the stress, my clothes began to fit very loosely on me. People would have thought that I was doing drugs by how skinny I had become. I wasn't myself; my countenance gave it away. Pretending wasn't one of my strong suits.

"You don't look happy. What's wrong with you?" Pee said looking at me.

"I am not happy," I told him.

"What would make you happy?" he asked.

I wanted to say *"Getting away from you,"* because at that moment I envisioned myself getting away from him. It was pure agony to endure sexual contact when I didn't want to. If I didn't, he would start accusing me of being with someone else. I just wanted to keep the peace, so I had to pretend to like it. At the same time, I couldn't wait for it to be over. Misery loves company, and his misery had nothing to do with me. I was just there. I thought several times in the process of this abusive relationship, *"Why me?"* He said that he loved me, but he just wanted to beat me. I kept my mother's extended welcome to come back home in the back of mind. I had to get away from him.

Amidst the drama with Pee, it was on November 8, 1986 when I received the horrible news that my mom had died in her sleep. Words cannot express how I felt on that day. We, my sister, our boyfriends, and I, rushed to the apartment quickly. I was still numb from hearing the news because I couldn't fathom the reality that she was gone. When we arrived, our mother was lying in the bed as I touched her cold body. My stepfather tried to explain what had happened as tears were flowing from his eyes. We were all heartbroken and in despair, as we cried uncontrollably. We couldn't believe she was gone. I had just talked to her last month about Thanksgiving Day, going over the arrangements which she was excited about. In my distress, I repeatedly stated in my mind, *"I didn't leave you when you asked me not to leave you. Mommy, you're gone forever."* I was so angry because we were finally getting along. I was crying and asking her, "Why did you leave me so soon?"

> *"We are confident, I say, and willing rather to be absent from the body, and to be present with the Lord."* (2 Corinthians 5:8 AMP)

Our relatives, far and near were contacted about her passing. We hadn't seen our relatives in years, due to my mother's desire to be as far away from them as possible.

She hadn't spoken to her older sister, Aunt Lola in years because she couldn't stand her, and I'm not sure why. My mom would call her a witch; in so many words, it's complicated to explain why she called her this.

I remembered my mother, and I had gone to visit her primary care doctor a few years back. She spotted Aunt Lola and tried to hide from her, so she looked at me and whispered, "Don't you say anything." Then, when my aunt left the doctor's office, my mother told me, "I didn't want her to see me like this- overweight." There was a rivalry between them, and one rivalry between my Aunt Nellie, my stepfather's sister, and my mom. Aunt Nellie and Aunt Lola were two women that my mom stayed away from. She even forbade us to mention their names while around her.

Despite their differences, Aunt Nellie and Aunt Lola oversaw the funeral arrangements. Although my mom's insurance policy had elapsed, Aunt Lola called my uncles who notified my biological father of what happened and the funeral arrangements. She paid for the funeral, along with Aunt Nellie who tried selling some of my mom's clothes to make up the difference. She raised money towards the funeral and money for us as well. They were stunned at the many tagged and beautiful clothes she had, though she couldn't wear them. She had three furs, various coats, pants and blouses, dresses and suits, shoes, and more; whatever, we could think of, she had it. Her apparel was costly and nothing but the best. Aunt Nellie tried to persuade me to take some of the clothes that were left.

"No thank you. My mom wouldn't want me to have them," I said sadly.

"Child, you better take some of those clothes. Your mother is gone, and she can't take them with her as you could see, so please take some clothes," she pushed.

"For we have brought nothing into the world, so [it is clear that] we cannot take anything out of it, either. "(1 Timothy 6:7 AMP)

In obedience, I took a few pieces but that was it.

Many family members were calling and stopping by to pay their respects. I visited my family's home every day to greet any family members or friends that had stopped by. Additionally, I wanted to be there for my stepfather.

Within that week, there was a knock at the door and standing there were my two uncles and my biological father, Charlie Crawford Slaughter. I was happy to see him, but my sister wasn't because we hadn't seen him in years. It was very awkward, and we didn't really know what to say to him. On the other hand, we were real comfortable talking to our uncles. During their visit, we learned interesting information; my biological father never divorced my mom.

"It was until death do us part. I would not have had it any other way," he told us. He made that clear.

"I say to you, whoever divorces his wife, except for sexual immorality, and marries another woman commits adultery[a]." (Matthew 19:9 AMP)

After that statement, we just stared at him. What could we have said? We were unaware of the entire situation. He even added that he had loved her, and that he always would, despite her leaving him. Everyone was astonished at his words, but I knew the real story; I knew what he said in the past and how he felt about her.

The funeral was the next day, so we prepared for it, and there weren't any additional things to be done because Aunt Lola had taken care of everything. We would be forever grateful for what she had done for us.

The next morning, we rose for the funeral, and there were two family cars waiting for us: her immediate family and siblings. Those who were not immediate members had followed us. Once we arrived, the ushers escorted us in the sanctuary to be seated. As I glanced at her body in the casket, our mother looked as if she were asleep with not a care in the world. My Aunt Lola discovered that her death while sleeping was due to an accidental overdose of prescription drugs mixed with alcohol reportedly caused her heart to burst open. This mixture was not a shock to me because she tended to take her medication while drinking alcohol, so that she could sleep. My stepfather had repeatedly express to her the dangers of doing so. But she would ignore the knowledge, proceed sneakily and do it anyway. If I had caught her, I would have reminded her, but who am I? I was only her child. She would say, "Shhhhh don't say nothing. I am only taking *one* pill. That's not going to hurt." I would look at her sadly.

One time, when I was fifteen, she gave me a half of a volume and sent me downtown. I was so high; I felt like I was on cloud ninety-nine. It was so hard to stay awake on the bus that I had to hold on to things to keep consciousness. To this day, I don't know how I accomplished the task and returned home safely, but I do know that I prayed like crazy.

"LORD, KEEP ME IN MY RIGHT MIND. HELP ME TO GET BACK HOME SO I CAN SLEEP THIS OFF...never again," I pleaded.

"Thou wilt keep him in perfect peace, whose mind is stayed on thee: because he trusteth in thee." (Isaiah 26:3 KJV)

I was so nauseous, and I felt like vomiting. That tiny half of a pill was too powerful for me. When I arrived back home, I told my mom what had happened and all she did was laugh.

"Never again, because it was scary," I assured her.

To this day, I don't remember why she had given it to me in the first place.

Getting back to the funeral, it was very melancholy and somber. I believe it was hard for all of us, but I took it the hardest because I was so angry that she left me in the middle of us building an actual relationship. ***"How could she leave," I thought.***

"We are confident, I say, and willing rather to be absent from the body, and to be present with the Lord." (2 Corinthians 5:8 AMP)

After the funeral, my biological father and uncles invited Denise and I to come with them. She declined their invitation, but I said I would give it some thought. They told me that they were leaving in the morning, and if I wanted to move to South Carolina it would be no problem. I began to think about who was going to take care of my brothers and sisters.

Therefore, I called their hotel and said, "I've decided to stay in New York."

"You could always call if you change your mind," my dad told me.

"Okay, Dad," I said.

Tell me, what do you do after the funeral when everyone has gone their separate ways? I realized, once again, that life still goes on with pain and memories that reside within us.

> *"Now we do not want you to be uninformed, believers, about those who are asleep [in death], so that you will not grieve [for them] as the others do who have no hope [beyond this present life]." (1 Thessalonians 4:13AMP)*

Chapter 31
Taking a Stand

As soon as Pee and I returned home, he started a stupid trivial argument. Maybe he didn't know what to say in my time grief, so he decided to say something stupid.

"Pee, I'm tired, and you're being insensitive." I said in a stressful tone.

My mother had died for heaven sakes, and he was being uncompassionate and inconsiderate of my feelings right now. I knew that he had a motive, and so did I at this point.

During the week of the funeral, I had to go to the doctor because I was having pain in and on the outside of my vagina-like blisters. I sat in a tub of warm water, and that didn't help; therefore, it was time to visit the emergency room.

"You bet not have nothing," Pee blurted out obnoxiously as we waited in the emergency room.

He had *the audacity* to say that to *me*. It was obvious that he was insinuating that I was cheating on him.

"Are you crazy? When would I have the time? Negro, you are the guilty one. You're the one who does the disappearing acts. Do not let *me* find out that you are cheating. I can show you better than I could tell you." I exclaimed.

Eventually, the doctor came up with my results and said to me, "Ms. Crawford you have Chlamydia, a disease transmitted through sexual contact. If someone had multiple partners, this is how it is transmitted, and you have a tube infection as well. In addition, your tubes are damaged, and you may not be able to have any children."

That news shattered my heart. I was prescribed medication, as well as Pee. Now what could he say? Nothing. What he didn't know was that I was having dreams that he was cheating on me right under my nose. I began to become more aware and suspicious that something was going on which would explain why he continued visiting this man's house from time to time; maybe he was bringing girls there.

In the dream, Pee was cheating with his brother, Tee's girlfriend. She slept in the next bedroom while Tee went to work at night. One night, I woke up and caught Pee out of the bed. Her door was cracked open with the television on, so I peeped inside. I had startled her, and I rushed in and looked around.

"Is something wrong?" she asked

"No. I'm just looking for Pee," I told her while peeking my head around her.

She told me that she hadn't seen him, but I felt that she was lying; I had missed it. They were finished before I got there. I saw him pass by her room, but I didn't say anything. I kept quiet because I was making plans to get away. When I asked him about it later, he wanted to act innocent.

"For there is nothing hidden that will not become, nor anything secret that will not be known and come out into the open." (Luke 8:17 AMP)

Later, I ask Denise and Speed some questions about the man that Pee sometimes stayed with.

"Oh, we thought you knew, the man is gay, and he pays Pee to have anal sex with him," they said confusingly not looking at me directly.

They knew that I had no idea... "*lies, lies, and more lies.*" *I though furiously.*

> *"If a man lies [intimately] with a male as if he were a woman, both men have committed a detestable (perverse, unnatural) act; they shall most certainly be put to death; their blood is on them." (Leviticus 20:13 AMP)*

> *"Then the LORD said to Cain, "Where is Abel your brother?" And he [lied and] said, "I do not know. Am I my brother's keeper?" (Genesis 4:9 AMP)*

I was sick to my stomach and heartbroken because everybody knew, except me. The danger that I was apart of. My own sister didn't tell me. I knew then it was time for me to go far, far away from all of them. There was nothing left for me in New York since my mother was gone. I was ready to go to the south.

I always knew as a little girl that I didn't belong in New York City. I would tell my mom, "When I grow up, I'm leaving here. I'm going to the south." This desire never changed because as I grew in age, I constantly reminded her of this.

"Why do you want to leave?" she would asked me.

"I belong in the south," I told her knowingly

"Don't leave me," she pleaded.

"I won't leave you," I would tell her, but now that she's gone, I could leave. She would have been the only reason that I stayed if she were still alive.

> *"The steps of a [good and righteous] man is directed and established by the LORD,*
>
> *And He delights in his way [and blesses his path]." (Psalm 37:23 AMP)*

While Pee was at work, I decided to follow through with my plan. I didn't take any clothes and I didn't have any money; I just ran down the steps and down a block or two and called out for a taxi. I jumped into the cab and gave the driver the address to Uncle William and Aunt Odessa's home which was the projects across town. During the funeral, my aunt told me that I could come anytime I wanted to; therefore, I accepted her invitation by going. When the driver drove up and stopped, I had to tell a lie; I told him that I didn't have any money and that my aunt and my uncle would pay him. I walked to the entrance of the door, ran up the stairs, got to a window, and watched the cab driver drive away. He already knew I wasn't coming back. I was sweating and scared that the cab driver would come looking for me.

When I knocked on the door, Aunt Odessa was home but was just about to leave. She was going across the way, in walking distance, to see her mother because she was her caretaker. Nonetheless, she was so happy to see me. As we were walking over, I told her everything.

"Could I stay with you and Uncle William until I can get in touch with my father to see if his offer still stands?" I asked her, and she was okay with it but she had to get the approval from my Uncle William as well.

She was such a sweetheart and so was Uncle William. Uncle William was my stepfather's brother, the brother that my mother was once in love with. I was looking forward to seeing him, and he had finally come home from work.

"Hey there, Trish," he smiled while giving me a hug.

"Come in the back. I need to talk to you," she told him.

I was so nervous awaiting the outcome of their conversation. I heard them coming back as my stomach was turning.

"Yes, you can stay as long as you pull your weight around here and help your Aunt Odessa," he told me.

"Yes sir," I nodded.

I was so overjoyed and hugged them both. In addition, I just knew it was time for me to leave New York City, and this was the first step.

"For I know the thoughts and plans that I have for you, says the Lord, thoughts and plans for welfare and peace and not for evil, to give you hope in your final outcome." (Jeremiah 29:11 AMP)

I knew that this would be the one place where Pee would not find me.

Therefore, I settled in at their home, and that evening, being sure he was home from work, we called my biological father, and he answered.

"Hey Dad, does your offer still stand?" I asked eagerly on the phone.

"Yes, I will send you the money to take the bus down here," he told me. Aunt Odessa proceeded to give him the address where he could send the money. I was so anxious and excited to leave New York.

"Do not be anxious or worried about anything, but in everything [every circumstance and situation] by prayer and petition with thanksgiving, continue to make your [specific] requests known to God." (Philippians 4:6 AMP)

Every other day, Aunt Odessa and I would check the mailbox, but there wasn't anything there.

"Don't fret. Let's give him the benefit of the doubt and wait a few more days," she told me.

"Okay Auntie," I said as we smiled at each other.

So, we checked a week later, but there was still nothing. We decided to call him that evening and he said,

"I don't know what could have happened, so I'll make arrangements to send it through *Western Union* on Friday when I get paid."

Friday arrived, and we checked Western Union, but nothing had arrived. I became very distraught. Why the lying, the running around, and the deceit? We were furious, so he tried to call him, but he didn't answer. I cried my eyes out.

"Don't worry, Trisha," Aunt Odessa consoled me. "We'll figure something out."

Most of all, I was so embarrassed. I began to see what my mother was talking about when it came to my father: he was a habitual liar and a coward.

*"Lying lips are extremely disgusting to the L*ORD*, but those who deal faithfully are His delight." (Proverbs 12:22 AMP)*

"But as for the cowards and unbelieving and abominable [who are devoid of character and personal integrity and practice or tolerate immorality], and murderers, and sorcerers [with intoxicating drugs], and idolaters and occultists [who practice and teach false religions], and all the liars [who knowingly deceive and twist truth], their part will be in the lake that blazes with fire and brimstone, which is the second death." (Revelation 21:8 AMP)

Out of the blue, in the middle of December, my spirits were lifted when Aunt Nellie informed us that she was visiting Lewiston, North Carolina over the Christmas holiday. Instantly, I asked her could I go with her, and it was nothing but a word; she said "sure" with a smile. With overwhelming excitement, I called my sister and let her know that I was going out of town. Denise sounded like she was happy for me. Afterall, I didn't feel needed because I wasn't included in any of her plans to take care of our brothers. She and Speed had everything figured out.

"I need a break from New York, Denise" I told her.

She tried to talk me out of it, but it didn't work; my mind was made up. I told her I would call when I return. Well, I thought she would be happy for me.

Later that evening, there was a knock at the door of my aunt and uncle's apartment. On the other side, it was Pee, asking if he could speak to me when my uncle answered the door.

"Should I go get my gun?" Uncle William asked, already knowing who Pee was.

"No, I will go out and talk to him," I said.

At the same time, I wondered who told him where I was staying. I didn't want to believe that it was my sister, but her and Speed was the only one who knew. So, I walked out the door, into the hall, and there he was.

"I'm sorry," he said repeatedly. "I want you to come home."

"No. It's over! You slept with a man, cheated on me with other women, and gave me an STD [a sexually transmitted disease]! Are you crazy?!"

He began to deny everything, as I turned to walked away.

"You take one more step, and I will shoot you," he threatened while pointing the gun at me. "If I can't have you, no one can."

I turned my back and started walking.

"Pee, you go right on ahead and pull the trigger. Kill me! I have nothing else to live for. My mom just died, so what do I have left. I'd rather die than go with you, so go on ahead and shoot me," I shouted boldly without a blink of the eye or stutter.

Then, I walked away with satisfaction, saying to myself *"This fool ain't crazy."*

"Girl, you're crazy," he said while shaking his head and leaving.

"Pee, I am crazy," I said to myself. I walked in my aunt and uncle's apartment with a smile on my face. I felt a sense of freedom.

"Is everything okay?" My uncle asked.

"Now it is," I smiled.

Now, I had a bone to pick [a conflict; issue] with my sister. She's supposed to be my sister, and she told him where I was after everything that had happened; Unbelievable!

"So, submit to [the authority of] God. Resist the devil [stand firm against him] and he will flee from you." (James 4:7 AMP)

I was so irate. *"How could she do something like this to me?"* I asked myself. There was only one way to find out- to call and ask her why.

"I really didn't want you to go because something was telling me you won't be coming back. I just didn't want you to leave me like you did before. I was scared you might do better where you are going, but I am sorry" Denise said honestly.

"You almost had a dead sister. You were only thinking about yourself and not the welfare of your sister. Remember, I was trying to get away from him and furthermore, you don't need me. You and Speed have everything under control, plus, you should want me to be better and do better," I said.

"You're right, Trisha, and I love you. Again, I am sorry for what I did." She said apologetically.

I just felt that she was being selfish which was nothing new; she was very spoiled. She asked when I was going to leave, and I told her the weekend of Christmas, so she needed to let our brothers know that I was going out of town.

"I'm going to make sure they stay in school, and we are going to keep the apartment," she assured me.

"See there, you already know what to do. You don't need me. I love you all, and I'll talk to you when I get back," I said.

It was nice to know that she was taking over guardian-ship to help our stepfather because of his drinking habit.

Chapter 32
Transitioning By Faith

"What is the benefit, my fellow believers, if someone claims to have faith but has no [good] works [as evidence]? Can that [kind of] faith save him? [No, a mere claim of faith is not sufficient—genuine faith produces good works.]" (James 2:14 AMP)

I was so excited as I prepared to leave, and I couldn't wait to meet a plethora of relatives that I hadn't met before on my stepfather's side of the family.

Aunt Natalie had changed her mind of the day she had plan to leave because she wanted to extend our stay. Instead of Friday, we ended up leaving Thursday morning. Our journey to Lewiston, North Carolina was a little quiet at first. I even slept a bit, then later we engaged in a little conversation. After several hours, we finally arrived at Aunt Thelma's house where I met Uncle Buggar, Aunt Thelma, and Cousin Jackie, who was the baby girl out of the five sisters and two brothers. They welcomed and embraced me like they've known me forever.

Aunt Thelma cooked such a wonderful breakfast, where we talked about how she met my mother and brothers when they were younger. At the same time, I kept looking at myself noticing that my clothes barely fit me, and my hair was all over the place. I had lost so much weight and went from a size five to a size one, and I was smoking cigarette after cigarettes. That's how bad my nerves were from being with that boy, Pee.

"While you're here, we are going to try to help put some meat on your bones," Aunt Thelma chuckled.

"That's fine with me. I love to eat," I said.

"You eat as much as you want," she said cheerfully.

"Yes, ma'am and thank you," I responded gratefully.

Later, I met Cousin Jen and her husband Patrick, Cousin Barb and Cousin Carol. I didn't meet Cousin Connie right away because she lived in another state, but I was going to meet her and her family soon. When meeting everyone, I was so overwhelmed by the love. For some reason, I kept my eye on Cousin Carol because I didn't see her with a husband nor children. She took me riding around with her; showing me the scenery which wasn't much to see since it was the country. I noticed that she loved to laugh just like me; she was funny. Being here, I realized that I didn't want to leave North Carolina and go back to New York; I knew in my heart that I would have died there, if I stayed.

I figured that if Cousin Carol allowed me to live with her and get a job, I could make Lewiston my permanent home, a new start. Just thinking about it made me excited, and I hadn't even asked her yet. Aunt Nellie was planning to leave the day after Christmas, so I had to put my plan into effect and find the perfect time to ask Cousin Carol. Thereafter I did. I asked her if I could live with her. Also, I told her that I would apply for employment to help as well, so I could save and get a place of my own.

"Let me think about it," she said.

"Okay." I replied.

I waited until the night before Christmas to ask her again, and this time she said yes.

When I told Aunt Nellie that I was staying in North Carolina with Cousin Carol, she was absolutely pleased. I can't begin to tell anyone about the overwhelming, exhilarating feeling that I had knowing that I was finally staying where I belonged. I thought that I was supposed to be with my biological father, but I was here with my stepfather's part of the family. It was amazing to me that this was all happening. I called my sister to let her know that her instincts were correct-I wasn't coming back.

"I knew it. I understand. You deserve to be happy too," she said.

"Death and life are in the power of the tongue, and those who love it and indulge it will eat its fruit and bear the consequences of their words." (Proverbs 18:21 AMP)

A tradition on Christmas Day, all the family members would gather at one of the family member's house to celebrate. This Christmas, it was at Cousin Jen's house, where I met my Aunt Bess and her children, Uncle Charlie and his family. I also met Aunt Thelma's other daughters: Barb, Connie, families. I was just surrounded by an abundance of family, and they treated me like I was a part although I wasn't their blood relative. This was the highlight of the evening for me.

After the gifts under the Christmas tree were given out with their names on it, sweet Cousin Carol went back under the tree, got a gift and gave it to me. She was such a giver, and Christmas was her favorite time of the year.

"I always have extra gifts just in case someone came unexpectedly, so they wouldn't be left out," she said kindly.

The wrapped gift was a pair of gloves which was something that I needed. The tears were rolling down my eyes because someone thought about me. This was a memorable moment for me; something I could never forget. I was grateful and I let her know that.

"[As for me] I am poor and needy, yet the Lord takes thought and plans for me. You are my Help and my Deliverer. O my God, do not tarry!" (Psalms 40:17 Amp Classic)

The next day, Aunt Nellie left to return to New Jersey, and I settled into Cousin Carol's single-story, family home which was very nice and cozy. She gave me a tour showing me where my bedroom of three was and the washer and dryer which were in the garage. The nice spacious kitchen was beside the living room. I was so overjoyed! I had my own room! It was amazing. I never had my own room that I could say was mine although its temporal. I could even decorate it.

"We are going to do something about your hair," she said looking at my hair.

My hair was in its natural state, but I always wanted a perm (chemical- hair product used to straighten the hair of black people). My hair was very long, tangled, thick and dirty. I couldn't do anything with it, so she insisted that she did it. I was once in a vulnerable state, and I had let myself go; this wasn't me. I was always dressed to impress, wearing the latest fashions. My shoes always matched what I wore, and my hair was always kept up. I never missed a beat until I became involved in an abusive, reckless relationship. It's so crazy that I allowed it to happen. I promised myself this would be a new start for me. I would be in **no committed relationships, no time soon because I needed to take my time and not rush into anything so soon.**

At the same time, I was so embarrassed by my appearance, and I was ashamed. I had to give Cousin Carol her props; she worked with my hair until it was a masterpiece. My hair was stunning, straight, shining, and long. I looked like a new person. Being that I didn't have many clothes, she had clothes that she could no longer wear and kindly gave them to me. I was so appreciative for what she had done thus far. I couldn't have thanked her enough. Secretly, I would cry while looking at myself in the mirror, wondering how I could have allowed someone to bring me down like that. I was so upset with myself, but I would wipe my tears and say that I couldn't let it bother me; I'm moving on. *My motto was "A new place and a new slate".*

Chapter 33
Learning A New Environment

In my new place, January 10th arrived, and I turned nineteen years old. At this point, I had been in Lewiston for only ten days, and there were some things being uncovered that I had no knowledge of. Cousin Carol had to teach me how to wash clothes in the washing machine. When I needed some clean clothing, I washed them in the tub because I didn't know how to use the washing machine. When she came home from work, I had clothes hanging in the bathroom.

She questioned me and said, "Patricia, why did you wash your clothes in the tub by hand? That's too much work *gurl*! I know *we live in the country, but we are not that country*," in a playful tone while chuckling.

"I was use to washing clothes by hand I didn't know how to use the washing machine and dryer," I said with embarrassment. Oh boy, she chuckled, then she took the time to explain and show me how to use the appliances.

"No need to feel embarrassed. If you don't know, you don't know," she said.

I wasn't use to her type of response. If I had gotten a stain on the sheets from my menstrual cycle which something I couldn't help. My mother would have scolded me. I felt so relieved when she said that. I thought I was going to be in trouble. Instead, she was the opposite of past experiences and what I expected. She was very understanding, and all I could say was thank you to her.

There was another situation where I couldn't sleep in the bedroom. I would try to stay up and sneak into the living room to sleep on the couch, or I would stay up and watch television. I was so afraid to sleep in the bedroom because I had a dream about my mom, and it frightened me. It woke me up. Then, I was scared to close my eyes thinking that she would revisit me. I finally told Cousin Carol after she caught me.

I'll never forget what she said to me: "Your mother is dead. She cannot harm you. She probably just wanted to say something to you. I want you to go back into that room and stand up to whatever is in there. **Pray and call on Jesus.**" She was also a church goer.

> *"Therefore humble yourselves under the mighty hand of God [set aside self-righteous pride], so that He may exalt you [to a place of honor in His service] at the appropriate time, ⁷ casting all your cares [all your anxieties, all your worries, and all your concerns, once and for all] on Him, for He cares about you [with deepest affection, and watches over you very carefully]." (1 Peter 5:6-7 AMP)*

"Okay. I'll give it a try," I said with fear.

> *"For God hath not given us the spirit of fear; but of power, and of love, and of a sound mind." (2 Timothy 1:7 KJV)*

I took her advice, and I went to bed to see what the outcome was going to be; the dream didn't come back.

However, when I shared with Cousin Carol that it was my birthday, she wanted to celebrate my birthday by taking me out to the club with her and her friends. She took me to a club called *LTD*. It was the most extravagant, classy club that was well known; they even had a bodyguard at the door, so no one couldn't go in there acting crazy. It had a big dance floor, with a shiny ball in the ceiling and flashy lights. This was my kind of club. I couldn't stop looking around; I was so fascinated by it. Also, they had a bar and a booth where we could sit and enjoy our drinks.

After moments of us sitting and drinking, the club was packed. Once it was filled to its capacity, the bodyguard turned people away. I'm sure this was because of safety reasons. This was a night I wasn't going to forget. I had truly enjoyed myself. Especially when the men asked me to dance, I felt special. I stayed on the dance floor, and these men didn't know what they got themselves into by dancing with me. I knew all the latest dances, and some I made up along the way.

Amid this, Cousin Carol said, "I forgot to tell you that someone wants to meet you."

"I'm not ready to meet anyone. I just want to be by myself for a while because I just got out of a stressful relationship," I said.

"Well, could you just meet him, so he could stop worrying me to death about meeting you?" she asked me.

"Well, how does he look?" I said curiously.

"Let's just say he is a very nice person," Cousin Carol replied with a tight lip smile.

"Ohhh, it's like that?" I said raised my eyebrows then, we giggled.

"We'll see," I said smiling.

Honestly, my mind was on searching for a job on Monday. I wasn't thinking about meeting or dating anyone; I needed to stay focus.

For the remainder of the night, I danced until closing which was 2:00 a.m. Also, I was a little tipsy. I kept my drinking at a minimum, so I wouldn't be overly intoxicated. When we returned home from leaving the club, we went straight to bed. And I thanked her again, for the wonderful time we had, my hairdo, and the clothes. I was so happy to be in a new environment and meeting new people. I felt refreshed. Meaning, I could go on just a little while longer.

"But those who wait for the LORD [who expect, look for, and hope in Him] Will gain new strength and renew their power; They will lift up their wings [and rise up close to God] like eagles [rising toward the sun]; They will run and not become weary, They will walk and not grow tired." (Isaiah 40:31 AMP)

The next morning, Cousin Carol woke me to ask if I wanted to attend church with her. I really didn't want to go, but she did tell me that she would be asking me from time to time. She wasn't going to make me go, but she was expecting me to go sometimes. I accepted her invitation and went to Mount Olive Baptist Church with her.

Truthfully, I wasn't ready for God, I only went to appease her. Not only did I fall asleep in church, but I was still angry at God. I blamed him for what I went through with my parents, and I blamed him for allowing my mother to die.

"[a]My God, my God, why have You forsaken me? Why are You so far from helping me, and from the words of my groaning?" (Psalms 22:1 AMP)

"How did you like the service?" Cousin Carol asked when it was over.

"It was okay," I shrugged.

Then, we made our way to Aunt Thelma's house to visit her, and we had Sunday dinner with her. She was such an awesome cook. At these dinners, she would prepare two meats, two vegetables, two starches, and a homemade cake: what a Sunday meal! At dinner, she also asked me how church was, but I simply told her that it was fine. I didn't openly talk much unless someone spoke to me, I was more of an observer. I talked more when I drank beer or liquor. Also, I had to feel my way through this family because I didn't know too much about them; therefore, again, I did more observing than anything. Overall, they were all sweet and treated me like family.

I was able to ride around with my Cousin Jackie, Cousin Carol's baby sister, and she showed me around the one light town of Lewiston, North Carolina. She was funny just like Cousin Carol. They were close. I noticed that if Cousin Carol wanted anything done, she called on Cousin Jackie. In fact, everybody called on Jackie, and she didn't mind doing what they needed her to do. She never com-plained-at least not to them. She only complained to me. I remember that she had just gave birth to her baby after I arrived in Lewiston.

Cousin Jackie and I rode around so that I could be familiar with the area. There was a store sitting a quarter mile up the road along with the town's grocery store and a few other small stores. I just loved the country it was a breath of fresh air. It was nice, quiet and not at all equivalent to the hustle and bustle of the crowded streets of the city.

"Did Carol tell you about *Perdue*?" she asked me.

"No," I shook my head.

"It's right down the road from yawl," she informed, "It's a chicken plant. This is where most people work at. Well, you can't work at other places unless you have a college degree."

"Well, that counts me out I don't even have a diploma," I told her.

"Well, you don't have to worry about not getting hired at *Perdue*. They will take anybody who is willing to work," she assured me.

I went on to tell her about how I was planning to get my G.E.D.

"Maybe you could talk to your Cousin Carol. She knows some folks," she shared.

Later, I took Cousin Jackie's advice and talked to Cousin Carol about it.

"How about taking some night classes to get your diploma?" Cousin Carol suggested.

"Okay, I'll give it a try," I said in agreement.

The next week, she introduced me to Mr. Coley, the director of the night school program at *Bertie High School* who would be my transportation as well. He was an older distinguished-looking man with a clean-shaven baldhead, and he also smelled good. After riding with Mr. Coley for a couple of weeks, I was losing the desire to attend night school because I began to feel uncomfortable with Mr. Coley. He would ask many questions about myself which was fine until he asked if I liked older men. He would express how he could take care of me, and I knew he had money, but I declined his *offer*. I told him that I just wanted to go to school and get a job. After this, I began calling out of class and not attending. I just didn't want him to get fresh [flirt] with me.

I expressed to Cousin Carol that I'd rather just take the G.E.D test to see how I'd do. On the overall test, I had to get certain score to receive my G.E.D. The test was divided by academic sections; for example, I could take the reading test now and take science, math, social studies another time, as long as I completed all five. She was to arrange this for me, and she also knew someone that could help me get hired at Perdue.

Chapter 34
My Own Plans

I just wanted to work because I got tired of being at home watching T.V. all day. I still had dreams and plans for myself, and they did not consist of living with my cousin for the rest of my life. Therefore, I wanted to start saving money, so I could have a house of my own.

> *"Trust in and rely confidently on the LORD with all your heart*
> *And do not rely on your own insight or understanding.[6] [a]*
> *In all your ways know and acknowledge and recognize Him,*
> *And He will make your paths straight and smooth [removing*
> *obstacles that block your way] (Proverbs 3:5-6 AMP)*

> *"A man's mind plans his way [as he journeys through life],*
> *But the LORD directs his steps and establishes them."*
> *(Proverbs 16:9 AMP)*

I took the reading test first because I love to read. When the results came back that I passed with a high score, I jumped up and down with excitement and couldn't wait to tell Cousin Carol.

"Oh, you can read?" she said sarcastically.

"Uh, yes," I said while thinking, *"Is she looking down on me because of my upbringing and my downfalls?"*

I was hurt, but I brushed it off and kept it moving. I thought she would have been happy for me. She was a college graduate herself and worked at the Department of Social Services, so why couldn't she be happy that I had passed one test? She certainly had a whole lot more than I had.

> *"Rejoice with those who rejoice [sharing others' joy], and weep with those who weep [sharing others' grief]. (Romans 12:15AMP)*

Later, I found out some very upsetting news while visiting Cousin Jen, another one of Cousin Carol's sisters.

"I know that Carol says hurtful things to you at times," Jen spoke suddenly while we were hanging clothes on the clothes' line.

"Yes, but I usually just brush it off," I responded.

"I know because she says hurtful things to me too," She stated.

I was stunned shaking my head.

"Why the insults or sarcasm?" I asked her.

"I don't know, but she has always done that since we were children," she said shrugging her shoulders.

> *"Live in harmony with one another; do not be haughty [conceited, self-important, exclusive], but associate with humble people [those with a realistic self-view]. Do not overestimate yourself." (Romans 12:16 AMP)*

> *"Set me as a seal upon thine heart, as a seal upon thine arm: for love is strong as death; jealousy is cruel as the grave: the coals thereof are coals of fire, which hath a most vehement flame." (Song of Solomon 8:6 KJV)*

I didn't allow Cousin Carol's negative remarks deter me from the big dreams and plans I had. I just wanted to work, save money, and get out of her house; this was my plan.

Although I wanted to work, going back to school, and attending college were still on the agenda. Meaning, I had a made up mind,and I was determined to go further in life than where I was. I asked Cousin Carol every week if she could speak to her friend about what he could do, so I could apply for a position.

> *"⁹And my God will liberally supply (fill until full) your every need according to His riches in glory in Christ Jesus. (Philippians 4:19 AMP)*

Previously, I mentioned that at club LTD, Cousin Carol wanted me to meet someone who was dying to be introduced to me. Apparently, this someone wasn't a looker (good looking), but he was nice; at least, this is how she made it seem. She asked if I was ready to meet him, and I told her sure because I was bored. I had been here for about nine months; I guess it was time to meet someone while I was waiting to get hired at Perdue.

She was glad that I finally agreed because my family was tired of him pestering them about meeting me or asking them to put in a good word for him. Lee and I met over at my aunt's house where he usually hung out at because Lee and Jackie were good friends. They went to school together. He was about twenty-two years old and worked construction I believe. Cousin Carol was right about him: he wasn't all that good looking, but he was nice. As I continued to speak with him, I really couldn't see him as my boyfriend. I would have to drink a beer or two, or three or four; in order, for him to be attractive to me. However, I was told about the many girls that had broken his heart because they only wanted him for his money. Well, he didn't have to worry about that with me. I just wanted to have a good time and that's it.

"Could I take you out on a date and call you? Maybe visit you some time?" he asked.

"You can take me out and call me, but you can't visit me," I said strongly.

The following weekend he took me out to eat and to a club. He was doing very well for himself; he had a car and his own place. Lee had a nice grain of wavy hair, and he was well groomed and smelled good. After talking with him further, I learned that he was very humorous. After having so many beers, he was beginning to look attractive to me. "*Oh, my God, what I am thinking,*" I said to myself, but he was a gentleman and very sweet. After our date was over, he took me home and asked if he could take me out again, but I had to think about it.

"Please, can I call you?" he begged.

"Sure, so you won't bother anyone else about me," we chuckled.

"I know it's too early to ask for a kiss," he said bashfully.

"Yes, it is," I said with a straight face.

"How about a hug?" he asked.

"Sure," I told him. We then embraced each other in a hug.

"Ooh you're so soft and beautiful with your gorgeous hazel eyed self," he said.

"Thank you," I said with a generous smile.

He talked real country and that's what really made me laugh. Our second date was a little different. After we went to the club, he invited me to his place. I forgot to mention that he wasn't a good dancer at all. Well, he warned me. When we slow danced, he held me so tight; he didn't do that well either. He was still a sweet guy... for someone else. Anyhow, he had invited me to his place of residence.

"As long as we have some beer and my cigarettes," I said.

"No problem, you can have anything you want," he responded.

The more beer I drank the better he began to look. He asked could he kiss me, and I let him.

"Come on and spend the night with me," he whispered in my ear.

"I'll stay for a few hours, but you have to take me home before daylight," I told him.

"Bet," he said, and we both smiled.

He was so happy about that, and I was as drunk as a sailor. We went to his trailer that he owned and the land it was on. I could see that he was doing quite well for himself. I was truly impressed and happy for him because he had his own. This is what made me want my own home even more. If he could do it, so could I.

We started kissing and caressing each other. I was so turned on because it had been awhile since I had been with someone, and it had been a long time for him too.

He pulled back from the kiss and said, "There is something you need to know."

"What is it?" I asked curiously.

"God didn't bless me to be *enormously endowed*," he said anxiously.

"I bet you will be fine," I said.

"Don't say I didn't warn you. I want you... bad," he said.

I rolled my eyes in the back of head and said to myself, "*Oh Lord.*"

We undressed ourselves, and I got under the covers because I was still shy about my body. I told him to turn off the light before he got in the bed. Thereafter, I was ready, and he was ready; he began entering in.

As I felt it, I said to myself "*Why does it keep slipping out? Ooh! Oh my God, it is really, really short!*" he was right. I had to keep my composure and pretend that everything was okay. Also, he didn't take him long to ejaculate.

"I'm sorry. It's been a long time," he said apologetically.

He repeatedly apologized for his performance.

"It's okay," I told him.

I didn't want to hurt his feelings.

What I did know was that this would be the first and last time that this would ever happen again- sober or not. This was about me wanting to be loved and feeling wanted.

> *"For this is the will of God, that you be sanctified [separated and set apart from sin]: that you abstain and back away from sexual immorality; [4] that each of you know how to control his own body in holiness and honor [being available for God's purpose and separated from things profane], [5] not [to be used] in lustful passion, like the Gentiles who do not know God and are ignorant of His will;" (1 Thess. 4:3-5 AMP)*

Having sex with him was the most outrageous thing I had ever experienced; I agreed with him that God just didn't bless him in that area which is why he probably couldn't keep a girlfriend. Shame on those girls because he was a sweet guy, but as for me, I didn't want a boyfriend because of the trauma I left behind in New York City. I wasn't ready to be in a committed relationship. I just wanted to have fun, and in doing so, I made sure that I used protection. My plan was to not bring any children into the world until I was married.

Later that night, we laid there for a little while; then, I was ready for him to take me home although he didn't want me to leave.

"Are we going to see each other again?" he asked me.

"I'm sure that we will in passing, but that's it. I don't want to string you along and use you; that's not me," I said.

"Use me? Girl, you look good, and you're good but I understand." We both laughed. "You're beautiful- inside and out," He said.

"Thank you, but I don't believe that or feel that way," I said.

"Well, you are!" he said then, we embraced each other, but he didn't want to let go.

Lee finally took me home and walked me to my door, giving me a kiss on my cheek. I entered my cousin's home with a smile as he was leaving. That night, I went straight to bed.

The next morning, Cousin Carol asked me if I had a good time, and if I "gave him some."

"Yes," I nodded with a laugh.

I already heard rumors about him, prior to our encounter, so I knew the basis of her questions.

"I don't have to say anything," I told her and we began laughing.

"You must have been tipsy," she said knowingly with a chuckle.

"Yes, I was. It wasn't going to happen any other way," I said as I nodded.

"He started looking good to you?" she laughed.

"You know it, or it wouldn't have happened. I promise you," I replied seriously.

After the talk about Lee, I asked her if she had heard anything from her friend at the *Perdue* plant.

"Oh Trish, yes. He said that you could go and fill out an application. He works at night, so you can go tonight if you like. Jackie will take you."

"Yes!" I said happily.

It was a factory, so I didn't have to dress business conservative to fill out the application; I just needed to look presentable. Jackie took me to fill out the application and brought me back home. When I finally received a call from Perdue Inc, the person explained that I was overqualified.

"Overqualified? What do you mean by that?" I asked in confusion.

"You never worked at a factory before," they told me.

"I could learn," I told them desperately.

"I'm sorry. We don't have anything here for you," they said.

I couldn't believe what I was hearing. When Cousin Carol came home from work, I asked her could she talk to her friend again to see what he could do to get me hired. I just wanted to earn my own money and not depend on anyone else.

"I will ask if he could pull your application and see what he could do for you," she said.

After a couple of weeks, I don't know what he did, but they called me for an interview and hired me on the spot. I was overwhelmed with excitement. The only positions available were during the nightshift, but honey, I didn't care at this point; I had a job.

> *"¹⁰ For even while we were with you, we used to give you this order: if anyone is not willing to work, then he is [a] not to eat, either." (2 Thessalonians 3:10 AMP)*

Chapter 35
Fulfilling Bad Choices

My first night at the chicken plant was very interesting; they took me around the plant while I was wearing my apron, boots, gloves, ear plugs, and hairnet. The area that I was going to be working was very cold so, I had to wear: a warm coat, a couple of pairs of socks, and long johns (similar to leggings) under my jeans; in order, to keep warm. I was told about this ahead of time, and I was glad that I followed the instructions because I didn't like the cold. It was like a freezer in that place.

While I was observing the facility from the catwalk with one of the managers, there were some men watching me; I was the new kid on the block. Everyone was very friendly nodding or waving at me as they passed by. I had the pleasure of meeting three lovely ladies: **Amelia, Evelien** (eve-va-leen), **Angela, Tanya** (and eventually their family and friends as well). In the pages and chapters to come one by one, I will share my adventures and moments with each of them.

I was formally introduced to the supervisor, **Amelia** who would be training me to be a machine operator in the *Weldatron* department. We grabbed the trays of chicken off the conveyor belt and fed the machines, so that the machine could wrap and seal the trays which slid down the ramp.

The receiver at the end would catch it and put it in a dolly to be pushed off to a belt to be packed. I was being trained for both positions because we had to take turns through the night. Amelia informed me that the conveyor belt with the chicken trays may run slow or fast some nights. There would also be times where no chicken would be on the belt, and we had to be fast when the chicken did run. I caught on very quickly because I was always good with my hands, so being speedy wasn't a problem for me. The problem was making sure that the product I was picking up wouldn't go pass me unless they had another machine picking up the same product.

As Amelia trained me, she and I would converse about many things.

"Who is your family, and where are you from?" she asked.

Surprisingly, she knew my family because they were related to Cousin Carol father's side of the family. It was nice to meet someone other than just my female cousins while living down there. She introduced me to Eunice who was going to start training me the next day. I noticed that there was a conveyor belt with many workers and machines that was on the side that was extended across from me. They were doing what I was doing but with different parts of the chicken. We also had maintenance men who were around if the machine broke down. We were to turn on the light if that were to occur. Speaking of maintenance men, there was one maintenance man who was very polite. He spoke to me in passing, so I smiled and spoke back.

If my memory serves me correct, I believed I was hired around September; the temperature was a little warm. I remembered that morning when we got off, I walked out with Amelia, and she offered to take me home since she had to pass where I lived. Amelia became my transportation for a good while. Anyway, there was something that she said to me on that day that stood out.

"You better stop grinning in these men's faces like that," She said in a serious way.

I didn't know what she was talking about. I mean, I had only said hello to whomever said hello to me. I looked at her in a curious way.

"What do you mean by that?" I asked her.

"Some of these men ain't studdin' you like that. Some of them just want to get in your pants. I'm warning you now, be careful," she said.

> *"My son, do not forget my [a] teaching, But let your heart keep my commandments;[2] For length of days and years of life [worth living]And tranquility and prosperity [the wholeness of life's blessings] they will add to you.[3] Do not let mercy and kindness and truth leave you [instead let these qualities define you];Bind them [securely] around your neck, Write them on the tablet of your heart" (Proverbs 3:1-3 AMP)*

"Okay. Thank you for everything and I will see you tonight," I told her.

I was puzzled as to why she would say something like that to me. It never occurred to me that she was looking out for me. In my mind, I thought, *"Who does she think she is? I'm grown, and you can't tell me what to do. That's my business and not yours."* I was just fussing on the inside. I wasn't used to anyone caring about what I did like the way she did. I took it in a negative way because I always received negativity from some women for no reason. However, little did she know, I just wanted someone to love me.

> *"For rebellion is as the sin of witchcraft, and stubbornness is as iniquity and idolatry. Because thou hast rejected the word of the LORD, he hath also rejected thee from being king." (1 Samuel 15:23 KJV)*

Cousin Carol was at work when I came home in the morning, so she called me to see how my night went.

"It was an experience. It was so slow, so it made the night seem longer but other than that I like the job," I told her.

"Good," she replied.

I knew that soon we would be discussing how much my rent would be. Although, I wanted to be able to save money to buy my own home, I didn't have a problem paying for my stay. I was grateful that she opened her home to me - a stranger.

> *"For I was hungry, and ye gave me meat: I was thirsty, and ye gave me drink: I was a stranger, and ye took me in:³⁶ Naked, and ye clothed me: I was sick, and ye visited me: I was in prison, and ye came unto me." (Mathew 25:35-36 KJV)*

The only complaint that I had it was difficult for me to sleep during the day because of the light coming through the window of my bedroom. I took a blanket and draped it over the window until I could buy a shade for the window.

Fortunately, I was glad that Cousin Carol kept beer in the refrigerator because I drunk one before I went to sleep. I drank beer every day and smoked my Newport cigarettes. The one thing that I did like about working at the *Perdue* plant was that smokers could smoke, so there would be no problem with me smoking. Not only did I have a job that

I liked, but I began to gain the weight back; I was now a size three.

Anyway, I woke up around the time that Cousin Carol came back from work and laid there until she prepared dinner. It was a perfect set up; she could cook, and I could eat. She always cooked enough, so I could have seconds. Afterwards, we would talk for a bit; then, I would go back to sleep until the alarm went off for me to prepare for another night of work. Soon after, I would finish getting ready, and Amelia would pick me up.

"How was your day?" she asked with a smile.

"Fine. I had a hard time sleeping," I told her with a sigh.

"You'll get used to it," she exclaimed.

"I don't think I'll ever get used to this," I said while shaking my head.

The graveyard shift wasn't no joke, but I was willing to stick it out. I had to wait two weeks before I got paid. It seemed like it would take forever, and I didn't like that.

When I arrived at work, Eunice was late, but she was only there to train me for a little while. I could see that she didn't talk much. In Weldatron, she was the line leader under the guidance of Amelia. She made sure the line was running properly and that we were doing our jobs. We stayed on our P's and Q's because no one wanted to get written up for not doing their job.

Anyway, the next person I had the pleasure of meeting was **Evelien,** who was introduced to me by Amelia. She helped me with the trays when they came down fast on the conveyor belt. She was quick at what she did, so I watched her closely because I wanted to be the best at what I was trained to do. I never had to worry about falling asleep with Evelien; she could talk. She made me laugh, not just with her country accent, but also because of her personality. Amelia must have also known that I would get a kick out of Evelien [meaning enjoy Evelien]. We talked about many things, including the fact that she was saved [to be a follower and believer of Jesus Christ]. I must say that everyone I met had a sense of humor. This was a plus because I loved to laugh.

After two weeks of working at Perdue, a young lady who I passed by on break to go to the restroom every night, she stopped me and introduced herself to me then we began to conversate.

"Do you like working here so far?" she yelled.

She talked loud and fast because the machines in Weldatron were running and made a lot of noise, hence the reason we wore earplugs.

"Yes," I shouted back.

With no hesitation, she invited me to a lingerie party that she was giving soon and asked me would I be interested in being one of her models. She told me that if I didn't want to model, she still wanted me to come. I didn't have to answer then; she gave me time to think about it.

I was amazed at the fact that she just met me and didn't know anything about me, but she still invited me to her lingerie party.

However, my first two weeks of working were up, and I finally got paid, but it wasn't much. Cousin Carol was lenient towards me since my check was short, so she waited until I had a full paycheck. She didn't ask for much besides giving her a fee every week to pay for my: long-distance phone calls, help buy food, pay for gas, and pay half the water bill, I became very mindful of my usage of certain things. It was nice to have my own money and not have to depend on anyone else for certain things. Since I had money, I could go out if I wanted to.

Amid meeting new girlfriends, there were others that wanted to get acquainted with me as well, meaning the opposite sex. Every night at work, James, one of the maintenance men would stare at me and shake his head. Certain times, he would whisper in my ear and say, "You're beautiful someone would get killed over those gorgeous eyes. D---! You make me nervous," with a grin. I'd just blush and smile back at him. I could surely see his nervousness, especially when he had his eyes on me and not on what he was doing; he'd use the wrong size film to wrap the trays. It was hilarious. Then, he'd blame his actions on my *'beauty, and big, pretty hazel eyes.'*

> *"-but I say to you that everyone who [so much as] looks at a woman with lust for her has already committed adultery with her in his heart." (Matthew 5:28 AMP)*

James wasn't bad looking himself. He was light-skinned with a tall stature and small, muscular build. His pretty, curly hair, long dark eyelashes, and beautiful smile made him something to look at. He asked me out on a date.

"Patricia, would you like to go out with me?" he asked me one night.

"Let me think about it," I said. Walking way, he nodded.

I played hard to get for weeks, and he continued to entreat me to go out with him. No matter what area he was working in Weldatron, his eyes were always on me; I could feel him staring at me. *"I hadn't even giving him some or kissed him, yet I would hate to see how his actions would be then,"* I thought to myself. The real reason that I hadn't given him an answer was because I found out that he was married. He didn't wear his wedding ring, so I asked him about it.

"We've been separated for six months. I'm sorry for not telling you that, but we are talking about getting a divorce," he assured me.

"Hm...okay, well I'll let you know my answer by the end of the week," I told him.

Through the week, I strongly pondered it, and because they were separated, I didn't see any harm in it.

"Marriage is to be held in honor among all [that is, regarded as something of great value], and the marriage bed undefiled [by immorality or by any sexual sin]; for God will judge the sexually immoral and adulterous." (Hebrew 13:4 AMP)

James and I went out on our first date. He looked handsome, and I had on my best attire. During the dinner, we talked and laughed, enjoying each other's company. After the date, he asked could he drop by sometimes. I told him sure. Since he passed Cousin Carol's house on the way home; we lived in the cut. He came to see me one morning, and we ended up having sex; it was okay. Things were going strong between us until I saw him out with a woman who I believed was his wife. He had spotted me too, and he knew by my expression that it was over. I was furious, but I held my peace. My ears couldn't wait to hear his explanation. I saw that he was a liar and a deceiver.

"You are of your father the devil, and it is your will to practice the desires [which are characteristic] of your father. He was

a murderer from the beginning and does not stand in the truth because there is no truth in him. When he lies, he speaks what is natural to him, for he is a liar and the father of lies and half-truths." (John 8:44 AMP)

When we returned to work on that Sunday night, I couldn't bear to look at him. I just wanted to cuss him out and punch him in his face. He didn't come near me at all during the first part of the night. I stayed focus on the job that I was hired for. The last part of night, he tried to grab my arm, but I yanked away from him.

"I'll be by your house in the morning," he spoke in a stern tone.

"Fine!" I said sassily. I couldn't wait to see him, so I could break up with him.

Monday morning, there was a knock at the door, and I let him in. He began to explain to me that his wife was six months pregnant.

"This tells me you're horny and ain't getting none at home so you're preying on women, so you can get off (receive pleasure)," I said bluntly.

"That's cold. It's not like that," he said with a frown. "We were separated, but we decided to work it out."

"When were you going to tell me?" I said with my arms crossed. "I hope you know this is it no more me and you," I spoke while motioning my fingers back and forth between us.

He tried to talk me out of it, but I stood my ground.

"Nope. Let's just be friends and only friends. Keep working it out with your wife," I said sternly.

> *"Therefore, what God has united and joined together, man must not separate [by divorce]." (Mark 10:9 AMP)*

Thereafter, James would give me pitiful looks at work, or he would talk to other women with clear intentions to make me jealous, but it didn't work. "*He'll be alright,*" I said to myself. Unbeknownst to him, when I'm through with someone, **I am through**. There is no coming back. Whether it's a boyfriend, friend, or associate; no matter the title, there is no coming back or working it out. Once you hurt me-that's it. No one will have the option of hurting me a second time. That was my motto at this point.

Chapter 36
It shoulda' Been Me

The plan was for me to be married by twenty-five, no children until then, and to own a house and car. I was certain that I could move up the ladder [be successful] if I put in the time. I would go back to school, get my G.E.D, and further my education.

> *"Commit your works to the LORD [submit and trust them to Him], And your plans will succeed [if you respond to His will and guidance]." (Proverbs 16:3 AMP)*

> *"But first and most importantly seek (aim at, strive after) His kingdom and His righteousness [His way of doing and being right—the attitude and character of God], and all these things will be given to you also." (Matthew 6:33 AMP)*

In the meantime, I needed to start saving money to visit New York. Amelia told me that I could save money by allowing Perdue to subtract it from my check. I thought about how I wanted to see my sister and brothers and go shopping while I was there, so I took Amelia's advice.

Christmas weekend was near, so I wanted to go out. Cousin Carol didn't want to go out, but there were some sisters who lived next door: Jennifer, Bernadette, and Popeye. They were known around the neighborhood because of their beauty. I had already been introduced to them; Cousin Carol called to ask if they were going out. They were going to a club called the *Coliseum* and said that I was welcomed to come along with them, and we would be riding with someone.

"I would love to go," I told them.

At 11:00 p.m., I was ready and excited to go. They picked me up, and we were on our way. In the car it was me, Jennifer, Bernadette, and one of their boyfriends, who was driving. Once we arrived, we paid the fee and entered. Popeye worked the bar that was in front where we sat and had drinks. The dancing area was in the far back, and it was nice and spacious. All I needed was a couple of beers, and then I was ready to dance. After dancing for a bit alone, I sat back down and had a few drinks.

After a while, someone asked me to dance. At first, we were one of the only dancers on the floor, but then it quickly became crowded. Many of the people in the crowd were jovial and friendly, but I kept my eyes on my ride because I kept getting this strange feeling that something wasn't right. Jennifer told me she would be back and said don't worry my other sister is still here.

"Okay," I told her before she left, but I still had that feeling that something wasn't right.

"The heart of the discerning acquires knowledge, for the ears of the wise seek it out." (Proverbs 18:15 NIV)

Due to my skepticism, I began to watch how much I had to drink. I kept on enjoying myself with the young man who I was dancing with. He was nice looking. Apparently, he knew Jennifer, Popeye, and Bernadette as well. We talked with each other at the bar, and he was nice enough to buy me a beer.

While we were talking Popeye came up to me and said, "My sisters had to rush and leave with Bernadette's boyfriend. I'm not going home, so you'll be okay getting home right?" Here I was-stranded; they were not reliable people. I was so sick to my stomach because I knew something terrible was going to occur.

While standing there, Popeye recognized the young man I was with as Tony.

"Tony, could you drive Patricia home?" she asked him.

"No problem," he said, and she proceeded to give him directions. I had no other choice but to ride with him.

On the ride home, Tony and I were playing and talking smack to each other.

"I can take care of myself," I told him playfully.

"Oh, you can humm," he said while glancing his eyes from me to the road.

"Yes, I can," I said with a smile.

Looking around, I began to realize that he was taking me down a dirt path, off the road we were on. He had locked all the doors and my stomach dropped to my feet. I began to feel fear overtaking me.

"Why did you turn this way? This is not the way," I asked in a concerned panic.

"But you said you can take care of yourself with a perfect stranger. I just got out of jail, and I haven't had none in a long time," he spoke eager tone.

He forcefully laid my chair back and quickly laid on top of me with his lips puckered. I began to think and **PRAY, "LORD, show me what to do and say," I said to myself.**

"You don't want to do this. I could have a disease-I could have AIDS or something." I said when I pushed him back.

He sat back in his chair and thought about what I said.

"What about giving me head?" he said.

Inwardly, I became nauseated when he said that.

"No! That ain't going to work either. How about I use my hand to jerk you off, then will you take me home?" I suggested as I almost gagged.

"Yes," he responded.

Jerking him off was very quick; the disgusting mess was all over my hand. To ensure that he takes me home, I told him that maybe we could go out next weekend, and he liked that idea. I was just irate with myself for being so naive and believing that these n----- down here were any different from the ones in New York. Now I knew that *this is what Amelia meant, but I had to find out the hard way.*

In my head, I called him every name but a child of God. Finally, he took me home, and I had played his narrow behind the whole time. I couldn't wait to get in the house.

"I'll see you next weekend," I told him with a phony smile.

When I entered my home and closed the door, I looked out the door window and whispered "**Lord**, I thank you for showing me what to do and say. It kept me from getting **RAPED.**" All I thought about was that *I should have been raped* because of my immature thinking, but; instead, I was released. This taught me a valuable lesson: **be cautious and**

don't be so naïve, especially in a new state. *Danger lurks everywhere; same evil, different people.*

> *"O wretched man that I am! who shall deliver me from the body of this death? I thank God through Jesus Christ our Lord. So then with the mind I myself serve the law of God; but with the flesh the law of sin." (Romans 7:24-25 KJV)*

> *"Do not be far from me, for trouble is near; And there is no one to help." (Psalm 22:11 AMP)*

> *"No temptation [regardless of its source] has overtaken or enticed you that is not common to human experience [nor is any temptation unusual or beyond human resistance]; but God is faithful [to His word—He is compassionate and trustworthy], and He will not let you be tempted beyond your ability [to resist], but along with the temptation He [has in the past and is now and] will [always] provide the way out as well, so that you will be able to endure it [without yielding, and will overcome temptation with joy]." (1 Corinthians 10:13 AMP)*

The next morning, Cousin Carol asked me how everything went, and I told her every detail that happened that night.

"I know that n---- isn't t crazy enough to come back here. But remember, you may have sounded mighty convincing in the portrayal that you truly wanted to get to know him," she told me.

When we visited her mom, Aunt Thelma, they had a high time laughing at me especially at how I handled the situation.

Of course, I didn't look at everyone as being evil but when Toni returned that weekend, I was paranoid because he was evil.

"If you don't get away from my door, I'm going to call the police," I threatened when he returned.

I really thought that he wasn't going to show up - crazy fool. He tried to say something before he left, but I didn't want to hear anything he had to say.

"Leave and don't you ever come back," I told him and that was the end of that.

"The thief comes only in order to steal and kill and destroy. I came that they may have and enjoy life, and have it in abundance [to the full, till it overflows]." (John 10:10 AMP)

Cousin Carol wasn't at home when he showed up at the door; she was out of town for the weekend. When she arrived home that Sunday, I told her that he came. She was out done, and she laughed some more. It was funny but not in the moment that it had occurred.

After that, it was a while before I went to a club again. The *Coliseum* was far from my mind.

Chapter 37
Going through life motions

My plans for my twentieth birthday was eliminated by the 5-6 feet of snow that covered Lewiston grounds, and how sick I felt. My body was aching like crazy; the snow and freezing temperatures added to that. Because my plans were destroyed by this; therefore, I just stayed home and rested. There was no other choice. Cousin Carol took very good care of me, so I could get better. I just hated getting sick because it takes a complete toll on my body. As a child there was always something wrong with me. I had pain in my stomach mostly, but my mother always thought that I was pretending. She believed that I complained to seek attention, but that wasn't true. It was really something wrong with me. After following Cousin Carol's instructions, I became well in a few days just in time to go to work because the roads were cleared up. And now, that I was feeling better, I went back to drinking my cold beer. It was good and refreshing.

> *"Heal me, O LORD, and I will be healed; Save me and I will be saved for You are my praise." (Jeremiah 17:14 AMP)*

Amid, I daydreamed about my family; I was feeling a little homesick. So, I'd call my sister just wondering how everything was coming along. I wanted her to know that

I missed and loved them. Her unknowingly, I decided to make plans to visit them in the summer.

As I continued to work, I enjoyed meeting new people. On a norm, I kept to myself unless I was spoken to. Like I said previously, I was more of an observer not much of a conversationalist unless I was drinking. This was the life of a Capricorn; we are very laid back, and loyal, but don't cross us because you'll have something on your hands. Formerly in my life, I was very big on the zodiac signs, horoscopes and sometimes psychics when it came to my everyday life. Once, a lady read my palm, and I was amazed by it. Sometimes the things that I read or heard were true. If I saw a newspaper, that was the first thing I wanted to read and then the comics. It was a weekly routine when I was living in New York, and it was the same here. I would say to myself, "*I'm never mess with a Pisces, Gemini or Scorpio.*" I had my reasons for each of them. We were all into horoscopes, but I felt like I was addicted. The first thing individuals asked others in cordial conversations: what sign are you? This was funny because zodiac signs made a difference to others before entering into a relationship. I have seen people turn down others because of their sign.

> "*When you enter the land that* GOD, *your God is giving you, don't take on the abominable ways of life of the nations there. Don't you dare sacrifice your son or daughter in the fire. Don't practice divination, sorcery, fortunetelling, witchery, casting spells, holding séances, or channeling with the dead. People who do these things are an abomination to* GOD. *It's because of just such abominable practices that* GOD, *your God, is driving these nations out before you.*[13-14] *Be completely loyal to* GOD, *your God. These nations that you're about to run out of the country consort with sorcerers*

and witches. But not you. GOD, your God, forbids it."
(Deuteronomy 18:10-14 MSG)

"Blessed [fortunate, prosperous, and favored by God] is the man who does not walk in the counsel of the wicked [following their advice and example],Nor stand in the path of sinners, Nor sit [down to rest] in the seat of scoffers (ridiculers).[2] But his delight is in the law of the LORD, And on His law [His precepts and teachings] he [habitually] meditates day and night.[3] And he will be like a tree firmly planted [and fed] by streams of water ,Which yields its fruit in its season; Its leaf does not wither; And in whatever he does, he prospers [and comes to maturity]." (Psalm 1:1-3 AMP)

Remember Angela, my coworker that invited me to her lingerie party around December? Well, the party was in March, and she told me that if I didn't have a way to get there, she would pick me up.

"Yeah, I'm going to most likely need a ride," I told her when we talked.

"No problem, I'll pick you up," she told me, and we exchanged numbers.

"I'm still preparing for the party. You won't be scared if my husband comes to pick you up, will you?" She said on the day of the party.

"No, I don't mind." I said as I hesitated a bit.

"He won't bite I promise," she said with a chuckle, but I was nervous.

I was going to be riding with another strange man, and I didn't know how far they lived. Many negative things were going through my mind. I was in awe that she allowed her husband to come pick me up a strange woman that she didn't know that well. She was very confident and trusting.

"Strength and dignity are her clothing and her position is strong and secure; And she smiles at the future [knowing that she and her family are prepared]." (Proverbs 31:25 AMP)

However, I felt good because she seemed to have trusted me, but it just may have been that she trusted her husband. Honey, if so, that was a good thing.

When her husband arrived, he was very nice and polite. I barely said anything to him during the whole ride; I just couldn't wait to get to Angela. Finally, we arrived at their home, and Angela greeted me as she hurried to finish setting up. She had invited the right person because I didn't mind helping her out. Also, I met her best friend, Patricia Arrington, another friend named Clementine, and her sister, Carrie. We had such a wonderful time, a lot of laughs, and fun while trying on lingerie.

I noticed that Angela was very ambitious and liked beautiful things. She didn't mind working for what she wanted or needed to make things happen for her household. Her husband made sure that she was happy in every way. The more she invited me over the closer we became as friends. Her husband and I became drinking partners; Melvin was like a brother to me. We all got along wonderfully. I became a part of the family, and they all treated me this way even down to her mother, brother and sisters. We went out just about every weekend. Going out with them, I knew I had to get some new clothes. Yes, I liked to dress, and it ran through my bloodline. Who *doesn't* want to wear or have the finer things in life?

"Now, to Him who is able to [carry out His purpose and] do superabundantly more than all that we dare ask or think [infinitely beyond our greatest prayers, hopes, or dreams], according to His power that is at work within us," *(Ephesians 3:20 AMP)*

Chapter 38
It coulda' been me

It was time for me to go on my vacation to New York City. So while I was there, I could go shopping and visit my family for a few days. When I arrived, they all were happy to see me because I had been gone for a year and some months. My sister shared with me that our baby brother, Daniel, was barely going to school, Willie completely stopped going to school, and my stepfather still was drinking; that hadn't changed. Other than these things, everything was fine. Her boyfriend, Speed shared some terrible things about his brother, Pee, my ex-boyfriend that pulled a gun out on me. He explained that Pee was very sick and wasn't doing so well.

"What's wrong with him," I asked with concern.

"Trish my brother has full blown *AIDS*. He has lost a lot of weight, and he doesn't look like himself," he said while shaking his head.

"Oh, my God! I am so sorry to hear that! Where is he now?" I was in complete shock and felt sorry for him.

"He's living with our mom. He doesn't have much time; he's dying. Trish, did you ever get yourself checked out? I believe you left him right on time," he said.

"Yes, I did, and it came out negative. I did leave him right on time. Tell me, what happened to his partner?" I asked with curiosity.

"He died of *AIDS* six months ago. Boy, you are lucky. ***The man upstairs was looking out for you,*** " he told me.

> *"The LORD is gracious and full of compassion, Slow to anger and abounding in loving kindness. ⁹ The LORD is good to all, And His tender mercies are over all His works [the entirety of things created]." (Psalm 145:8-9 AMP)*

> *"Who is a God like You, who forgives wickedness And passes over the rebellious acts of the REMNANT of His possession? He does not retain His anger forever, Because He [constantly] delights in mercy and lovingkindness.¹⁹ He shall again have compassion on us; He will subdue and tread underfoot our wickedness [destroying sin's power].Yes, You will cast all our sins Into the depths of the sea" (Micah 7:18-19 AMP)*

"Yes, thank you Jesus," I said.

Later, I was by myself, and thought about how **it could have been me**; I was still here. However, I couldn't help to think about the day he pulled that gun out on me. *What if I was afraid enough to give into his manipulation and control? What if I left with him and forfeited my release from him? I would be dying too.* I thanked God for my boldness to walk away and still be alive.

> *"⁴³ But now, this is what the LORD, your Creator says, O Jacob, And He who formed you, O Israel Do not fear, for I have redeemed you [from captivity]; I have called you by name; you are MINE!" (Isaiah 43:1 AMP)*

> *"So, we take comfort and are encouraged and confidently say, "THE LORD IS MY HELPER [in time of need], I*

WILL NOT BE AFRAID. WHAT WILL MAN DO TO ME?"
(Hebrews 13:6 AMP)

"I would like to visit, and plus I would like to see your beautiful mom. Will you both escort me there?" I said hesitantly.

"Yes," Denise and Speed said.

When we arrived there, Speed's mom was so happy to see me. We talked for a little bit, then Speed asked his mom about Pee.

"He's in his bedroom and won't come out," she told us.

"'Trish is here to see you," Speed said while knocking on the door as he entered.

Pee wasn't up for any company but of course, I understood.

After I spent time with my family and did a little shopping, I was ready to return to where I called home. New York City would always be a place that I would visit and shop but never a place of residency again. On my journey back to Lewiston, North Carolina, I rode the Greyhound bus with enthusiasm and excitement to get back to my friends.

Chapter 39
Searching for Mr. Right

Returning home from New York, I did the usual: worked all week and was ready to go out on the weekend. Angela had invited me to spend the night at her home; therefore, I would pack up a few things to take with me on the weekend. Out of respect for Cousin Carol, I always let her know where I would be. So, the location was in Murfreesboro, North Carolina, about forty-five minutes away from where I lived. Angela picked me up, and we headed to her house. After that first time I visited her home, she loved the idea of me visiting because I would help her clean her house, though it wasn't all that dirty. I used to look at her and laugh because she was a little perfectionist which I understood. She liked everything nice, clean, and organized.

However, Saturday night was our night to go out, so I wore something that I had bought in New York. Honey, you couldn't tell us anything. *We looked... good*. The rest of our friends met up at Angela's house, so we could all leave for the club together. Dancing was an outlet for me that's how it's always been. Even on the dance floor, I envisioned about my future. But in the meantime, *I was going to have fun until I found Mr. Right*. I was definitely searching.

> ^{22}*He who finds a [true and faithful] wife finds a good thing*
> *And obtains favor and approval from the* LORD*." (Proverbs*
> *18:22 AMP)*

Everyone else didn't drink like I did. Someone had to stay sober, so why not them? After we hit the dance floor, all our hair curls dropped [when hair can no longer hold the form of a curl due to sweat]. We had a good old time. While I was dancing, I was in another place, but when it was over, and the alcohol wore off, reality kicked in.

> ^{46}*Do not be anxious or worried about anything, but in*
> *everything [every circumstance and situation] by prayer*
> *and petition with thanksgiving, continue to make your*
> *[specific] requests known to God.* ^{7}*And the peace of God*
> *[that peace which reassures the heart, that peace] which*
> *transcends all understanding, [that peace which] stands*
> *guard over your hearts and your minds in Christ Jesus [is*
> *yours]." (Philippians 4:6-7 AMP)*

I stayed over Angela's house more than I stayed at home some weekends. But I did stop at some point, I didn't want to whereout my welcome. When I was there, I was invited to a cookout or something of that nature. I loved her and her husband, Melvin. We would get a card game going (spades of course). They would let it be known they loved when I came over. Therefore, I let them know how much I enjoyed them having me.

After I slowed down my visits for a while, I would go back and visit because we all had planned to go out. One day their friend, Arthur Lee had stopped by while I was over. He was twenty-seven years old, but he certainly didn't look his age. Out of all the times I've been there, I had never met, heard, or knew about him. He was a tall, skinny, and light-skinned fella [guy] with jerry curls, thick eyebrows, and long eyelashes. He dressed in big name fashion brands and gold accessories, and he smelled good. The only thing that bothered me about him was his cussing; he had a nasty mouth. The only person that I knew that cussed as much as Arthur Lee did was Richard Pryor. Honey, I thought that I had met Richard Pryor's twin brother.

I could tell he was attracted to me because he was sarcastic and obnoxious towards me. We fussed the whole day. He overheard as we were planning to go out, so he wanted to go too. And deep on the inside, I wanted him to go too. That night was different from the day we had spent bickering. We began to talk cordial to each other. Watching him drink, I had thought I was a drinker, but he was a *drinker*. When he got drunk, he got *drunk*.

Nevertheless, his cussing was worse, but he tried to respect me as much as possible, by apologizing. Other than that, he was a cool dude. I don't remember what he did for a living, but he had his own place. Angela did tell me that he was in and out of jail. *Why do I always fall for the bad guys?* Internally, I really liked the suspense- the challenge of hood guy. If you're wondering if I slept with him; yes, I did. With the big mouth he had, I had to try him out, and he was alright. I had been drinking, and I wanted to feel loved. After the sex, let's just say his nose was wide open, but I wasn't crazy about him like he was about me. He had a lot going against him: a temper, jail, and hustling. I just didn't want to go down that road again.

"Like a dog that returns to his vomit Is a fool who repeats his foolishness. " (Proverb 26:11 AMP)

"A wise man suspects danger and cautiously avoids evil, but the fool is arrogant and careless. [17] A quick-tempered

man acts foolishly and without self-control. And a man of wicked schemes is hated. [18] The naive [are unsophisticated and easy to exploit and] inherit foolishness, but the sensible [are thoughtful and far-sighted and] are crowned with knowledge." (Proverbs 14:16-18 AMP)

After that evening, it had been awhile since I visited Angela's home. I didn't want to give Arthur Lee any ideas about us being a couple. Later, when I spoke to Angela at work, she told me about how he had asked about me continuously. He talked about he wanted to make change because of you. I didn't respond because I had a made up mind. One day, I asked her how he was doing, and she told me that he was in *jail*. I smiled inwardly because I made the right choice. I just felt safe in not being committed to someone.

"I call heaven and earth as witnesses against you today, that I have set before you, life and death, the blessing and the curse; therefore, you shall choose life in order that you may live, you and your descendants, [20] by loving the LORD your God, by obeying His voice, and by holding closely to Him; for He is your life [your good life, your abundant life, your fulfillment] and the length of your days, that you may live in the land which the LORD promised (swore) to give to your fathers, to Abraham, Isaac, and Jacob." (Deuteronomy 30:19-20 AMP)

Over the years, I observed Angela never wanting for anything, and I admired that about her. She and her husband were partners in building their own home. No matter what, she always said, "My blessings come from Jesus." They went from living in a single wide trailer to a double wide. Whatever she set her mind to, she did it, and I thought this was *amazing*. I knew that she believed in Jesus, and she went to church. I watched her as a wife when she didn't know I was watching. She loved her husband, Melvin. He was truly blessed and so was she.

> *"An excellent woman [one who is spiritual, capable, intelligent, and virtuous], who is he who can find her? Her value is more precious than jewels and her worth is far above rubies or pearls.[11] The heart of her husband trusts in her [with secure confidence], And he will have no lack of gain.[12] She comforts, encourages, and does him only good and not evil All the days of her life.[13] She looks for wool and flax And works with willing hands in delight.[14] She is like the merchant ships [abounding with treasure]; She brings her [household's] food from far away." (Proverbs 31:10-14 AMP)*

> *"He who finds a [true and faithful] wife finds a good thing And obtains favor and approval from the LORD." (Proverbs 18:22 AMP)*

Of course, their marriage wasn't perfect, and they still went through trials and tribulations, but because of God and the love in their marriage, they are still together to this day. In fact, when I had met them, they were already ten years in. To me, they were an actual example of what marriage should be like. Although my parents weren't married to each other; however, my mom did her wifely duties. She served my stepdad, and, at times, my stepdad served her. I didn't take these things lightly. Marriage was a part of my dream, so I was very observant of their actions and gained enlightenment of what marriage was.

> *"Therefore, what God has united and joined together, man must not separate [by divorce]." (Mark 10:9 AMP)*

After a while, I started hanging out in Windsor, North Carolina where my supervisor, Amelia resided. She would invite me over to spend the night, so I could go out with her and her friends. I remember that her family would make fun of her because she knew three ladies named Patricia, and I was the third; this was too funny. I had met the other two, and they worked at Perdue too.

Amelia had a big family, and she surely had some handsome brothers. All of them were older and married, except one, Oliver, who just had a divorce. Once they all got to know me and saw me often, they started to treat me like family including Amelia's humorous, beautiful mother. Amelia also had multiple sisters, who were all beautiful as well.

The clubs we would go to were *Disco 17* and the *Commodores*. We always had a good time no matter which one we went to. I went to the bar and got my beer, but Amelia's friends didn't drink often, and Amelia didn't drink at all; it was more for me. Sometimes, I started the dancing off because most people were standing on the wall which was a no, no for me. I paid to get in, so I could dance not stand on the wall. Meaning, if no one asked me to dance, I would get on the dance floor by myself. I was a party starter. And once I got it started, I didn't dance by myself another minute because someone joined me. We would dance until closing. Once we left the club, we would stop and get something to eat at *Hardees*.

Amelia and her family were close and tight knitted; they looked after one another. They exemplified what you'd dream for in your own family. I admired their closeness and love for each other. Though one or two members may have messed up, their doors were still open to them. Their mother showed tough love, but whole heartedly cherished them all. I was on the outside looking in studying their environment.

> *"Honor (respect, obey, care for) your father and your mother, so that your days may be prolonged in the land the LORD your God gives you." (Exodus 20:12 AMP)*

> *"bearing graciously with one another, and willingly forgiving each other if one has a cause for complaint against another; just as the Lord has forgiven you, so should you forgive." (Colossians 3:13 AMP)*

Every time I visited her mother's home, I looked forward to seeing Oliver, and he always did me the pleasure of showing up. He'd playfully pick on me and call me *"cat eyes."* It was never a boring moment at her house. Later, it became Amelia's house because her mom bought a big, beautiful house that sits on a hill. Don't get me wrong; the house that Amelia now resided in was big and beautiful too, especially after she had some work done to it. Everyone gathered at her mother's new house and stayed close because she was ill. She didn't paint the picture of an ill woman. We'd sit around laugh, talk, and run errands for her. Her mother was a businesswoman. Anytime a black woman owned two big houses, she's either knowledgeable, knows someone, or both.

> *"Her children rise up and call her blessed (happy, prosperous, to be admired); Her husband also, and he praises her, saying," (Proverbs 31:28 AMP)*

> *"A good man leaves an inheritance to his children's children, And the wealth of the sinner is stored up for [the hands of] the righteous." (Proverbs 13:22 AMP)*

I remember a party they threw where they sold dinners and chicken sandwiches. Their chicken sandwich was the best that I had ever tasted. It was evident Amelia and her sister, Sara, were really close even when working together in the kitchen. They deep fried the chicken the old fashion way: in a tall stainless-steel pot. Once the chicken was done, the leg quarters were seeping out the bread because of how big they were. A nice size chicken sandwich was fulfilling after drinking a couple of beers and dancing the night away.

When I stayed over, Amelia and I would go straight to work together on Sunday night, and she dropped me off Monday morning. I knew Cousin Carol had missed me because she would make remarks here and there like "*Hello stranger,*" and we would both chuckle before she would ask about my weekend. It never took me long to make friends and us enjoying each other's company.

> "*The man of too many friends [chosen indiscriminately] will be broken in pieces and come to ruin, but there is a [true, loving] friend who [is reliable and] sticks closer than a brother*" (Proverbs 18:24 AMP)

I always saw myself as someone who got along with everybody. I loved people, and most people loved me once they got to know me. Of course, I had been pre- judged, but that's not relevant because in many of those incidents, they found themselves to be wrong about me.

> "*Do not judge and criticize and condemn [others unfairly with an attitude of self-righteous superiority as though assuming the office of a judge], so that you will not be judged [unfairly].*" (Matthew 7:1 AMP)

In between going out with Amelia and Angela, Cousin Carol introduced me to Raymond. I believe he was in college at the time, and he was tall and very handsome with mahogany skin. Once, we went to a club together in his shiny, candy apple red, two-seater. He didn't smoke or drink, but I drank enough for the both of us. He was so sweet and a perfect gentleman. While we were on our way home from the club, he told me that I could sleep; since my head was nodding from side to side every so often. The next thing I knew, the car was spinning out of control. I woke up in fear and screaming, as it continuously flipped over.

"Calm down! It's okay, Patricia! Calm down. It's going to be okay," he told me while trying to calm me down.

It was a one car-accident, and we didn't know what happened nor did the police know after the investigation. They had to pull me out of the damaged upside-down car. I had blood flowing from my head and nose, and it was all over my clothes. It was so dark out there, and they didn't find anything on the road. It was the strangest thing. There was no evidence of speeding, and I knew for a fact that Raymond wasn't speeding.

> *"He will cover you and completely protect you with His pinions, and under His wings you will find refuge; His faithfulness is a shield and a wall. ⁵ You will not be afraid of the terror of night, nor of the arrow that flies by day,"* *(Psalms 91:4-5 AMP)*

The ambulance took us to the hospital, and when I woke up in the bed, there was a brace around my neck, but other than that, I was fine. They took a blood test from both of us and discovered that I had been drinking. I was over the limit that was required in North Carolina, and they believed that it saved my life.

> *"For He will command His angels in regard to you, To protect and defend and guard you in all your ways [of obedience and service].¹² They will lift you up in their hands, So that*

you do not [even] strike your foot against a stone." (Psalms 91:11-12 AMP)

Cousin Carol and Aunt Thelma showed up at the hospital to pick me up, and I was completely drunk.

"Girl, you are lucky. What happened?" Cousin Carol asked me. So, we explained everything to her.

Raymond was very pensive and sorrowful. He even suggested that I sue his insurance, so they can pay the expense of my hospital bills.

"No, no Raymond. It's okay. I'm okay," I told him as he continuously suggested.

Afterwards, we all went home because I just wanted to sleep. I couldn't wait to get in my bed.

When I woke up the next morning, I was crying because I couldn't move. The pain in my neck and back were out of this world. Cousin Carol and Aunt Thelma took me back to the hospital, and I had x-rays taken. There were muscles spasm from my neck down, so I had to wear a back brace and go to therapy. The recovery process caused me to be out of work for a little over two months. Soon after, I decided to get a lawyer.

Therapy and taking medicine helped with the pain and my rehabilitation. Every part of my body healed wonderfully, and now, returning to work was the goal.

"But He was wounded for our transgressions, He was crushed for our wickedness [our sin, our injustice, our wrongdoing]; The punishment [required] for our well-being fell on Him, And by His stripes (wounds) we are healed." (Isaiah 53:5 AMP)

I was ready to go back to work and cash in with the insurance company through my lawyer. Once the lawyers paid all the medical expenses and took their percentage, I was a little disappointed because there wasn't much left. This was okay because I just placed most of it in a savings account. I wanted to buy a piece of land, so I could put a double wide on it.

Thankfully, I was back to myself again. I was able to buy more clothes with some of the insurance money. Different color hooded- sweat suits were in style during this time, and I had many with song lyrics on the back, front, and down my pants leg that read things such as: "*Can't touch this,*" "*Don't start nothin,' It won't be nothin,*" and "*To legit to quit,*" and I stood by them. I wore these outfits to work because they were thick and warm. I loved them, and so did everyone else.

Speaking of everyone, I caught Mr. L's eye, the maintenance man in the same department watching me. I began to get nervous because of the way he looked at me. Sometimes he would come to my side to work on a machine that was down, if no one else was available.

"I wanna talk to you," he said calling me over and whispered in my ear.

We had a conversation, and I found out that he had liked me. I thought that he was very attractive. He was of a milk chocolate complexion, with thick eyelashes, and he had curly haired with a rattail (a small braid in the back of the head). Also, he was bowlegged with a muscular build and a nice smile. Immediately, he said that he was married but separated and had two sons who were his heart.

"Why are you and your wife separated?" I asked him.

"We haven't been getting along, and I believe that she's cheating on me," he informed me.

"Well, I'll think about it; you and I," I told him before getting back to work.

With a little investigation of my own, I found out that his wife worked the second shift and was indeed cheating on him. Her fast behind was all up in other men's faces; this woman did not care one bit. Therefore, I made-up my mind.

"I'd love to go out with you," I told him.

I felt that if his wife was seeing other people, why shouldn't he? This was the only reason why I said yes.

"For we know Him who said, "VENGEANCE IS MINE [retribution and the deliverance of justice rest with Me], I WILL REPAY [the wrongdoer]." And again, "THE LORD WILL JUDGE HIS PEOPLE." (Hebrews 10:30 AMP)

"We all had our eyes on you when you started working at Perdue. When you gave James a shot, and I found out that you broke up with him, I said to myself, *'she'll never give me a chance because I'm married'* and I am *truly* separated," he expressed while on our date.

He was right in thinking this before, but after I saw his wife getting in cars with other men, I changed my mind. From here, he would stop by my home almost every morning before he went home. Although James transferred to the day shift, he asked about Mr. L and I.

"Why are you worrying about what I'm doing, James? Worry about your wife," I spat. Boy, you should have seen his face; jealousy was not a good look on him

"You're only with him because you are trying to make me jealous," he said cockily.

"Negro, please! This is not about you. You were not all of that," I told him with a dry chuckle.

I told Mr. L about this conversation between James and I.

"I wasn't his friend then, and I'm not his friend now. I rarely say anything to him, and I want to keep it that way," he spat.

One thing about Mr. L was that he was real and kept it real; that's what I liked about him. He was an "*on the up and up*": a put it all on the table kind a man. He allowed me to choose what I wanted to do and was very giving. I could ask him for just about anything, and he would give it to me. I was truly into jewelry, and a gold ring was just about on every finger. I had a ring on my pointer finger with my initial "P" but there was a ring that I wanted to order out of a book, and he purchase it for me. When I needed lunch money, he would give it to me. He wasn't stingy at all. If he could do it, he did it, and he wasn't such a bad lover either. We had our share of intimacy, but most of the time when he came to see me, we would sit and talk. We enjoyed each other's company.

One night, my mother appeared to me in a dream. I almost became frightened until I remembered what my Cousin Carol told me, so I faced her. My mother was dressed in all white, looking beautiful, and she expressed that she didn't want me involved with a married man because I knew better. I nodded my head, and said "yes, I do". Then, she left after giving a smile of love. After I woke up, I didn't know what to do because I truly liked him and breaking up with him was truly going to be hard.

"'FOR THE LORD DISCIPLINES and CORRECTS THOSE WHOM HE LOVES, AND HE PUNISHES EVERY SON WHOM HE RECEIVES and WELCOMES [TO HIS HEART].'" (Hebrew 12:6 AMP)

Later, Mr. L told me that his wife found out about me and began to question him about me. Apparently, she wanted to work things out with him. We know that good things must come to an end, especially when the wife finds out about you and is bold enough to stop by your home. I believe she told whoever she was riding with to beep their horn, so I could come outside. Once I came to the door and opened it, she began shouting at me to leave her husband alone.

"When you stop the mess you are doing, so will I," I said boldly while getting in her face.

"You are such a hoe, (whore)" she said while looking me up and down.

"Right back at you...hoe," I said before rolling my eyes and slamming the door in her face.

"For there is nothing hidden that will not become evident, nor anything secret that will not be known and come out into the open." (Luke 8:17 AMP)

She stood outside belligerently fussing and cussing, but I didn't care. I just looked through the window and laughed at her.

"If you don't move off my property, I will call the police," I yelled from the window, and then, they hurriedly drove off. As soon as they left, I paged Mr. L's beeper, but he didn't return my calls right away. I said to myself, *"he must be going through right about now."*

Later that evening, he finally called and said what *she* wanted him to say.

"It is over between us," he said with a sigh.

"Okay, if that's what you want. That's fine," I shrugged. I knew she was listening on the other end.

For some reason, I wasn't sad at all. I knew that once I saw him again, he was going to communicate with me better than what he did over the phone. I couldn't wait to get to work on Sunday night. I got there early, so I was able to talk to him, and he explained everything in a better way. He had to do what she said because she was threatening to take his boys from him; therefore, he chose to work it out. She had people spying on the job; he had to be very careful. I told him that was fine, and he apologized to me. He was always genuine – a no nonsense man. We walked away as good friends with no hard feelings; everything happened for a reason.

After a few months, I barely saw him because he was working a different shift. Honey, this was better for me because I had fallen for him, but he didn't know it. As time went by, I got better and better and losing feelings. I was glad that I had never shed a tear over him. Although, it was very hard not to fall in love with him, life goes on. I tried to not let this get to me.

"He heals the brokenhearted. And binds up their wounds [healing their pain and comforting their sorrow]." (Psalms 14:3 AMP)

Chapter 40
Dancing the Pain Away

It was the weekend, and I was ready to party. After the situation with Mr. L, I met Tanya. She and I hit it off, so she introduced me to her mother who worked at *Perdue* as well but in a different department. They invited me to their home to spend the weekend with them, so we could go out. Tanya lived in Plymouth, North Carolina which was about fifty minutes away from where I lived. They stayed with Tanya's grandmother, along with Tanya's baby sister, Beany. Tanya's grandmother had a big, two-story house with a juke joint (a small bar where people listen to music) that had a pool table, and anyone could buy a shot (drink). It was different, and I had a mighty good time there too. Her family was another family that made me feel at home.

Tanya and I grew so close that I had invited her to go with me on my trip to Brooklyn, New York. I believe Denise was giving Speed a birthday party at the time. No matter where Tanya and I went, we had a good time if she wasn't with her boyfriend, Mike. When she did spend time with him, it didn't stop the show. I would hang out with her mother, and she would take me to the shot houses that she knew about. There were mostly older people who loved to gamble, but I didn't mind. They were nice people with a great sense of humor and hospitality. I liked being around older people because you learn what to do and what not to do. They had a lot of wisdom.

> *"Remember the days of old, Consider the years of many generations. Ask your father, and he will inform you, Your elders, and they will tell you." (Deuteronomy 32:7 AMP)*

Tanya's mom drank *Budweiser, Bacardi, and Coke*: Tanya drank a little *Bacardi and Coke*; her sister drank *Heinekens, Bacardi, and Coke;* and I drank *beer, Gin and Grapefruit juice.* By this time, I was a hardcore drinker. I loved some *Gin and juice* because *Bacardi and Coke* never agreed with my system; I vomited every time I drank it.

Plymouth, North Carolina had become my second home. When I did go home, Cousin Carol would have a list of who called me: Angela and Amelia. Of course, I would return their calls because they were my friends, and they made me laugh when they'd say things like *"You're a hard person to catch up with since you been hanging out in Plymouth. You just forgot about us."* Then, we all would burst out laughing, as I denied their playful allegations and told them that it wasn't like that. They were still my friends, but they had their own lives too: Angela was married, and Amelia had a boyfriend. I would visit Angela every now and then when I was invited over, and Amelia and I would ride and visit her boyfriend's home. During visits to his home, I met his brother, Bally who just got out of jail. He was a handsome fella, with a six pack and was very smart, but he didn't have a job. We talked a few times, but when he asked me for money this was a *Big Turn Off* for me. I am not the one to ask especially when you're a "*MAN*"; you have got to be kidding. He really had some things going against him.

> *"And do not give the devil an opportunity [to lead you into sin by holding a grudge, or nurturing anger, or harboring resentment, or cultivating bitterness]. ²⁸ The thief [who has become a believer] must no longer steal, but instead he must work hard [making an honest living], producing that which is good with his own hands, so that he will have something to share with those in need. " (Ephesians 4:27-28 AMP)*

I never believed that a woman should take care of a man especially if they weren't married. Certainly, things had to have happened that couldn't be helped. I just met him, and he was already asking me for money. I must have had *"dummy"* written on my forehead. I guess some men just put themselves on a pedestal thinking that they are all that and a bag of chips. Don't get me wrong, he was fine (handsome) but not fine enough to get away with using me. Like I said with Arthur Lee, I wasn't going to put myself through any grief again because a lesson was learned. Experiences always teach us something and I decided to take heed.

> *"The things which you have learned and received and heard and seen in me, practice these things [in daily life], and the God [who is the source] of peace and well-being will be with you." (Philippians 4:9 AMP)*

When I told Amelia how I felt about the situation, she burst out laughing. She agreed with me. I may have been wrong, but that was just me.

> *"For My thoughts are not your thoughts, nor are your ways My ways," declares the LORD." (Isaiah 55:8 AMP)*

Anyway, getting back to Tanya and me, everywhere we traveled in Plymouth, people thought we were sisters. We got tired of telling people that we weren't sisters, so we decided to let them believe this. *We were sisters;* and her mother would introduce me as her daughter. Honey, we partied just about every weekend. Ms. Joyce, their mother, and I would find somewhere to go early Saturday or Sunday morning to drink beer and talk smack. She knew where all the liquor houses were, and we indulged in plenty of laughter and fun. I had so much fun with them during the weekend that I hated for it to end on Sunday evening. We would all ride together and go to work Sunday night. In the morning, they would drop me off home.

Cousin Carol would already be gone for work when I got home, so she'd leave me a note telling me to call her at work. I would do just that. Our conversation was the usual, and she added,

"You're not allowing any grass grow under your feet," and we both started laughing.

"I will see you when I get home," she said before we ended the call.

"Hi stranger, long time no see," Aunt Thelma said when she called.

I would feel kind of bad because I hadn't been around to visit. I would tell her that I will be around to see her soon, and of course, I would keep my word.

> *"For we have regard for what is honorable [and above suspicion], not only in the sight of the Lord, but also in the sight of men." (2 Corinthians 8:21 AMP)*

Chapter 41
Relationship After Relationships

A few months after the breakup between Mr. L and I, there was a fella named Ronnie who was a maintenance man at Perdue as well. He was an interesting character. If you were low-spirited, you would not be low-spirited for long around him because of his humorous personality. He was a sweetheart and a gentleman. He stood at about 5'4 which was my height and he was light skinned with a bearded mustache; he was cute and from Scotland Neck, North Carolina. He would clown around and dance like George Jefferson, and I would be in tears from laughing at him so hard. He was married with three children, but he and his wife had been separated for some time. As a matter of fact, she didn't live in North Carolina anymore, and she wanted a divorce. After three years of working at Perdue, he noticed me and asked me if he could take me out. I was surprise he hadn't asked me out sooner. But he expressed that he pondered on asking, he got scared because he thought I would reject him. I probably would have because he was so silly for a twenty-eight year-old. However, I was able to see the serious side of him, and I liked it. He reassured me that everything was over with the last relationship, a young lady that was nineteen years-old; I thought that was very young.

"Yes, that relationship is over and wasn't really anything serious. She had gone back to her boyfriend and they are getting married," he told me.

From his description of her, she was very fast- tailed. Furthermore, Ronnie expressed that there is no worries, and that it was completely over.

"Good," I said sternly.

Then, Ronnie and I began to become more acquainted with one another. From the start, we had a pretty good relationship. Everybody, I knew adored Ronnie. When we were out having fun, he liked to be silly and make people laugh, including myself. He was a people person just like I was. In addition, my family liked him, and his family liked me. I must say that we had a few things in common: we both drank beer and smoked *Newport* Cigarettes, but he also indulged in a little weed smoking.

Ronnie was very close with his father, who married his stepmom after his mom passed. When we were introduced, they were glad that Ronnie had met someone nice, and they were hopeful that I'd help keep him on a straight and narrow path. He used to be on drugs but had quit. He told me that his drug addiction destroyed his marriage, so I understood why his family had concerns about him.

For our first date, he allowed me to choose where we went because he wanted me to be happy, so I chose the club. He could dance a little but I ask him to do the George Jefferson dance for me. I laughed so hard until tears flowed from my eyes; he was hilarious. After we left the club, we spent the night at his Aunt Louise house since I lived a little farther. We didn't have relations, and if we did, I would have felt uncomfortable. His aunt had breakfast ready for us in the morning: homemade biscuits, thick bacon, eggs, and grits with sharp cheese. Oh my God, everything was delicious. Ms. Louise would extend her hospitality by saying eat all you want, and she didn't have to tell me twice. She loved Ronnie, and I could see why he was her favorite nephew; he was very giving, helpful, and well-rounded.

As time went by, we became so close that he stayed with me from time to time, ate breakfast, and mowed our yard. We had boyfriend-girlfriend type of situation, and it had been a long time since I've been in a relationship like this. We would spend every weekend together, get our checks cashed, and he would get us a room in Roanoke Rapids, North Carolina. Roanoke Rapids was like a smaller version of New York City. We stayed there Friday through Sunday or however long our money could buy. Sometimes, his check was a little low because he had to pay child support, so he worked overtime as much as he could. Anyway, we would buy food, beer, cigarettes, and a little *Gin* for me. We would have everything we needed. We had a good time, and we did everything together.

After about two or three months. Ronnie's car started acting up, so he needed a new car. When he got his tax return, he went out searching for a used car that he could afford to make payments on. Finally, he found one that he liked and was affordable, but he needed a co-signer.

"Trish, would you be the co-signer for the car?" he asked me.

"Let me think about it," I said.

I thought about us and our situation; we needed a car. I didn't drive, but the car would be a great way for him to drive me to New York City. So, I told him yes on one condition:

"You have to keep up the payments on this car no matter what because my name is involved. **If they call looking for me to make the payments, the car and the title will become mine,**" and he agreed to this. The car was a two door, four-seater 1978 *Grand Prix* with brown crushed velvet seats. It was a nice car. I thought, *"New York City here we come."* We had planned to go during the summer.

"It is better that you should not vow than that you should vow and not pay." (Ecclesiastes 5:5 AMP)

I remember it being scorching hot that summer; thank God for air conditioning. Ronnie and I had a nice drive to New York City, and when we arrived, my family was so happy to see us. They loved him. He and my family talked like they had known each other for years. It was amazing.

While we were there, a mishap had occurred: someone shattered our car window. We had just got the car and a tragedy had already struck. We thought what if it had rained. We saw some people that were outside and asked if anyone saw what happened, but everyone said no.

"Do any of you know someone who can fix a car window at a reasonable price," Ronnie asked them.

"Who you all are visiting," one of them asked.

"Denise and Speed...right up there," I said while pointing at the apartment building.

In New York's apartment buildings, it is known that everyone knew each other.

They took a liking to Ronnie, who was talking a good game like he knew his way around, and he didn't talk like a country boy either. They told Ronnie once the car was fixed, they'll keep an eye on it. They found someone; I just smiled because he only charged Ronnie thirty dollars for the window and didn't charge him for the labor.

"Are you two visiting from out of town," he asked us.

"Yes," we said.

"Alright, no worries. I got you all backs," he said.

I was so happy because I thought we would have to pay an arm and a leg.

"For His anger is but for a moment, [1]His favor is for a lifetime. Weeping may endure for a night, but a shout of joy comes in the morning." (Psalm 30:5 AMP)

Even Ronnie was amazed at the price. All I could say was thank you, Jesus.

"Do not be anxious or worried about anything, but in everything [every circumstance and situation] by prayer and petition with thanksgiving, continue to make your [specific] requests known to God." (Philippians 4:6 AMP)

"Praise the LORD! (Hallelujah!) Oh, give thanks to the LORD, for He is good; For His mercy and loving kindness endure forever!" (Psalms 106:1 AMP)

We stayed in New York City for a few days, and then we left: besides, there's no place like home. When we arrived back, Ronnie received the divorce papers from his wife, and the correspondence for seeing his children. She brought the children to see him from time to time, and I even had the pleasure of meeting them. They were beautiful children that favored him and their mother.

Ronnie and I were now six or seven months into our relationship. One day, Cousin Carol wasn't home, and Ronnie and I were watching television and laying on the living room floor. I had worked so hard that night that my body ached all over including my back. I had no idea what was going on. Ronnie took me to the hospital right away because I was in pain and could barely walk. He had to practically carry me to the car. He was strong for a short man. When we reached the hospital, the diagnoses were muscle spasms from overworking my muscles at work. The doctor relieved me from work. I needed to get papers from my job to fill out, and I had to see their doctor. I was able to get paid during my time off because of worker's compensation.

Ronnie visited me in the morning after he got off from work or called me to see how I was doing which I truly appreciated that. However, three weeks had passed, but this particular week I hardly heard from him. I called his beeper and there was no answer, so I called his Aunt Louise. She hadn't seen him, but his father told me that I had just missed him. "*Maybe I will see him later*," I said to myself. I continued to rest like the doctor said to do, and while I was a sleep, **I had a dream about Ronnie: he was cheating on me with Shantel, and a small voice said to me, "*He drove her in the car you cosigned for*."**

I remember telling Ronnie at the beginning of our relationship if he ever cheats on me, I will know about it.

"*If you become interested in someone else, I would rather you just break up with me than cheat on me. If you cheat on me, you're going to wish you hadn't,*" *I told him seriously.*

"Aww girl please! I'm not going to cheat on you," he said while brushing me off.

I sat up from the dream and said out loud, "*That n----is cheating on me!*"

"But God came to Abimelech in a dream during the night, and said, "Behold, you are a dead man because of the woman whom you have taken [as your wife], for she is another man's wife." (Genesis 20:3 AMP)

"And the LORD said to them, "Now listen to what I say: "If there were prophets among you, I the LORD, would reveal myself in visions. I would speak to them in dreams." (Numbers 12:6 NLT)

I was furious, but I had a plan to find out the truth because he was going to lie about it. Coincidently, it was nearing Valentine's Day, he showed up with a dozen of roses and candy. "He looks guilty as h---," I thought to myself. I had a few choice words for him, but I waited patiently. I played along, but I began to question his whereabouts, and why he didn't return my calls. His lame excuse was I went straight to bed, and I wanted to give you some time to heal. I just looked at him with contempt because I could see right through him. I barely let him touch or kiss me.

Sunday night, I was released to go back to work. Ronnie had arrived to work earlier than me, but I told him to pick me up, and I'll just sit in the car. While we were riding to work, I started interrogating him.

"Ronnie did you cheat on me?" I asked him.

"No, I didn't cheat on you," he said.

"You're lying. Didn't I tell you that if you cheat on me, you are going to wish you hadn't? Then, you're going to sit here and tell me a bold-faced lie? Honey, I got my ways of finding out. Some folks here at this plant know."

You should have seen the look on his face. It was the look you had when your parents caught you doing something that you had no business doing, and you knew you had a whipping coming.

"Okay Patricia, you are not going to find out anything because I didn't do anything. All I did was take the girl home because she didn't have a ride, and that's it," He said brushing me off.

"So, it had to be you? Hmm. So, you expect me to believe that's all that happened? Well, I don't believe you. I know there is more to the story. You did tell me the truth about her being in the car because I knew that too," I said obnoxiously.

"Truthful lips will be established forever, but a lying tongue is [credited] only for a moment." (Proverbs 12:19 AMP)

He parked the car, and we went into Perdue. I waited for some more people to come in to work, so I could begin my investigation.

The first person I questioned was Tanya. I asked her if she had saw or heard anything, and I will keep this between her and I. She heard about some things concerning Ronnie and that girl, Shantel. She told me what she heard, and said,

"But I don't know if it's true or not."

"Oh, no. It's true," I said.

"How did you know?" she asked in a surprised tone.

"I just know," I told her.

Also, I asked Sandra who was an acquaintance of ours, but she just didn't want to get involved. I told her I understood, but she did tell me that I was on the right track and that's all she was going to say. The last person I approached was Shantel, who also worked in Weldatron. She had just come back from having her baby and was already pregnant when her and Ronnie were having their fling. She didn't mind telling me the truth.

"I was waiting on the ride, but the ride didn't show up, so Ronnie offered to take me home. He stayed around for a good little while and *one thing led to another*," she said honestly.

"Oh really, so you're telling me you both had sex?" I said as I crossed my arms fired up on the inside (mad as h---).

"Yes," she said nodding her head.

"Thank you for telling me the truth," I said before walking away.

I couldn't wait to talk to Ronnie when I went on break or when he went on break. When he saw me in passing, he asked me what was wrong while trying to grab my hand.

"Don't you touch me, liar," I said as I jerked my hand from him.

"Can I talk to you?" he asked.

"Oh, we are going to talk because I have a lot to say," I told him.

I was hurt, but I tried not to show it. I just laughed angrily to myself when I got to my machine. I really thought that we had something good, and he had messed up a good thing. I didn't take it very well when men cheated on me, and they lied about it. I was faithful to him, and I truly expected him to be faithful to me. This is the way that I looked at it: I was his loss and someone else's treasure.

> *"An excellent woman [one who is spiritual, capable, intelligent, and virtuous], who is he who can find her? Her value is more precious than jewels and her worth is far above rubies or pearls." (Proverbs 31:10 AMP)*

He waited around until I got off and brought me home. We got out of the car, and he followed me into the garage. I didn't want to go into the house because Cousin Carol was still home. The next thing I knew I laid him out (cussed him out). He tried to lie his way out of it, but he couldn't. Finally, he came clean and confessed that he had messed up. With those words, I began smacking and punching him.

"Okay, I deserved that," he said pitifully.

Then, he grabbed my arms to keep me from continuously hitting him. I screamed out hysterically and told him to let go of me while calling him a liar and a cheater.

"You are d---- right you messed up. It's over between us," I yelled… I told you I would know if you ever cheated on me, but you didn't believe it. You wanted to test the waters."

> *"But there is nothing [so carefully] concealed that it will not be revealed, nor so hidden that it will not be made known." (Luke 12:2 AMP)*

"You're going to let almost a year of our relationship go down the drain like that? I promise I won't do it again," he pleaded.

"You let it go down the drain when you put your penis in her vagina, n----. Now, you think you're going to put your penis in me. Hmm, I don't think so! You can go back to her. Oh, I forgot she doesn't want you either, Her and the baby's father are working it out, and she is getting married. She left *you* looking stupid. I trusted you to be faithful to me like I was to you." I said tauntingly while pushing and hitting him.

"It is better to take refuge in the Lord than to trust in man." (Psalm 118:8 AMP)

"Lying lips are extremely disgusting to the Lord, But those who deal faithfully are His delight." (Proverbs 12:22 AMP)

"I'm sorry for hurting you. I love you. Shantel didn't mean anything to me."

"N----please, you don't know what love is. And you don't love me, you love yourself. Plus, I wouldn't be able to trust you. I don't want to hear no more. Get the h--- out of my yard." I said cutting him off.

"Beloved, let us [unselfishly] [a]love and seek the best for one another, for love is from God; and everyone who loves [others] is born of God and knows God [through personal experience]. 8 The one who does not love has not become acquainted with God [does not and never did know Him], for God is love. [He is the originator of love, and it is an enduring attribute of His nature.]" (1 John 4:7-8 AMP)

"Love is to be sincere and active [the real thing—without guile and hypocrisy]. Hate what is evil [detest all ungodliness, do not tolerate wickedness]; hold on tightly to what is good. 10 Be devoted to one another with [authentic] brotherly affection [as members of one family], give preference to one another in honor;" (Romans 12:9-10 AMP)

I kept pushing him, then Cousin Carol came out and grabbed me to keep me from hitting him. I felt so much better after that. She began telling Ronnie to please leave. Later, after I calmed down, I called him to talk about the car. He called me back quick and in a hurry. I told him I only called him to discuss my expectation that he would make the payments on the car as he promised. I was the co-signer, if they called telling me that he stopped making the payments, then arrangements would have to be made. If I make the payments, then it becomes mine. He agreed with the arrangements since my credit score was at stake.

> *"Don't agree to guarantee another person's debtor put up security for someone else.*[27] *If you can't pay it, even your bed will be snatched from under you." (Proverbs 22:26-27 NLT)*

However, I ended up finding myself another ride to work. When we were at work, it was a little awkward, but when I saw him, I kept it moving. He looked terrible. He hadn't been shaving his face, and he looked gloomy. I heard that the guys at work were picking and laughing at him because he was under the machine shedding tears. Even Mr. L heard about it on the dayshift and pulled me aside about it. "*Wow the word gets around*," I said to myself.

"They said that he was really crying, and that he should not have messed up.

Shoot. I'm surprised that it lasted that long," Mr. L laughed.

"Well, it would have lasted longer if he didn't cheat," I told him.

> *"So, any person who knows what is right to do but does not do it, to him it is sin." (James 4:17 AMP)*

As days went by, I continued resume with my life. I noticed Ronnie wasn't coming to work that much. When he did come to work, he wasn't his joking self. He would fix the machine and then hide. He became very standoffish.

Ending things with Ronnie left me vulnerable; when a man said kind words to me or paid any attention to me, I was drawn to them. This was around the time that I met Bridgett. He worked in the supply room where we went to renew our work uniforms. He was a tall dark-skinned man with a mustache and Jerri curls. He was sweet and funny; he just knew how to make me laugh at the time I needed it the most. Bridgett wanted an opportunity to get to know me, but he was separated from his wife. He told me this, and I found it to be true. He would visit me sometimes, and we would have a few drinks and talk, but this didn't last long. He was only a temporary fling because I didn't have serious feelings for him. In all honesty, he was more like a rebound.

I went back to hanging out with Tanya and her family again. Amid, Tanya, her sister, Beany, and her mom decided to get a place together after Tanya 's grandmother died. Sometimes, I would go to their house just to get away. We didn't always go out, though; we would lounge around the house and play Spades. No matter what we did, I always had fun. When Ms. Joyce, Tanya's mother did cook, she was a wonderful cook; otherwise, we had to cook for ourselves.

Tanya and her family always made sure that everything was okay with me because of what happened between Ronnie and I. They were truly good friends, but I didn't want to wear out my welcome. It was time to give it a rest and allow them to miss me.

"Don't visit your neighbors too often, or you will wear out your welcome." (Proverbs 25:17 NLT)

Chapter 42
Hometown

I didn't spend a lot of time in my own hometown as you've already read, but I'm not sure why I didn't; I was literally surrounded by family. There was my Cousin Sandra, known as Shug, living on the right side of us, Aunt Bess lived on the left of us, and Aunt Bess's oldest daughter, Margie, and her four sons were directly across from us. I began to visit and talk to them a little more because most of the time I would only speak in passing. Out of everyone, I was closest to Shug, but she didn't go out with me. She told me that her going out days were over. Regardless, Shug was the cousin who made me laugh all the time, and she was a sweetheart as well as her sister, Miranda when she wasn't asleep from working the graveyard shift at *Perdue*.

Yes, just about everyone worked at *Perdue*; yes, sir and yes, ma'am. That would be the place to get you started until something better came along.

"Where there is no vision, the people perish: but he that keepeth the law, happy is he." (Proverbs 29:18 KJV)

For some time, I had been looking at a lot that was right next door. It was a wonderful spot to put a double wide trailer. I talked to Shug, and she shared with me that she spoke to the owner about her lot. She gave me the owner's name and number, and he informed me that he was interested in selling for three thousand dollars. I had to give him a down payment, and after that, I had two years to pay it off. After I paid it off, he was going to give me the deed to the property; so, I agreed to this deal. I was so excited that I was on my way out because it was starting to become a little crowded. Now that, Cousin Carol had a boyfriend, Mr. R., and she was pregnant. Mr. R was a nice guy, and I was glad that she had someone who treated her wonderfully.

Anyway, I would take many walks into town, and one time, a car stopped me as I was walking.

"Aren't you new around here?" the woman asked me.

"Yes, then again, no not really. I've been here for a few years now, but I haven't been hanging around here," I told her.

"I saw you at the *Hide Away [Club]* over the weekend, but when I turned around, you were gone," she said.

"Yeah. I asked the person who brought me to take me home because somebody scared me away," I said while chuckling.

"There was nothing to be afraid of; it's a nice place to have a good time. My name is Charlotte," she introduced herself.

"I'm Patricia," I replied.

"Can I call you Trish for short?"

"Yes, you can," I said with a smile.

I didn't know that she would, later, become one of my best friends.

Charlotte was so beautiful; she was brown skinned, with Native American like features, beautiful long hair and a nose ring. Also, she had a beautiful, little daughter. Although, I was two years older than her, we were like two peas in a pod once we got to know each other. Our first time hanging out together, it felt like we had known each other forever. She and her boyfriend, Andre, known as Achy lackey were such a comical couple and loved each other very much. When I say he was tall, he was tall-at least seven feet. He even had to duck his head when walking through a doorway. He and I were cool with each other as well; a friend of Charlotte was a friend of his.

She lived past town, in the projects, but close enough that I could walk to her house. Charlotte and her mother stayed with her grandmother. They were beautiful people and treated me like family. Also, Charlotte knew Cousin Carol, but they didn't have good things to say about one another. However, their issues had nothing to do with me. Cousin Carol was still my family, and Charlotte was still my friend. I didn't allow anyone to deter me from others because of the way *they* felt about them. If you have had a bad experience with someone that's none of my business. The issue is between you and the other person. I judge people by *my* experiences with them.

> *"To speak evil of no man, to be no brawlers, but gentle, shewing all meekness unto all men." (Titus 3:2 KJV)*

I didn't talk about Charlotte to Cousin Carol that much. She didn't like me hanging with her, but I did anyhow. Cousin Carol was a social worker so this had a lot to do with her care and concern. I would tell Cousin Carol that she needed to give her a chance because she was sweet and was nice to me.

Charlotte, Achy lackey, and I went to the *Hideaway*. This time, I wasn't afraid because I was with them. As our relationship grew, we were dressed to impress even if we had to buy something new. *Cato's* was our shopping ground. We would dress up in a suit or a whole-body jumper. Charlotte would buy the pants set while I'd buy the skirt set. She would wear flats because she was tall, and I would wear patent leather pumps. Oh, I can't forget about my black hat that I wore cocked to the side. All my friends would get a kick (laugh) out of me wearing my black hat. Please, don't sleep on a sista; we could dress. Ackee lackey was a sharp dresser as well.

Anyway, when we arrive to the *Hideaway*, the crazy looking boisterous man that I had saw the last time was walking towards us.

"You know him?" I asked her.

"Yeah, why?" she replied.

"That's who scared me away last time. He was loud and acted like a crazy man," I told her as we watched him.

Once he approached us, then Charlotte introduced us before telling him what I said. He apologized, and he was very polite. He was known as DJ B, the DJ (disc jockey) of the club. He told me that his craziness was all in fun and to make people laugh.

"Oh okay," I replied in relief.

The inside of club *Hide Away* was big and had two sections to it. The bar was near the front, and there was a sitting area with a big pool table. The second part had tables that were placed around the sides of the wall, and the dance floor was like a platformed stage. Lastly, there was a big, colorful ball that hung from the ceiling with flashing lights. Once it opened on Friday and Saturday nights, people were ready to enter around midnight. We sat around, talked, and I had a few Colt 45s, since Charlotte and Achy Lackey weren't drinkers. After a while, we got on the dance floor, and DJ B started dancing with me as the music played. He was very popular, and everyone knew him-young and old. He was short, light skinned, round headed, muscular built with a little fat, and chubby cheeks that framed his beautiful smile. He was cute, and what made him even cuter was the way he treated me.

> *"For such people do not serve our Lord Christ, but their own appetites and base desires. By smooth and flattering speech they deceive the hearts of the unsuspecting [the innocent and the naive]." (Romans 16:18 AMP)*

After having a good time, DJ B asked, "Do yawl want to ride out of town with me to this club I have to play at tomorrow."

"Sure," Charlotte and Achy Lackey said.

"Where are we going to stay?" I asked since I wasn't so quick to reply.

"It will be enough room for all of us where we're staying," he said.

"Okay," I said.

I believe that he was anticipating the trip since I agreed to come along.

The plan was to meet and leave from Charlotte's house. He picked us all up from her house in his truck, and during the ride, we enjoyed each other's company. DJ B teased and messed with me for a bit to get me laughing and talking. In our conversation, he asked who my family was.

"Keys and Bazemores," I told him.

"Oh so, Ms. Bess, Ms. Thelma, and Carol are your relatives," he said.

"Yup, that's them," I confirmed.

"You know your Cousin Carol is my cousin on her daddy's side of the family," he told me.

"Oh really? I'm related on her mama's side of the family," I told him.

"Good we're not related," he said with a slight smile.

I just laughed.

"Well, Cousin Carol said that you both are cousins, but she said you all were distant cousins," I told him.

"Hm, Carol and 'nem is on the uppity side of the family. We're the crazy side," As we continued to converse, he said with his lip turned up.

I was thinking in my head, "*Well she did say that they were the crazy side of her family and that they didn't engage with each other.*"

When we arrived, he checked us in, and we walked into a very nice suite which had a kitchen and one bedroom.

"I wonder who's going to sleep on the couch (pullout bed)." I said with a puzzling look on my face.

"It won't be me. I paid for the room," he said.

"Well, I guess it will be me then," I said with a shrug and a sigh.

"Don't worry about that now. We will discuss that when we get back here," he said.

"Hmmm, okay we'll see," I said.

We were preparing ourselves to get ready for that evening. Before it was time to go, we ordered food and lounged around a bit. Despite my feelings about the sleeping arrangements, we had a good time at the club where he played. He was a phenomenal DJ. I heard that everywhere he played the crowd would come especially the ladies. When we returned to the suite, we had to decide where I was going to sleep. Automatically, Charlotte and Achy Lackey had their room to sleep in, since they were a couple.

"You could share the pullout couch I don't bite," he joked.

I just looked at him circumspectly, as he explained that the bed was big enough for the both of us.

"Okay, but as soon as I feel some hands I'm jumping out of the bed," I said sternly.

"Woman please, I'm not going to touch you especially if you don't want me to," he said.

We laid down in the bed together, and we laughed and talked until we fell asleep.

In the morning, after we got ourselves together, we stopped for breakfast on the way back home. Charlotte whispered and asked how our night was together.

"Oh, he was a perfect gentleman and very respectful to me," I told her.

"Hmmm that's different," she said.

"Does he have a girlfriend," I asked her.

"I don't know. Last I heard was that he was living with a woman, and he lived with her for a long time. Oh, and I know she has a child by him," she told me.

Amid this conversation, we arrived at her house.

"Tell your girlfriend I said, 'hello,'" I said smartly as I got out of his truck.

"I use to have one, but she kicked me out," he said with his eyes bulging out of his head.

"Why did she kick you out?" I asked him.

"Because I didn't know how to come home some nights. We had an arrangement where I stayed there because of my son," he said.

"Oh, okay that's all I wanted to know," I told him.

"When will I see you again?" he asked.

I'll be around. Charlotte knows how to get in touch with me," I said.

The next weekend, we went to the *Hideaway* again, and I was introduced to Gail, DJ B's baby sister. She was a beautiful, kind and full-figured woman who was also humorous.

"I heard we're almost related," she said.

"H--l! No, we are not," he said and we started laughing.

Gail and I started talking about certain things like my living situation.

"You know I stay by myself. You could come stay with me if you want," she offered.

"Give me your number, I might have to take you up on that. I believe it's about time for me to leave," I told her.

I always knew things like this. I couldn't figure out what it was, but I always knew when my time was up, and when I should leave.

"For the gifts and calling of God are without repentance." *(Romans 11:29 KJV)*

"To another the working of miracles; to another prophecy; to another discerning of spirits;" (1 Corinthians 12:10 KJV)

I probably knew it was time for me to leave because Cousin Carol's boyfriend made a pass at me. I thought he adored her, and this surprised me. *"Why would he do that,"* **I asked myself.** *I couldn't even imagine or see myself with* *him* **nor did I look at him in that manner. He started telling me about what he had and what he could do for me. Although it was tempting, it wasn't worth risking or downgrading my character.** I was not attracted to him, and if I were, the answer still would have been no. I didn't want anything he had, and I would never do anything to hurt my cousin. Of course, she got on my nerves at times, but that's neither here nor there; she was family. I was appalled by his action, and I thought, *"Maybe it was a set up to see if I would agree to it."* **In any case, it was time to go because at this point, I was feeling very uncomfortable. I really didn't expect that from him.**

Later, that week, I didn't like the idea that Cousin Carol raised the amount of money that I was paying to stay with her. I thought she was crazy. *"If I paid her that much I would never get out of her house,"* I thought to myself. I was furious when she confronted me with that. At the price she was asking for, I would be practically paying her mortgage.

"You better be glad you got that baby in your arms," I said in a furious tone.

If she hadn't been holding her child, I would have smacked her. The price was preposterous.

"I'm rarely here to even use anything," I exclaimed.

"Well. your clothes are here" she said.

"Something is seriously wrong with you," I said with a dry chuckle.

She was money hungry. I was so angry; smoke was coming out of my nose.

> *"For the love of money [that is, the greedy desire for it and the willingness to gain it unethically] is a root of all sorts of evil, and some by longing for it have wandered away from the faith and pierced themselves [through and through] with many sorrows." (1 Timothy 6:10 AMP)*

"Trish, you've been drinking," she said.

"Even if I weren't drinking, I would have still said what I had to say. I will move out before I pay you that much money." I said yelling.

"Leave? Where are you going to go?" she said.

"Wouldn't you like to know! That's none of your business," I said as I was packing and rolling my eyes.

I called DJ B and asked him to come get me; it was nothing but a word to him.

Then, I had gotten a phone call that Ronnie missed two car payments, and they were looking for me to take responsibility for it. I remembered once before he missed a payment, but he paid it because I called and got on him. I told him that if he couldn't handle the payments any longer, just bring the car to me. Well, I called him, and his stance was I could come get the car because he had no way of getting the car over there. I agreed then he expressed that he missed me.

"Ronnie, I only called to talk about the car," I told him.

"I know," he said while laughing.

"It is better that you should not vow than that you should vow and not pay." (Ecclesiastes 5:5 AMP)

When I got situated at Gail's, we made plans to get the car after I moved in, and DJ B helped us. He and some friends packed my stuff into his van, and they took it to Gail's. I was so excited because she didn't charge me as much as Cousin Carol. She was truly being a help to me. I'm not discrediting Cousin Carol's help; in the interim, Gail was an enormous help to my need in that moment. Also, I was still able to pay on my loan for my lot. I could finally see myself getting somewhere.

Later, Gail and I went to get the car, and one of her friends followed us, so they could drive my car back since I didn't know how to drive yet. Ronnie handed the car over with no problems.

"Driving the car wasn't the same because I was used to having you sitting right beside me," he said with sorrow.

He looked like a sad puppy, but he knew he messed up a good thing.

The Grand Prix came in handy when Gail's car broke down and had to get fixed. Other than those times, it stayed parked in the yard.

The arrangement that we had was perfect: I worked at night, and she worked during the day. Gail and I clicked.

She treated me like I was a part of her family. When we weren't working, we hung out with each other. We would go out to the club and hang out with Charlotte and Achy lackey. At the club, I met Linda, who was introduced to me by Charlotte. She and I hit it off as well. We, Charlotte, Gail, and I, were all friends or let's just say I had befriended them. I was *the friend* in the middle who kept the peace. Charlotte and Linda had their differences and opinions about each other, but they had one thing in common: *me* which was a good thing. I liked them both.

> *"Blessed [spiritually calm with life-joy in God's favor] are the makers and maintainers of peace, for they will [express His character and] be called the sons of God," (Matthew 5:9 AMP)*

We always called each other during the weekend to see where we were going out. If we didn't party on Fridays, we partied on Saturdays, or on both nights.

This particular night, we went to the *Hideaway*, and I got on the dance floor after having a few drinks. The strangest thing happened while I was dancing.

"Come out, I want to show you something better," the voice spoke into my ear.

"No God, I am not ready yet," I said and smiled as the voice left me.

I continued dancing as if nothing ever happened.

> *"So, COME OUT FROM AMONG UNBELIEVERS AND BE SEPARATE," says the Lord, "AND DO NOT TOUCH WHAT IS UNCLEAN; And I will graciously receive you and welcome you [with favor]," (2 Corinthians 6:17 AMP)*

I didn't say anything to anyone about the voice because I didn't want anyone to think I was crazy. Thereafter, I began having dreams of being chased. I was always running from a light or dreaming about falling off a building and wake up before hitting the ground. These dreams were frightening to me, but I would brush it off and try to convince myself that they were the results of being drunk or too much drinking.

"Where can I go from Your Spirit? Or where can I flee from Your presence?" (Psalms 139:7 AMP)

"The Lord does not delay [as though He were unable to act] and is not slow about His promise, as some count slowness, but is [extraordinarily] patient toward you, not wishing any to perish but all to come to repentance." (2 Peter 3:9 AMP)

Chapter 43
Becoming Familiar with Others

At times, It was a riot (so to speak) living with Gail. She was so hilarious that you couldn't stay mad at her for long. For instance, one day, I decided that I was going to prepare a nice Sunday dinner, and I made baked macaroni cheese as one of the dishes in a big round casserole bowl. It was just the two of us, so it would last us for a few days. I went to work that night but the whole night, I was thinking about how delicious the macaroni and cheese was and envisioned myself eating some for breakfast. When I got off from work that morning, I walked into the trailer, took my coat off and while washing my hands, I saw the empty casserole bowl in the dish water. "*Maybe she moved it into another container,*" I said to myself. I looked in the refrigerator and there wasn't any macaroni and cheese in the containers. "*NO, SHE DIDN'T!*" *I said furiously out loud.* I hated to think that she would be that selfish to do something like that. Though she was a heavier woman, I still didn't want to believe that she could eat the whole bowl of macaroni and cheese and not save me a corner. So, when she got home, I asked her,

"Gail, please tell me that you didn't eat that whole bowl of macaroni and cheese?"

"Trish don't be mad at me. Yes, I did. I am sorry but you shouldn't have made it so good. I took a fork and never got a plate; I just started eating," She confessed sorrowfully.

> *"Then He said to them, "Watch out and guard yourselves against every form of greed; for not even when one has an overflowing abundance does his life consist of nor is it derived from his possessions." (Luke 12:15 AMP)*

"You didn't think about me not one bit," I told her

"How can I make it up to you?" she asked.

"For one, you are going to have to ask your mama to make me some of her homemade biscuits. Secondly, I am going to help you by not making any more macaroni and cheese, and I forgive you." I said happily.

"Deal!" she said seriously.

All I did was laugh to keep from crying while my mouth was left watering. Despite this, we truly enjoyed each other's company when we were home at the same time.

When I moved in with Gail, DJ B would come by to see me. I loved the way he treated me. I guess that's how all the ladies felt about him. You will soon find out, why I specifically said, "*All* the ladies."

One evening he spent the night with me, but that morning, I heard Gail running to the front window to see who was driving up. It was a young lady who seemed very disturbed, and DJ B rushed outside.

"Who's that," I asked Gail with my eyebrow raised as we looked out the window.

"That's the woman he's staying with," she told me.

"He's still with her? What? So, he lied!" I said furiously.

"It is an off and on thing because they have a son together," she informed me.

I was so upset. I couldn't wait to see him again.

"I'll show him," I said.

"Trish, you are going to cuss him out ain't you? The next time you see him," she said while chuckling.

"Just as sure as my name is Patricia, but right now I'm making plans to get up out of here. I don't sit around and wait on no man, especially if he is not truly mine," I told her.

"Guide me in Your truth and teach me, For You are the God of my salvation; For You [and only You] I wait [expectantly] all the day long." (Psalm 25:5 AMP)

"Wait for and confidently expect the Lord; Be strong and let your heart take courage; Yes, wait for and confidently expect the Lord." (Psalm 27:14 AMP)

"I hear you, Trish. He may be my brother, but I don't blame you. I wouldn't wait around here either, Trish," she told me.

I don't know if she was trying to patronize me or what, but it didn't matter. I was going to do me.

Later, I called Charlotte and told her what happened.

"Trish, I already knew, but I wanted you to find out on your own," she told me.

"What else don't I know," I asked while getting irritated.

"That man has nine children by different women. All the young girls just loved him and I don't see what yawl see in him," she said.

"Well, I can only speak for me. He just has a way of making you feel important just by listening to you," I told her.

"I just wanted to let you know that I'm going out of town just to get back at him. It's not like we're committed to each other or anything. I just wanted the truth," I told her over the phone.

With fury, I paced the floor, smoking one cigarette after another; my nerves were terrible. I called Tanya to see if she could come and get me, and luckily, she was able to. Hurriedly, I packed my clothes for the weekend.

An earlier time, while visiting with Tanya and her family, I was introduced to a tall, bowlegged, dark skinned, man named Woodrow with close-cut hair. He had a habit of being sarcastic with me and checking me out at the same time. He was a little older than me: he was thirty-two, while I was twenty-four. Age wasn't the issue, but the way he dressed turned me off. He always wore high watered pants and a silk, flared, half buttoned shirts from the 1970s. I didn't give him the time of day, but that didn't stop him from pursuing me. This time while visiting, Woodrow caught me at a bad time: I was on edge with DJB. I asked Tanya and her sister if they had ever seen him dressed up. They never saw him dressed up, but as far as they knew he was a nice guy. He came around to visit the family and spotted me. We were cordial with each other.

> *"Guide me in Your truth and teach me, For You are the God of my salvation; For You [and only You] I wait [expectantly] all the day long." (Psalm 25:5 AMP)*

"Would you like to go to dinner and a hotel with me... just to get away," Woodrow asked me.

"I don't know you like that, and I'm not interested," I told him.

He had been aggravating me my entire visit. I was going out with my friends anyway. I wasn't going to entertain or give him the time of day because of the way he was dressed.

On Sunday night, after I broke his heart, he knocked on the door, and when I opened it, I was stunned. Woodrow looked distinguished and sharp; my eyes nearly popped out of my head. I knew then that I didn't have a chance. I messed up my chance by being superficial and judging him by his exterior before giving him a fair chance. He let me know he was really into me, and that for him it was love at first sight; but it wasn't that for me. Now, I was hurt because I hurt his feelings and my chances with him. I went home just disgusted all the way around. I had learned a valuable lesson.

"But the LORD said to Samuel, "Do not look at his appearance or at the height of his stature, because I have rejected him. For the LORD sees not as man sees; for man looks [a] at the outward appearance, but the LORD looks at the heart." (1 Samuel 16:1 AMP)

Thereafter, when I would visit Tanya, I would go looking for him. If he found out I was in town, he would come and see me. We would kick it together, and we would have breakfast together. I was cool with this for right now.

Now that I was back home, I couldn't wait to see DJB and burst his bubble. There would be no more of him sleeping with me up in here. By the end of the week, he came by. I had to let him know I wasn't one of his winky dink chicks who was probably scared of him. I had heard how he called these girls out of their name right after he slept with them. He came by as if nothing had happened, then he tried to play me with his twisted words and lies. Honey, I laid him out, and he thought I was crazy. He was shock.

"I didn't know you had all that in you," he said surprisingly.

"I'm not scared of you," I said bluntly.

"You are a feisty little thing. I guess that's why I like you." Right then and there we decided to be friends and that's it,"

"I heard how many children you have. You don't ever have to worry about me. I do not want any children by you. I will not give you child number ten." I told him.

"Trish, you wouldn't have my baby?" he said playfully.

I said, "H--l No!"

"You're smart," he said.

"I know I am," I said confidently.

"We are friends, right?" he said.

"Yes, we are. No hard feelings now even though I fussed you out." I said smiling.

Then, he walked through the door shaking his head and chuckling, whispering "*Woman, you're crazy.*"

The next time I spoke to Charlotte, I told her what happened, but she already knew because DJ B told her boyfriend, and he relayed it back to her. She laughed and said,

"That's good for him... trying to play you."

"The righteousness of the blameless will smooth their way and keep it straight, But the wicked will fall by his own wickedness.' (Proverbs 11:5 AMP)

*"Truthful lips will be established forever, But a lying tongue
is [credited] only for a moment" (Proverbs 12:19 AMP)*

We always wondered why men lie when they know we
are going to find out the truth. She had some of that same
problem with her own boyfriend. We started laughing
amongst ourselves and said that they should tell the truth.
Things would turn out better by just dealing with the
consequences.

However, we decided to change gears and go to another
club that weekend. I didn't want to go where DJ B was
playing. So, we went to a club called *"Forest Inn"* all the
way back in the boonies. This club was very nice. We were
having a good time until they started shooting. This club
only had one door and no back door. People were running
and trampling over each other. People were jumping into
cars head-first. I, on the other hand, stopped to look for my
shoe in the dark, while I was just as drunk as I wanted to be.
Charlotte and Achy were calling on me by the time I ran
to the car, the person who drove us down there took-off. I
was left behind. I thought, *"Oh my God, how in the world
am I going to get home." So,* I went back into the building,
and the only people who were still inside were the DJ and
his crew; they were all men. I told the DJ my situation, and
he was more than willing to take me home, even though it
was out of his way. They were my angels.

*"The name of the LORD is a strong tower; The righteous runs
to it and is safe and set on high [far above evil]." (Proverb
18:10 AMP)*

I told them to stop me at the town store because I knew
that's where my friends would be. When we pulled up to
the store, my friends were standing there concerned about

me and waiting on me. They felt bad and were hoping that I was right behind them. They had never been so happy to see me. They all hugged me and thanked the DJ for bringing me home safely. He happened to know Cousin Carol as well, and before leaving, he gave me his card and asked for my number. He was a short, handsome fellow, but I already knew that I didn't want to get involved with any more DJs. There were too many girls on their trails, and he also knew DJ B.

While we were at the store, my friends and I got something to eat, and then we went home. On my way home, I thought about what could have happened under the circumstances. I was so drunk, but I played it cool. The men could have taken advantage of me, but they didn't, and I wasn't afraid at all. I just kept smiling. Although I lost my shoe in the process, I had a good night.

Chapter 44
Fashion & Dance Contest

I didn't pass up the opportunity of being a part of a Fashion Contest at *Perdue*. The contest consisted of three to four categories, all of which separated the men and women. While I prepared for the Fashion Show, this young man named Anthony approached me.

"You look nice in your suit," Anthony said.

"Thank you, did you sign up for the contest?" I spoke.

"Yes," he said nodding his head.

Anthony was very handsome with nice brown skin. He had a top-fade haircut like Play (from the duo Kid-n'-Play) and a warm smile with pretty, pearly white teeth. He was also slightly taller than me and dressed GQ style.

Anthony and I were standing in line when a young lady came out with the same pants suit as me. The only difference between us was that I wore a black hat and heels; whereas, she wore flat shoes and no hat. Anthony encouraged me the entire time saying, "You're going to win." The judges went by the applause of the people in the audience, and I received more applause than she did.

"Girl, you're wearing that hat, and the suit looks better on you," he said complimenting me when I came backstage.

Before it was time to go on, I was so concerned about us having on the same thing, but in the end I won. This was the very reason why I liked to shop in New York: to avoid having the same clothes as other people.

Anthony hugged me, and he smelled so good. He was happy for me, and I was happy for him as well. Later, I found out that Cousin Carol knew him and his mother. I also learned that he was only working at Perdue temporarily because he was on his way to North Carolina A&T University in the fall to become an engineer.

"Do you have a girlfriend?" I asked him.

"Nah. We just broke up. I still have feelings for her," he told me.

I knew then that he wasn't ready for any relationship, and he made that very clear. Besides, he didn't see me that way; we became buddies- sister and brother.

Not long after, *Perdue* had another contest - a dance contest. We already know that this contest was calling on me. We had the opportunity to pick partners, and my partner was Tim. We were one of the three pairs. I asked him to be my partner because he was an excellent dancer, and he was gay; therefore, I didn't have to worry about him touching my butt or getting inappropriate with me. We had seen each other dance before at the club, so we knew what to expect from one another.

Anthony was standing out in the audience since I had invited him to come and watch. Tim and I danced so hard on the dance floor; eventually, one of the couples dropped out. They could not contend much longer with Tim and I. The next thing I know the crowd was cheering us on so hard that the other couple started taking off pieces of their clothes. Tim and I looked at each other and stopped. I just couldn't do it, and neither could he. Something on the inside just wouldn't let me expose my body like that. I didn't want to win that bad. They looked like they were having sex on the dance floor. They ended up winning, but I didn't think it was fair.

"I didn't know you could dance," Anthony said after it was over.

"Yeah. I love to dance," I told him.

"Yeah, I do too but listen: Can I take you out some-times?" he asked.

"Sure. I would love to. Are you sure you can keep up with me?" I said jokingly.

"I believe I can," he said while grinning.

After the dance contest at Perdue, I was in another one at a club, but this was a single dance contest-no partner. Well, I *threw down*, and I didn't have to take my clothes off to win either. I won twenty-five dollars, and I was so happy. After I won the contest, Tim told me that I would make a great stripper, but I told him that would never happen because it was not in me.

"Maybe not, but you're still a wonderful dancer," he said.

"Let us conduct ourselves properly and honorably as in the [light of] day, not in carousing and drunkenness, not in sexual promiscuity and irresponsibility, not in quarreling and jealousy." (Romans 13:13 AMP)

Everywhere I went people loved to see me dance espe-cially when I did the James Brown move. My feet would glide across the dance floor, and I would go all the way down and come back up. I was very light on my feet. This is something that Anthony didn't know about.

> *"Let them praise His name with dancing; Let them sing praises to Him with the tambourine and lyre." (Psalms 149:3 AMP)*

Nonetheless, Anthony and I went to a club in Greenville, North Carolina, and finally he had his chance to show me his moves. Honey, we got on the dance floor, and this man could dance; he was light on his feet too. We had such a good time. Of course, I did all the drinking; someone had to be the designated driver, so he limited his drinking intake.

Overall, he and I became good friends-very good friends. Every time he was on break from school, he would call me, and we would plan to get together. There was one time when we had a serious conversation about our lives. He had shared with me that his mom abused him as a child. It occurred to me that we had similar stories. Overtime, I sensed that he had a little bit of a short temper, but he had always been kind to me.

When he came down from school, I introduced him to Tanya. We all went out together, and I knew he felt special because he had two ladies on his arms. When we danced, he danced with the both of us. Honey, we laughed, danced, and drank; we had a ball (a good time). Once we dropped Tanya off that night, Anthony was singing a new tune (talking differently) on the way to take me back home to Gail's. He was in shocked that I moved out of Cousin Carol's home, so I explained to him what had occurred. I told him it was time for me to move out. Gail was barely home, and I was working on getting my own place.

"It sounds like you have a plan," he said being impressed with my stances to go forward.

"Yes, I do," I said.

"I like that," he said.

> *"Commit your works to the LORD [submit and trust them to Him], And your plans will succeed [if you respond to His will and guidance]." (Proverbs 16:3AMP)*

Then, he began to express his change of heart towards me as we reached Gail's house.

Chapter 45
Strictly Platonic

"**You're so** beautiful, and I was a fool to only like you as a friend," he told me seriously.

He had turned the tables on me, but I didn't like him like that. He wanted to make love to me, but I really didn't want to.

"I wanna make love to you, Trish," he told me as he stared into my eyes with passion.

I didn't want to hurt him, so I just pretended like I wanted to as well. God of heaven must have truly known my heart because when I went to the bathroom, my menstrual cycle started. Oh my God, I was so happy.

"Anthony we can't do anything because my period just came on," I told him.

"Okay maybe it wasn't meant to be," he said.

"Yeah, you are probably right." I kissed him and said.

After that, he stayed for a while then he left. I was so happy. I just wanted to be friends with him because the only person I had on my mind was Woodrow. When Anthony was on his way back to school after the break, he would call or stop by before he left; I always appreciated that. I don't know why, but once he told me what he had gone through as a child, it put a little fear in my heart. I didn't know how much of an effect it had on him, and I didn't want to find out. I already had to deal with my own skeletons.

"You hypocrite (play-actor, pretender), first get the log out of your own eye, and then you will see clearly to take the speck out of your brother's eye."(Matthew 7:5 Amp)

Once he left, I was back to hanging out in Plymouth, on and off every weekend. Tanya, her sister, Beanie, her mother, Ms. Joyce, and I would party out at the club and hangout in the juke joints. At one club we went to, the woman who was the owner of the club, kept staring at me especially while I danced.

"The owner over there is asking questions about you," Ms. Joyce whispered to me.

When she told me what the woman was asking, I told Ms. Joyce to tell the woman that I'm not interested. Apparently, the woman was a lesbian.

"Yawl I'm ready to go," I told them.

I was feeling very uncomfortable.

The woman walked up to the car as we were about to drive off.

"Wait...hold on don't leave," she said.

She began to come on to me and tell me that if I gave her a chance, then she would give me anything I wanted.

"No thank you. I don't want anything from you. I like men ma'am. After tonight you will never see me again," I told her.

We drove off, and they laughed hysterically. They got a kick out of laughing at my facial expression when the woman propositions me. I was appalled at what she offered me; it was crazy.

> *"Just as Sodom and Gomorrah and the adjacent cities, since they in the same way as these angels indulged in gross immoral freedom and unnatural vice and sensual perversity. They are exhibited [in plain sight] as an example in undergoing the punishment of everlasting fire."* (Jude 1:7 AMP)

The next week, things were slow. Ms. Joyce and I got up early Sunday morning and went to one of her drinking houses where they played cards. While we were there, I met Woodrow's cousin, Willie, but they called him by his nickname, Tawookee. He was winning in the card game, and he put me up. I had come with no money and ended up with money in my pocket. I knew a little something about playing cards. I used to play *Pitty Pat, Poker, and Blackjack* with my sister and brothers.

> *"He who loves money will not be satisfied with money, nor he who loves abundance with its gain. This too is vanity (emptiness)."* (Ecclesiastes 5:10 AMP)

As children, we knew all types of card games from watching our mom and step-dad. I promised myself a long time ago that I would never touch any cards dealing with playing for money. Once, when I was downtown paying a bill for my mom, I ran across a friend that I knew from school, and they had a game called *Three Card Malley*. There was two black cards and one red card. They explained to the crowd of people you had to find the red card. Being inquisitive, I stopped and watched. Then, I decided to play. I strongly believed that I knew where the card was. When we bet twenty dollars, and that twenty dollars would get you forty dollars. Boy, that sounded good to me. So, I bet my mom's money and won the first around. Then, they said if you bet forty dollars and find the red card that would get you eighty dollars. I got excited, so I played the bet, but I ended up losing all my mom's money.

> *"But each one is tempted when he is dragged away, enticed and baited [to commit sin] by his own [worldly] desire (lust, passion)." (James 1:14 AMP)*

> *"Let your character [your moral essence, your inner nature] be free from the love of money [shun greed—be financially ethical], being content with what you have; for He has said, "I WILL NEVER [under any circumstances] DESERT YOU [nor give you up nor leave you without support, nor will I in any degree leave you helpless], NOR WILL I FORSAKE or LET YOU DOWN or RELAX MY HOLD ON YOU [assuredly not]!" (Hebrews 13:5 AMP)*

I was devastated. I couldn't breathe, and my stomach was turning at the thought of the chastisement of my actions. I had to think of a lie and a plan; I thank God that I had a summer job at the time.

"Someone had pick-pocketed me on the bus. If you gave me a chance, I can pay you back the money when I get paid," I said anxiously.

"Okay," she said, "And, are you sure that you didn't stop at that Three Card Malley game and play my money?"

My eyes got wide,

"No, I didn't," I said while avoiding eye contact.

"What in the world! How did she know? Is she a psychic or something?" I thought. I was stunned at the mere fact that she knew.

"For the gifts and calling of God are without repentance"
(Romans 11:29 KJV)

"You can pay me back, but I still think you did something with my money. I just can't prove it," she said while squinting at me.

I walked away scotch free, and I paid her back her money. From that day, I made a declaration that I would never gamble again because I didn't like losing money.

Anyway, Tawookee offered to put up his money since I didn't have any, and that was the only reason why I played. After we played, he bought me a drink, and said that he hoped to see me again.

Well, that next weekend, Tanya, Beanie, Ms. Joyce, and I went out to the club, and we bumped into Tawookee. Honey, I thought I could dance, but *he* had some moves on him-moves I had never seen before. He walked in dancing and everyone knew him. When he spotted me, he made his way directly towards me. He stared me dead in my eyes and said, "D—n You're gorgeous with those beautiful eyes." He took my hand and led me to the dance floor. I was so flattered and blushed uncontrollably. Oh, we danced so well together. He danced like Patrick Swayze in *Dirty dancing*: this was my type of dancing. Oh man, and he was also a bad (great) dresser, I can't even explain it: it was better than GQ... my goodness. Also, he wasn't that much older than me.

In the face, he wasn't all that attractive. To be as young as he was, he didn't have any teeth in the front of his mouth. *"He had all this money. Why in the world he hadn't gotten his teeth fixed,"* I thought to myself. After that night, he started chasing me down while his ex-girlfriends were chasing him down.

"When I saw you, girl…it was love at first sight," he told me.

"That's probably what you tell all the girls." I said as I sucked my teeth and turned my head sideways.

He had his baby momma coming after him, but honey, he had those girls under his control. Those girls wanted to come after me, and for what? He wasn't my boyfriend or anything like that; I just liked dancing with him. Eventually, my dealings with Tawookee got back to Woodrow. He was furious with me, but he had it all wrong. Tawookee was going around talking about how he wanted me to be his lady, but I wanted to be friends- purely platonic.

One evening, Tawookee asked me if we could get a room, and I told him okay. No matter, how much I drank that night; I just couldn't take it there with him. The room was gorgeous, but I didn't know why I said yes. He told me if I didn't want to lay with him, he understood, and he would take me right home.

"Take me home." I said.

"It's my Cousin Woodrow? Isn't it" he said in dismay.

"Yes," I said truthfully.

"Well, I guess he won," he said.

"It doesn't have to do with anyone winning. Woodrow was here anyway before you got in the picture," I told him.

It was obvious he was in competition with his cousin; regardless, he was very nice about it and respected my wishes.

"You know you broke my heart," he told me.

"Well, I didn't mean to, but I'm sure you'll bounce right back," I stated sincerely.

In my defense, he did tell Woodrow that nothing happened between us and that we were just friends. Why was Woodrow so worried? Maybe deep inside, I wanted to make Woodrow jealous. Well, it worked because he certainly confronted me and that was the end of that.

Thereafter, I started laying low from Plymouth and allowing stuff to calm down. I started back hanging in my hometown again.

Chapter 46
Meeting Mr. Right

I reconnected with Charlotte and Achy Lackey, and they were glad to see me as always.

"You finally found your way back home," Charlotte said.

"Yes. I missed yawl too," I told her with a smile.

The next club we decided to hit was the *Cierra Lounge*. They had their grand reopening. It was said that the *Cierra Lounge* was *the place* once upon a time. I asked what happened. They said that some years ago someone had gotten shot and died there; thereafter, they closed the place down.

"You shall not commit murder (unjustified, deliberate homicide)." (Exodus 20:13 AMP)

Most people that we knew were going to revisit the club, but this was going to be my first time ever seeing the place. I was pretty excited about going to a new place. To my surprise, Gail told me that DJ B was going to be playing there.

All of us went to the club, including Gail. People came from all over; the crowd was big. Linda and her sister were there. You remember I told you a little about Linda who I met through Charlotte? We had become more acquainted. Did I mention that Linda had a child by my uncle? I thought that this was great. She had such a beautiful daughter; she looked just like the Bazemores. I would visit her home from time to time. When we went out, we had a good old time at the club and a whole lot of laughs. We never had any confusion; there was peace which was the way I liked it. I tried to spend equal time with all my friends and never leave them out, but I never wanted to wear out my welcome.

While we were at the club, I spotted someone I knew, and he spotted me as well. Our eyes met each other, and I recognized him. Wes, I used to see him around at *Perdue*, but I first met him in Plymouth. A couple of years ago, he used to mess around with Beanie while her boyfriend was living in New York. Wes was just something for Beanie to do- nothing serious.

We talked for a little bit, and he asked me to dance. He was actually a great dancer. I asked myself, *"Why in the world do I always fall for a player (womanizer)? Every man I bump into down here has to have more than one woman."* After I got to know him better, I learned that he was a little sneaky and sly when dealing with other women. I guess these men just didn't want to be committed, but I was getting a little tired of this mindset. Wes and I played around a bit - nothing major. I was getting older and my time was winding down. I had to find Mr. Right.

I would ask myself, *"Where could he be?"* These were the times when I was alone or with Gail, and I'd express that I was ready for something serious. I was twenty-four, soon to be twenty-five years old; this was getting old. I was ready to get married and have children.

This particular day, I was hanging out with Gail at her parent's house. We were in the backyard hanging up clothes when a brown skinned, broad shouldered, bowlegged man with a nice smile stopped by to speak to Gail. I didn't know him, but then he came out of the blue and asked who I was in a sarcastic tone. I didn't like his approach, and I let it be known.

"Oh, you're a feisty one," he said.

Then, we just started talking smack to one another. He was very humorous.

"Oh my God! Are you sure you both don't know each other?" Gail laughed.

"No, but now we do," we both said.

He introduced himself to me, and we'll call him RP. Putting all jokes aside, he asked me if he could take me out for drinks, and I said,

"Yes, sure why not?

"I live with Gail, so you can pick me up from there," I told him.

"No problem. Can I have your phone number?" he asked.

I nodded and gave him my phone number, and he gave me his beeper number.

On the day of our date, he called to let me know that he was going to be a little late, and I thought that was very considerate. I remember it was raining that evening, but that didn't stop us. When he arrived, I was ready to go. He was a gentleman and opened the door of his two-seater, grey *Trans Am* for me. I remember saying to myself, "*This car suits him.*" He was a debonair kind of guy.

He knew a place where we could have drinks, and the dancefloor was on the other side of the establishment.

"You're going to pay for the drinks, right?" he said when we got there.

"Hmmm. No, I am not." I said as I looked at him with my mouth open.

"I'm just messin' with you," he said.

"Oh okay, I was about to tell you to take me home," I told him.

He started laughing.

We talked and asked each other questions as we were getting more acquainted. Our birthdays came up in the conversation, and I said that my birthday was just around the corner; I was going to be twenty-five years old.

"I guess we'll have to do something on your birthday," he said.

"I would like that," I told him.

He was just cool and smooth. We both drank and smoked whether it was hard liquor or beer we had that in common.

He worked in Virginia, so he would travel and come home on the weekend, and I told him I worked at *Perdue*. He was from Aulander, North Carolina, not too far from Lewiston- about fifteen minutes away. We shared a little bit that night about each other; it was nice. After talking, we danced, and he was a smooth dancer honey. "*I think I have met my match,*" I said to myself, and I believe he had met his match as well. We had a wonderful time, and he took me home with a smile on my face. At the end of the night, he said he wanted to see me again, and I was okay with that.

Chapter 47
Courting Stages

During our courting stage, we celebrated our birthdays together. His was a month after mine, February 2, and he was an Aquarius: I was sold out on zodiac signs. A girlfriend of mine was an Aquarius as well and we got along beautifully, so I figured that RP and I would too.

> *"-and has gone and served other gods and worshiped them, or the sun or the moon or any of the heavenly host, [doing these things] which I have commanded not to do,"* (Deuteronomy 17:3 AMP)

We spoke to each other every day for a few months as if we were boyfriend and girlfriend, and I guess at this point, we were. I didn't have anyone and neither did he. We would hang out together, but I knew it was serious when he took me to his home to meet his family. He introduced me to his mom, and it was very pleasant to meet her. I also enjoyed meeting his cousin B, her daughter, KR, and her two sons. They were very friendly and humorous. You could tell that they were a close-knit family, and that RP was loved very much by them. He was youngest of eight children. Often, he brought me around his family, so that I could become more acquainted with them. We mostly saw each other on the weekend since he worked in the *Smithfield* plant in

Virginia which was one hour away from North Carolina if I remember correctly.

His mother stayed in the heart of Aulander, North Carolina, and everyone knew her. She was a short, little bowlegged, and pigeon-toed lady. She faithfully went to the church that was right up the street from where she lived.

> *"not forsaking our meeting together [as believers for worship and instruction], as is the habit of some, but encouraging one another; and all the more [faithfully] as you see the day [of Christ's return] approaching." (Hebrews 10:25 AMP)*

She was the type of person that would help anybody, and she would give her last to people especially RP. He was very spoiled, but she didn't take any nonsense. At times I wanted to laugh at her disciplinary actions, but I didn't. Once I remember, he didn't get his way in what he asked her for, so he got sassy with her. Honey, she turned back around and pointed her finger at him, and asked, "RP, who do you think you're talking to?" He apologized quickly, and she ended up giving him what he asked her for, but not before her saying, "Don't you *ever* disrespect me again."

"Yes, ma'am," he said

Later, I introduced RP to Charlotte and her new beau (boyfriend), Roger. She had broken up with Achy Lackey because she had grown tired of putting up with his mess over the years. She and Roger were like two peas in the pod when he wasn't working. I also introduced him to Linda and simply mentioned his name to my other friends. They had known him already because they went to high school with him, and I thought that was something.

RP and I weren't perfect: we had our spats here and there. One time, he and I got into it after we had been drinking. I hit him while we were arguing, but he didn't hit me back; instead, he tried to hold me back from hitting him.

"Don't you put your hands on me, Trish," he told me while we argued.

The next time we got in an argument, I hit him again. Although he told me again, not to hit him. I had hit him one, too many times, and he hit me back. I was in shock but after that I didn't hit him anymore.

"For I know that nothing good lives in me, that is, in my flesh [my human nature, my worldliness—my sinful capacity]. For the willingness [to do good] is present in me, but the doing of good is not." (Romans 7:18 AMP)

I was so used to a man hitting me first, so in my mind, I had to beat him before he did it to me. At that point, whatever I got, I deserved it because I should've never laid my hands on him, no matter how upset I was.

"Understand this, my beloved brothers and sisters. Let everyone be quick to hear [be a careful, thoughtful listener], slow to speak [a speaker of carefully chosen words and], slow to anger [patient, reflective, forgiving]; [20] for the [resentful, deep-seated] anger of man does not produce the righteousness of God [that standard of behavior which He requires from us]." (James 1:19-20 AMP)

After these incidents, things were okay between us. Even though. we only knew each other for a short period of time, it felt like we had known each other forever. I'd sit in his lap, and we would discuss our plans for a future together. He wanted to get a place together, but I told him in order for us to get a place together, he would have to marry me. I wasn't shacking up with anyone anymore.

> *"Marriage is to be held in honor among all [that is, regarded as something of great value], and the marriage bed undefiled [by immorality or by any sexual sin]; for God will judge the sexually immoral and adulterous." (Hebrews 13:4 AMP)*

"Well, I guess we're going to have to do something about that," he told me.

"Are you serious," I asked in shock.

"Yes, I mean, we don't have to have anything big," he said.

"We can go to the Justice of Peace (courthouse) to get married and have a reception," I suggested.

"That sounds good. My family would like that; they love gatherings. I think it's time for me to settle down anyway," he said.

Then, we embraced and kissed each other. We were so happy.

"I already have the land for a house, and all we have to do is put something on it," I said.

"That's good," he replied.

"The land is in Lewiston... next door to my cousins," I informed him.

I had cousins all around me in the dead-end circle. They were all family, aside from a couple of other neighbors that I had the pleasure of knowing.

I told him that I was still paying for the land, and he wanted to see the land. He liked the land itself, but he didn't like the idea that it was in Lewiston. He wanted to get something in Aulander that was closer to his mom and family. In my opinion, he was being a little inconsiderate for someone who didn't pay a dime on it.

Anyway, we started making plans for when the wedding would take place. First, we informed our family, friends, and I can't forget about RP's son, JD. I believe he was seven years old when I met him. He was so smart. He was adorable and looked just like RP.

The date of our marriage was set for June 5, 1992. I had told Charlotte that I wanted her to be my maid of honor, and I wanted Gail to be there as well. RP told his best friend that he wanted him to be there, and the family took care of the rest.

Chapter 48
I's Married Now

After dating for five months, we were ready to be married. We took care of all the requirements in order to get married. He bought the rings, and he got down on one knee and traditionally asked me. Of course, I said yes, but there were many doubts from his family.

"Is yawl sure? You don't think that this is happening too soon?" They would ask.

"Yes," we said.

"RP isn't ready to get married; he's a momma's boy. Trish, he is still in debt to me. I'm still paying on a car that he crashed." His mom told me.

I just listened.

Regardless, I just saw this as her not wanting him to lose him – her baby boy. I felt that this didn't have anything to do with me; that was between him and her. He truly wanted her blessing, and later, she changed her mind.

"Well, if you both love each other, so be it. I'll do everything I can to help," she said.

We were very happy that she gave us her blessing especially RP.

In contrast, my friends were a little more supportive from the beginning. If I was happy, they were happy. If they knew anything misleading about him, they certainly didn't speak up or tell me. DJ B had something to say about it, and I didn't even know they knew each other.

DJ B said, "You're marrying RP to make me jealous."

"Please... this had nothing to do with you," I scoffed.

"Trisha, I think you still got some feelings for me. I don't know why you're marrying him," DJ B stated.

"I'm marrying him because I love him," I told him.

Gail asked also if I was sure about marrying him. I was shocked by this because her and RP were close.

"Yes, I'm sure," I told her. She told DJ B, and he jokingly said, "Let me know where it is, so I can walk in and stop it."

I was so glad that I told RP about DJ B and I; I didn't want him to hear it from anyone else.

RP had bought his off-white suit with matching shoes, and I purchase an off-white, lace dress with pearl buttons, a pearl necklace and earrings to match my off-white shoes. My bouquet of wedding flowers was beautiful. Aside from the presence of our witnesses, we also had someone there to take pictures. After we got married, we walked out to the car from the courthouse.

"You's married now!" Charlotte stated.

"I's married Now!" I responded with joy. We embraced each other with laughter.

The car was dressed up and had "*Just Got Married*" written on it. Our friends out did themselves with the cans that were hanging on the back as we rode through town beeping the horn: thanks to RP's best friend and best man, Mr. W, who transported us.

Before we left, we talked to the family a bit, and his mother wished us well on our trip. For a whole week, we spent our honeymoon in Virginia in a room he had set up for us.

However, there were a couple of things that I found strange. He wanted to visit his friends and introduce me to them, but I thought it was odd to be visiting others while we were on our honeymoon. We should have been spending time together alone, but maybe he felt like it was unnecessary because he had already gotten the goodies before we got married.

> *"If a man seduces a virgin who is not betrothed, and lies with her, he must pay a dowry (marriage price) for her to be his wife." (Exodus 22:16 AMP)*

The next morning, he took me to meet a friend that was a very pretty and polite woman. Then, later, we visited and he introduced me to Pat, his friend from work, and his girlfriend, Mag. We all sat around and talked with one another. Later on, through the week, we visited some of his family members.

Though we visited others, we had a nice time together. We were able to spend some time sitting on the balcony of our hotel room watching the sunset and drinking Champagne. During the week, we went to the beach. He could swim but I couldn't. I did get in the water, but I didn't go as far as he did. I enjoyed him wrapping his big, strong arms around me, holding me close to him so that nothing wouldn't happen to me while I was in the water. We thoroughly enjoyed ourselves, and soon, we began preparing to go home. I knew once we got home, we had plenty of things to take care of.

Once we arrived home, we had to figure out where we were going to live. RP suggested that we stay with his mom, and she didn't mind us staying there when we asked her. Before, she didn't dare allow us to sleep together in her home without being married. I didn't want to anyway because I would have felt uncomfortable.

Remember the piece of land that I discussed? Now, that we were married, RP wanted to make demands. He assumed he would be able to make all of the decisions about the land that *I* had started paying on long before we were married. I was not in agreement with his decisions, but I didn't fuss about it. I tried to tell him about the details of the deal, but he didn't want to listen. RP wanted me to talk to the owner to see if we could work out a bargain, so I did. When it didn't work with me, he wanted to talk to owner himself. The owner told him that this deal was made way before he was in the picture. The owner was stubborn and said, "A deal is a deal." I felt that RP was being so ungrateful; I was embarrassed.

> *"For all that is in the world—the lust and sensual craving of the flesh and the lust and longing of the eyes and the boastful pride of life [pretentious confidence in one's resources or in the stability of earthly things]—these do not come from the Father, but are from the world." (1 John 2:16 AMP)*

Once we finished paying the land off which wasn't much, RP wanted to sell it. He wanted to take the money and buy some land in Aulander.

"Oh no we are not!" I exclaimed.

He told his mother about it and she said, "No, you stay right over there in Lewiston. You don't have to be in Aulander."

I was so happy she said that.

"For this reason a man shall leave his father and his mother, and shall be joined to his wife; and they shall become one flesh." (Genesis 2:24 AMP)

I had borrowed the money for the land from Cousin Carol's boyfriend, Mr. R. She told him my situation, and he lent me the money. We paid the owner and got the deed.

I always talked about wanting a house, but one of my girl-friends and I were talking, and she tried to change my mind.

"What are yawl trying to get?" she asked.

"A double-wide trailer." I told her,

"Don't you think that's a little too much to be just starting off?" she asked.

"No," I told her as I thought to myself, "*Don't you have a big house? Why can't I?*"

"You know Trisha, maybe it is best for you and RP to start with a single-wide: something you can afford in case something happens," she suggested.

Well, I believed that if something happened, I would be able to afford to live in my double wide. I was really upset when she said this. I realized that it isn't always worth telling everybody what you plan to do. She may not have meant any harm, but I didn't like what she said. It showed me that someone will always try to talk you out of what you desire. No one knew what we could or could not afford.

> *"Now faith is the assurance (title deed, confirmation) of things hoped for (divinely guaranteed), and the evidence of things not seen [the conviction of their reality—faith comprehends as fact what cannot be experienced by the physical senses]." (Hebrews 11:1 AMP)*

Furthermore, it's wasn't anyone's business. Her statement didn't stop us from getting what we desired. RP and I went out shopping, and we worked together to obtain money for the necessary things for our home. We were so excited about having our own home! We were on our grind (hard work; on top of things).

Fortunately, we found something that we liked. The grey doublewide was spacious and nice with three bedrooms, two bathrooms, burgundy shutters on the outside, and it had furniture (included in payments), so we didn't have to buy much. Then, we put the land up for collateral and had the land inspected. We did everything that was necessary in order to sit the double wide trailer on the land. As a wedding gift, my Uncle Charlie wired and inspected it without charge which was thoughtful of him. Also, we had to make sure that the septic tank was accessible, and it was. Everything was falling into place and going as planned. The only thing left to do was put a skirt around the bottom of the double-wide; in which, we planned to do later.

> [28]*For which one of you, when he wants to build a watchtower [for his guards], does not first sit down and calculate the cost, to see if he has enough to finish it? (Luke 14:28 AMP)*

> *"Many plans are in a man's mind, But it is the LORD's purpose for him that will stand (be carried out)." (Proverbs 19:21 AMP)*

While we were waiting to move in, we were preparing for our reception. We dressed comfortable since it was the peak of summer. His family planned for us to have the reception at a recreation building. It was very roomy inside but hot even with a fan. We had a cookout outside of the building, and there was a lot of people there. His family did a wonderful job with the preparations. Some of my friends came, but it was mostly his family that was there.

When it was time to cut the cake, we smudged the cake on each other's face in tradition. Then, out of the blue, RP, *my husband*, called me another woman's name.

"What did you call me?" I asked with seriousness.

He called me the name a second time, and that's when he caught himself. I couldn't believe it as my eyes began to swell with tears. Instead of making a scene, I walked away discreetly trying to keep anyone from noticing how distraught I was. Although I thought I was discreet, I heard little pitter- patters feet walking behind me until they were walking beside me: it was my step-son.

"Mrs. Patricia, are you alright?" JD asked me softly.

"Yes, I'm fine," I said while trying to hold my tears back.

"If you're fine, why are you crying? It's my dad. Did my dad say something to make you cry? Don't cry Mrs. Patricia. You want me to say something to him?" He said with his hand placed in mine with a puzzled look.

"No. Your daddy and I are going to be fine. Don't you worry about me. You go ahead and play with the rest of the children," I said with a tight-lipped smile.

"Okay," he said and I gave him a hug.

He made me feel so much better- such a sweetheart and smart. He knew that his daddy had done something to me, and he wanted to be my little hero.

> *"Out of the mouths of infants and nursing babes, you have established strength Because of Your adversaries, That You might silence the enemy and make the revengeful cease." (Psalms 8:2 AMP)*

RP did apologize; therefore, I tried not to let it bother me too much. I couldn't allow that to spoil our day. We partied and had a good time at the reception. We received many gifts for our home, but RP wanted to give some of our gifts to his family members. I was feeling some kind of way about that. They were *our* gifts. They weren't his gifts alone. "*He's already starting off wrong,*" I thought to myself.

> *"In the same way, you husbands, live with your wives in an understanding way [with great gentleness and tact, and with an intelligent regard for the marriage relationship], as with [a] someone physically weaker, since she is a woman. Show her honor and respect as a fellow heir of the grace of life, so that your prayers will not be hindered or ineffective." (1 Peter 3:7 AMP)*

"You need to discuss things like that with me before you take it upon yourself to make those decisions. You should care about how I feel, and vice versa," I told him.

"I didn't think you would mind," he stated.

"Oh really? Well, how would you have known that if you never asked me?" I replied with my arms folded.

These were the kind of issues that were going on at the beginning of our marriage. It was the misunderstanding the language of marriage. It was us: the "I" and "me" had become we. I understood that but at times, he didn't.

> *"AND THE TWO SHALL BECOME ONE FLESH; so that they are no longer two, but [are united as] one flesh."* (Mark 10:8 AMP)

For instance, the first time he got sick during our marriage, he had the audacity to go to his mother's house for *her* to take care of him. I was furious and hurt by this. "Who am I?" I asked him, "I am your wife. I want to be the one to take care of you when you're sick." I felt like he had robbed me of that. I went off! I didn't understand why his mother didn't send him home where he belonged. In fact, neither of them seemed to understand why I was upset. This is where I truly realized that I had married a momma's boy (a man that depends on his mother too much or in an unnecessary way). His mom never been married before so that explains it.

Other than these issues, we enjoyed our home together. I continued to decorate little by little. He bought a leather set for the sitting area from *Rent- to- Own*, and we had a jacuzzi in our master bathroom which we couldn't wait to try out.

As we continued to organize things, we moved the car from Gail's yard to our yard. RP's car was acting up, so he had purchase another one that was a straight shift. I couldn't drive yet, so he drove everywhere we went, and my car stayed parked. He'd drive my car sometimes so that it would keep running.

Moreover, I didn't like the idea that I worked at night, and he worked during the day. By the time I would get home, he was gone. We didn't get to spend much time with each other, and I was thinking about doing something about it on my next vacation. I talked to RP about me getting another job, and he agreed.

"If that's what you want to do, you should do it," he said.

In some instances, we still had our challenges. We would have arguments about JD spending the night on the weekend. He would use JD as a reason for me to stay home and an excuse for him to go out. JD was there to spend time with the both of us, not just me. I was furious at RP; he was being sneaky and underestimating my intelligence. Unbelievable! We would end up arguing because I knew what he was up to, but he would lie about it, of course.

"If any of you lacks wisdom [to guide him through a decision or circumstance], he is to ask of [our benevolent] God, who gives to everyone generously and without rebuke or blame, and it will be given to him." (James 1:5 AMP)

I found out the hard way that he would be out gambling and drinking. One time he didn't come home until the next day. He didn't call, and his mom hadn't seen him. I was truly worried about him. Once he came home, I was fired up (irate), but at least he came home with more money than he left with. He wasn't a stingy man. He gave me money for lunch and anything else that I may have needed, but I still fussed because he could have called to inform me of his whereabouts. That would have been considerate.

I loved when we went to the club together. When we danced together, it was outrageous. All our friends and strangers loved to watch us dance. There were times when we had the whole dance floor to ourselves. I don't even know how to explain it to you. We flowed together like no other; whether it was fast or slow. We always looked sharped together.

Overtime, we found ourselves arguing a lot. I guess because we were really getting to know each other. I remember one of his friends stopped by, and RP switched on me unexpectedly. He began to demand that I cook, and it appeared to me that he was trying to impress his company. I had been cooking all along, but he was acting as if he had to tell me to cook for him. I looked at him like he was foolish. I didn't say anything then, but when the company left, I had plenty to say.

"RP what in the heck was your problem? You tried to prove something in front of your company?" I asked him.

"I don't know what you are talking about," he shrugged.

"Oh, now you don't know what I am talking about. You cook your own d---- dinner," I spat. "You don't demand me to do nothing...talking to me any kind of way in front of people, trying to act like you're *the man*, and disrespecting me for no reason. You won't eat tonight if I got to cook it," I scoffed.

"I apologize. You right I shouldn't have done that. Since I did that, I will cook," he said.

"I accept your apology. We can cook together." I said and we hugged and kissed each other.

> *"Pay attention and always be on guard [looking out for one another]! If your brother sins and disregards God's precepts, solemnly warn him; and if he repents and changes, forgive him." (Luke 17:3 AMP)*

He was full of surprises-good and bad. His next surprise was when I had caught him snorting cocaine with some friends in the car. The white powder was on his nose. For some time, he had hidden that from me. What he was doing was an *expensive habit*.

"I didn't know that you do drugs," I said smartly.

"It's not a habit. I can stop anytime. I only do it once in a blue moon-only on special occasions," he told me.

"You need to stop completely," I said frankly, "because I know what drugs can do. Snorting cocaine is scary."

I didn't mind him drinking since I did it as well, but something had to give (something needed to change).

Chapter 49
Two Wrongs, Don't Make it Right

"Do you not know that your body is a temple of the Holy Spirit who is within you, whom you have [received as a gift] from God, and that you are not your own [property]?
(1 Corinthians 6:19 AMP)

"17 God will destroy anyone who destroys this temple. For God's temple is holy, and you are that temple."
(1 Corinthians 3:17 NLT)

During this time, things were getting a little rocky, so I wanted to spice things up a little bit.

"Have you ever had a birthday party," I asked him.

He shook his head and said, "No."

"Well, I want to give you one," I told him.

It had been seven months since we got married, and his birthday was coming. We began to plan, and all of our friends were invited. I invited my buddy, Steve and his wife; they were newlyweds as well. Boy, he was a riot (a funny dude). He owned a junk yard filled with cars, and people came there to buy parts for their cars. He was a mechanic, and he also bought cars that people didn't want.

When Steve came to the party, it was the first time that I was introduced to his wife, who he talked so much about. She was so beautiful inside and out. Her name was Georgetta, but she preferred to be called Dale. We hit it off as if we had known each other for years. I thought Steve was a riot, but he didn't have anything on Dale. She was hilarious and with her country accent-oh my God. She would have you bent over, laughing, with water coming out of your eyes. This was a start of a wonderful friendship for me and RP. Being friends with a married couple: we needed that. We all had things in common.

> *"With all humility [forsaking self-righteousness], and gentleness [maintaining self-control], with patience, bearing with one another [a] in [unselfish] love." (Ephesians 4:2 AMP)*

We worked hard to prepare for the party. Charlotte and my brothers- in-law, Lou and Pete, came as well and many others. Even Cousin Carol had stopped by. We had a DJ, a big trash can full of beer, and food. It was raining that evening; therefore, we had to put plastic covering near the entrance for the arrival of our guests since our double wide was still new.

We partied hard; however, in the midst of me parting, I was alert and very observant. I had to look for my husband: the birthday boy. It was his birthday party, and he was nowhere in sight. I looked around everywhere, until something said, "*Check the bedroom.*" I caught RP in the bathroom snorting cocaine with a couple of his buddies.

> *"For nothing is secret, that shall not be made manifest; neither anything hid, that shall not be known and come abroad." (Luke 8:17 AMP)*

"What are you doing? You told me that you weren't going to mess with that stuff anymore!" I exclaimed.

"Come on Patricia! It's my birthday. Loosen up- just this one time. After this, I won't touch it anymore. I haven't messed with it in a while," he said while chucklingly.

"I'm upset because you were being sneaky with it. I mean, you're already doing it. What's done is done. It's after the fact that I'm concerned about."

> *"Woe to the rebellious children, saith the LORD, that take counsel, but not of me; and that cover with a covering, but not of my spirit, that they may add sin to sin:" (Isaiah 30:1 KJV)*

"What did I say? Its only once in a blue moon" he said while holding me.

"You said the same thing last time," I told him.

"Well, I mean it this time, okay?" he replied.

"Okay," I said, giving him the benefit of the doubt.

"Come on let's go and join our friends. Don't be mad. It's my birthday," he said and then he kissed me.

"Okay," I said.

I tried to fix my face before I went out there in front of our guests.

We had the electric slide and the soul train line going on. I looked at RP, and he was really enjoying himself; that's all that mattered. We surrounded the table, sang happy birthday and gave him his gifts. My brother-in-law were so sweet; they started cleaning up without me asking them to help. In the meantime, I had to keep my eyes on Charlotte and the other brother-in-law. My brother-in-law was married, so I told Charlotte that nothing could happen between them.

"Girl, it's kind of hard because he's very tempting. I'll leave him alone only because you're my friend," I said.

"Thank you," I said to her.

I, then, told my brother-in-law to behave himself, as well.

I spent over five hundred dollars on this party, and it was worth it. But after affects of the party, we came in agreement that we would never have a party like that in our home again. That day, all we wanted to do is lay in bed and rest. When we finally got up, we had to clean up here and there.

When I went back to work, Steve told me that he and Dale had truly enjoyed themselves. Dale and I had exchange numbers at the party, so we could get together sometimes. They lived right up the road and around the corner from us. Their house and Steve's junk yard were walking distance, and I was so glad to hear that.

In addition, when I went on my vacation, I still wanted to find a new day job, so Dale and I applied at *Wranglers* to become machine operators. I heard about Wranglers through Patricia Arrington (now Patricia Wiggins). She had left *Perdue* and had been working at *Wranglers* for a while making good money through production. I was truly interested in working there, and they were hiring. I had worked nights at Perdue for six years, and it was time to leave. I always knew that I wouldn't be working at Perdue forever. I had too many dreams on the inside of me.

Before I left Perdue, I ran into Evelien, and she began to talking to me about Jesus. I told her that I didn't want to hear anything about God: I wasn't ready yet it would be a waste of her time.

"Well, I'll be praying for you," she said respecting my wishes.

"Okay," I said as I shrugged my shoulders.

"Let your light so shine before men, that they may see your good works, and glorify your Father which is in heaven." *(Matthew 5:16 AMP)*

"Fools, because of their rebellious way, and because of their sins, were afflicted.18 They detested all kinds of food, and they drew near to the gates of death." *(Psalms 107:17-18 AMP)*

Anyway, Dale and I was hired at Wrangler's around the same time, and we were so excited although we didn't work on the same line. They paid us hourly for six months, and then after the six months of training, our hourly pay became based on production by the bundles we did. We had to be fast with our hands, but I didn't care. I just liked the idea of working during the day. Although our jobs were different, we passed the training at the end of our six months. We always ate our lunch and rode together unless something happened.

Meanwhile, RP and I were learning to enjoy each other's company all the more, so I decided to make a surprise romantic dinner on our anniversary. He was already out, so I called and told him to stay out a little longer. My cousin, Shug was a great help to me: she took me to the store, so I could buy a couple of steaks. I already had the rest had my sides along with the candles.

"Can I come home now?" he said when he called because many hours had passed.

"Not yet give me some more time," I said.

I was waiting on the steaks to get done since the potatoes and everything else were ready. There was music playing, and I had the room set up with candles, also they were placed around the jacuzzi. I was a romantic. While I was setting up, I heard a car pull up: it was RP. He tried to sneak up on me and was being very suspicious; for what reason, I didn't know. He was the one that was out all day, and I stayed home trying to surprise him on our anniversary.

He came in the house drunk after I told him not to drink a lot, but of course, he did the opposite. I tried to enjoy the evening with him, but it was ruined because of his accusations. He was actually looking around to see if there was anyone in the house. This was the kicker: when we were sitting in the jacuzzi, he just splashed water in my face and that too was a turn off. He had spoiled everything by being drunk. I just called it a night and went to bed. The next morning, he apologized for his actions and thanked me for my thoughtfulness.

As time passed, I put that event behind me and continued to grow closer to him and his family. I loved visiting with his Cousin B. She and her family were very sweet, and I really enjoyed her cooking. I didn't care what she cooked; it was always delicious. She was also very humorous, and she didn't bite her tongue (she was outspoken). After we visited his mom, Cousin B was always the next stop in our travels; we visited very often.

RP and I had driven to New York City, so that he could meet my sister and brothers. RP was a driver that didn't like making many stops along the way; therefore, he would get upset with me when I had to use the bathroom. He wasn't sensitive about it at all. It was unbelievable how we would argue about me having to use the bathroom.

When we arrived in New York City, my family loved him. RP was a people person as well and could got along with everyone; it wasn't any different with my family. They would call him "brother-in-law" or by his nickname. We only stayed for a couple of days, but I was just glad that he was excited about meeting my family. I felt comfortable enough to share some things about me and my family, and it was unbelievable to him that I had such a dysfunctional childhood. He tried to make it seem like I made the whole thing up. All the bruises and wounds were on the inside; something that he couldn't see or even imagine. This is why it's good to keep some things to yourself. He couldn't help what was going on the inside of me, but what he did do was add more hurt.

> *"Come to Me, all who are weary and heavily burdened [by religious rituals that provide no peace], and I will give you rest [refreshing your souls with salvation]. [29] Take My yoke upon you and learn from Me [following Me as My disciple], for I am gentle and humble in heart, and YOU WILL FIND REST (renewal, blessed quiet) FOR YOUR SOULS. [30] For My yoke is easy [to bear] and My burden is light." (Matthew 11:28-30 AMP)*

After we returned to Lewiston, RP's job sponsored a trip to *Kings Dominion,* and they gave out free tickets to the employees when we got there. A few of his co-workers went, and we met up with some of them at the park. It was three men, two ladies, and then us. I quietly observed that RP had been acting really fickle-in a Dr. Jekyll and Mr. Hyde sort of way. He would start arguments for no reason, and then leave out. It seemed as though he did anything to get out of the house. We would go at it. He would purposely mess up things, so I would have to clean up. We both worked, and it was our home; therefore, we could both clean up. He'd say and do crazy stuff that made me become very suspicious. For instance, we were watching a movie one evening about a married couple. The couple fell on bad times, and the husband wanted his wife to sleep with a rich man for money to aid their situation.

"Hmm, I would expect you to do the same thing," he said as RP was getting up from the couch to get a drink.

"Me...your wife? You would want me to sleep with someone else for money?" I asked while looking at him with a raised eyebrow.

I couldn't believe what I was hearing. I was so hurt because he was serious. We were arguing about it, and he never took it back. I said to myself, "*Who in the heck did I marry?*"

We kept watching the movie without saying a word.

Then, there was a time when our lights got cut off, and when I asked him about it, he told me that he paid the bill. I always gave him the money for the light bill, and he took care of the mortgage and car insurance. We did the food, water bill, and telephone bill together. He was the partner that made sure it got paid. I was thinking to myself, "*If you paid it, the lights would be on.*" Thank God for candles.

He had to tell his mom what happened because he borrowed the money from her.

"RP, if you paid it, the lights would be on," she told him.

I wanted to laugh so bad. I had said the same thing to myself, but if I would have said this to RP, we would have been arguing. I didn't like that he had to borrow from his mom; he was a man.

On that Monday, he paid the bill, and the lights were back on. I didn't say any more about it; but I had my suspicions, and my senses were telling me that something wasn't right.

Now, getting back to the *King's Dominion trip*, I watched this young lady, named, Angel and my husband very closely. Although RP joked around with everyone, he joked around with her just a little too much. There was a bit of playful flirting going on. *"Maybe it's just me,"* I said to myself. Instead of being nonchalant, I became little more sociable, but my eyes were opened.

> *"Then the eyes of those who see will not be blinded, And the ears of those who hear will listen attentively." (Isaiah 32:3 AMP)*

I began to feel a little better about everything since they did include me in all the festivities, so I let it go. We had a lot of fun and at the end of the trip we said our goodbyes to his co-workers.

A couple of weeks after that, RP and I went out to club *LTD*. He tried to keep me home as usual but that didn't work. When we arrived, the music was pumping. After having a few drinks, RP pulled me by the hand: he was ready to dance and so was I. While we were dancing, I spotted three young ladies coming through the door, and one of those ladies was Angel. Oh, she and RP made eye contact; something was going on, and I felt it in my gut. He waved at them all, but his eyes stayed on her table. A particular jam (song) came on, and everyone got on the dance floor including us. Even while we were dancing, he kept watching her; especially, when she was dancing with someone else. I was boiling on the inside; I was ready to go home.

"Oh, this is why you wanted to go to the *LTD* without me. Yawl planned this, and I busted your bubble," I said.

"Patricia, please, I don't know what you're talking about," he said.

"As if you were really going to tell me the truth. Oh, you're telling me that it was a coincidence? I don't believe you; she saw us when she came in. She tried to act like she didn't see us, and you couldn't keep your eyes off of her. You're a bad liar." I said furiously.

I knew more than he thought. I had been having dreams about the both of them. He even had her riding in his car. This n---- was cheating on me, but I couldn't prove it. When you try to get in the shower with your husband or try make love to him, and he rejects you for no reason...something is wrong. He would say that he was *praying*. He was always praying after he has cussed me out or did something stupid.

"Who are you praying to- the devil? The way you talk to me and treat me...negro please, God isn't hearing anything you're saying." I said.

He had just got back in town, and I just wanted to see what his response would be if I tried because we hadn't made love in a while.

"The husband must fulfill his [marital] duty to his wife [with goodwill and kindness], and likewise the wife to her husband. [4] The wife does not have [exclusive] authority over her own body, but the husband shares with her; and likewise the husband does not have [exclusive] authority over his body, but the wife shares with him. Do not deprive each

other [of marital rights], except perhaps by mutual consent
for a time, so that you may devote yourselves [unhindered]
to prayer, but come together again so that Satan will not
tempt you [to sin] because of your lack of self-control."
(1 Corinthians 7:3 AMP)

Whatever was going on, this wasn't the marriage that I had expected. He would go away, visit friends, and stay over the weekend. I got lonely and wanted to go out with my friends. I would hang out with Charlotte and her husband, Roger, and we would go to the *Hide Away* and other places, so I wouldn't be by myself the entire weekend.

When RP came back, we started talking about having children. I was ready and up for it, so we started working on having a baby. Not only did I want a baby, but I also thought that a child would make things better. Also, I prayed that I would be nothing like my mother.

I was married, but lonesome. I didn't feel loved, nor did I get enough attention; RP was all over the place. When RP went off on his own, I knew he was cheating on me, and everyone else knew it too. He was one of those men who would talk and tell the truth in his sleep, but wide awake, he would tell a lie frontwards and backwards. He thought I was stupid and had dunce written on my forehead; so, this time when he went away, I cheated on him. What's good for the goose is good for the gander.

"See that no one repays another with evil for evil, but always
seek that which is good for one another and for all people."
(1 Thessalonians 5:15 AMP)

However, I told the person that I slept with that it couldn't happen again. This affair happened because there were some unresolved feelings, but I loved my husband, and

I wanted things to work out. The person was okay with that. The last time RP went away, he called, and I told him that I was going out since he wasn't present.

"I don't want you going out, Trish," he said over the phone.

"I'm going out because you are going out with your friends," I told him.

"If you go out...I'm going to beat your a--," he threatened.

"What?" I replied. I thought he was playing, but he didn't sound like he was playing. This made me believe that he had heard about the few times that I went out while he was away. He didn't want me to go out without him...oh, boy.

I was so bored once I got off the phone with him, so I called the *psychic* hotline because I wanted to know about my future with him. I just felt that RP and I weren't going to last. They said that I was proposed to by a tall, dark, distinguished looking man, and he was on one knee. She saw us standing next to each other. He was wearing a black tuxedo, and I was wearing a white wedding dress. The *psychic* told me that I was pregnant right now, but I didn't believe it.

I told the psychic that she was mistaken.

"No ma'am," she said

I was in awe. By the way, at this time, RP and I had been married way over a year. Afterwards, I hurried off the phone, so they wouldn't charge me so much.

> *"Do not turn to mediums [who pretend to consult the dead] or to spiritists [who have spirits of divination]; do not seek them out to be defiled by them. I am the LORD your God."*
> *(Leviticus 19:31 AMP)*

411

My mind shifted to the tall dark- skinned man. Where did he come from? *RP wasn't dark-skinned, and he wasn't all that tall.* I thought, "RP had on an off- white suit, and I had on an off- white dress." I was puzzled.

Later, my birthday approached, I was at work feeling happy but feeling sick at the same time. I was so dizzy that I grabbed my bundle, and before I knew it I started vomiting all over the place. My supervisor grabbed the trash can for me, and then some of the co-workers walked me to the bathroom. I was having cold sweats. I didn't know what was going on.

"Patricia, do you need to go home?" they asked with concern.

"Yes." I said nodding my head.

As soon I said yes, RP came walking in with balloons and a teddy bear for my birthday-surprising me.

"What's wrong, Trish," he asked with furrowed eyebrows. I told him what happened, and they let him take me home.

I went to the doctor, and they informed me that I was about three weeks pregnant. *"Oh my God the psychic was right,"* I thought to myself. Although my telephone bill was three hundred dollars, I paid it.

Finding out, I was pregnant on my birthday was a true gift. We were so excited. RP wanted a girl because he already had a son, but it didn't matter to me as long as the baby was healthy. When I returned back to work, I continued to get sick every day. Of course, I went back to the doctor. He gave me a note requesting that sick leave is required because my sickness continued. Meanwhile, I had some concerns about who the baby's father was because of the affair I had. The time that the baby was conceived was very close to both the affair I had, and the relations I had with my husband. I asked God for forgiveness and prayed like I'd never prayed before.

> *"If we [freely] admit that we have sinned and confess our sins, He is faithful and just [true to His own nature and promises], and will forgive our sins and cleanse us continually from all unrighteousness [our wrongdoing, everything not in conformity with His will and purpose]." (1 John 1:9 AMP)*

Thereafter, I had peace that this baby was RP's, but his mother would make little comments like "I hope the baby is his," but I would never respond to her comments. I'm sure that she was saying some things to him, but he never said anything to me. The person that I had the affair with would say things on the sly or sure the baby isn't mine. I would tell him, "No the baby is not yours, and you need to stop thinking and saying that." Remember, I told him that I would never have a baby by him; I spoke it, and I meant it.

> *"As it is written, I have made thee a father of many nations,) before him whom he believed, even God, who quickeneth the dead, and calleth those things which be not as though they were." (Romans 4:17 KJV)*

> *"Therefore, I say unto you, What things soever ye desire, when ye pray, believe that ye receive them, and ye shall have them." (Mark 11:24)*

In spite of the drama, I was having crazy cravings. For instance, combinations like pickles, cheese, and pretzels. I had to eat these things as a sandwich. I also craved Chinese food from a place that was across town. RP had to make the runs to go get it, and I was wearing him out. He wanted to help me eat it because it looked good to him too. Also, I remember craving seafood like crab salad, but we couldn't find any. It seemed that I also had sexual cravings. This was the funny part; we did it, but he was afraid that he was going to hurt the baby, and I told him that the baby was protected. Now, that was the best love making ever.

When I had to stay home from my job, my cousins and their friends would keep me company. We would indulge in playing *Spades*; I was an awesome spade player. They were teenagers, but RP trusted them to keep an eye on me while he was working. I would prepare a meal for keeping me company. Everyone loved my cooking.

"I don't usually eat other folks cooking, but I'll eat yours," said The youngster.

"That's sweet and it means a lot," I told him.

"I just don't trust everybody, and my mother told me not to, but I trust you," he stated.

I just smiled.

RP liked this arrangement, so he could be out there doing whatever he was doing: selling drugs or gambling. There was a whole lot of arguments because I didn't want him doing any of those things besides working. Due to whatever he was doing, he started losing weight. I was also having dreams of him becoming violent: putting his hands on me, and I said to myself, *"No, but why?" with my mouth opened.*

During my pregnancy, I had become very big because of the fluid. My feet were swollen so bad that I had to keep my feet up. From my neck down to my belly, I became very dark and my face was fat, but my hair did grow longer and beautiful. I must say, I vomited faithfully after every meal. Ironically, when I visited my family in New York while I was five months pregnant, it was worst experience of my life from riding on the bus to riding with my brother driving over pothole. I thought I was going to die. "*Never again while I am pregnant,*" I told myself; I was terrified.

While I was gone. RP made himself very scarce when I called which caused some concerns. When we did talk, and I question him, I felt like he was lying to me. When I arrived at the bus station, he was late picking me up and had lame excuses that didn't add up. I didn't want to accuse him of anything, so I kept quiet and continued to observe him.

"**Do not quarrel with a man without cause, if he has done you no harm.**" (**Proverbs 3:30 AMP**)

Chapter 50
Shattered Dreams

"Trust in and rely confidently on the LORD with all your heart
And do not rely on your own insight or understanding.[6] [a]
In all your ways know and acknowledge and recognize Him,
And He will make your paths straight and smooth [removing
obstacles that block your way]." Proverbs 3:5-6 AMP)

As wobbly and swollen as I was, I would visit my best friend. Dale and I were both pregnant at the same time and were having our babies in the same month. Dale was already a mother of two. Anyway, while I was there, we would catch up on what was going on with each other. I was home under the doctor's orders, but she was still working at *Wrangler's*. Dale wanted her own money, and she didn't want to depend on her husband. We still smoked our cigarettes while we were pregnant although it was bad for the baby. We just couldn't stop, but we just didn't smoke as much. Dale and I always felt a lot better when we spoke to one another we both had struggles. When she got tired of being at her house, she would come see me, and we had so many laughs.

Later, RP asked me if it was okay for his friend who he went to school with could come and stay with us. I had met her at the club a while back, and she was very sweet. She had just moved back home along with her daughter.

"Plus, she'd be great company for you while I'm at work," he informed. I could see his concern because I had about eight false alarms thinking that I was having contractions. I was terrible.

I knew that I got on his nerves because I got on my own nerves. I was disgusted. I didn't like pain. The last false alarm was the kicker: the ambulance had to pick me up from the grocery store, but it was another false alarm. The doctor told me to drink plenty of water which would help with the false contractions, so this is why RP didn't want me to be alone. I ended up saying yes because I liked her, and we wanted to be a help to her and her daughter; besides, it was only until she found a place. Everyone knew her including my mother-in-law, but Cousin B had something to say about it.

"For I hungered, and ye gave Me meat; I was thirsty, and ye gave Me drink; I was a stranger, and ye took Me in;"(Matthew 25:35 KJV)

"Are you sure you're alright with having another woman in your house?" she asked while laughing, "Don't pay me no mind. RP and she have been friends forever."

"Oh, Okay, okay," I said.

She was about to make me have second thoughts; nevertheless, we said yes to her moving in because I was close to going in. Because Naomi moved in, RP told my male cousins and their friends that they weren't needed anymore.

As days went by, I enjoyed Naomi's company. Sometimes, I would cook, and other times she would cook. It was just wonderful having help. One day, I asked RP for some money, and he acted like he was upset with me for asking. I mean, who was I supposed to ask? He was my husband, yet he didn't mind giving Naomi some money.

"Oh, that wasn't right." I said as he got in my face talking a whole bunch of junk.

"You're not going to tell me what to do with my d--- money. Come here!" he said calling me into the next room.

"No," I told him.

He pushed me into the room onto the bed, and he got on top of me as he drew his fist back. I was so frightened; I couldn't believe he was going to hit me while I was pregnant.

"Get off of me, before I call the police," I yelled out while struggling beneath him.

Naomi started calling his name for him to stop, but I knew she didn't want to get involved. He got off me, and I knew he was on something. I thought to myself, "*He's not himself or maybe he is.*" The dream that I had about him getting violent with me had manifested.

Frequently, I had been hearing rumors that RP and Naomi were doing drugs together, but I couldn't prove it. They were playing me, but I had to keep my cool until proof showed up. He would drive my car a lot, and she would ask if she could drive my car for *important business*. I didn't mind as long as she was trying to find a place to live.

I knew one thing; I couldn't wait to drop this baby (give birth) because I couldn't get around. I was truly big, and it was truly hot. I wore my house dresses at all times with my legs open; that's how hot I was although we had fans and central air.

Meanwhile, RP's family wanted to give me a baby shower, but it was postponed. I believe that they wanted to be sure that the baby was his. They had their suspicions. I knew that I was a part of their conversation.

Finally, the night had come, and it was the real thing. I was having contractions about twenty minutes apart. They were hitting my back in the most painful way; I had never felt anything like it. I awakened RP, and I told him that it was time.

"Patricia, are you sure?" he asked me.

"Yes!" I exclaimed.

The contractions were getting closer and closer, and I would cry as they came and went. I needed to get to my gynecologist, Dr. Brooks. Everyone knew him-with his fine self. Truthfully, he was so handsome. He had gorgeous, straight, curly hair slicked in a ponytail; he was tall, muscularly built. His pecan colored skin and beautiful white toothy smile topped it off.

Anyway, we called, and he was already there making rounds. He examined me and concluded that I only dilated two centimeters, and that I needed to dilate more. He didn't want to give me an epidural, but he did give me something to slow down the contractions a little. Other than that, I had to deal with the pain.

"Alright then Mrs. Patricia, I'll be back to check on you."

Later, during the night as hours passed by, the pain began to awake me. The contractions were becoming closer and almost unbearable. I would pull RP's hand to rub my back when the pain approached, but when it passed, I pushed his hands off me. I couldn't stand to look or talk to him; I was disgusted, and I blamed him.

> *To the woman He said, "I will greatly multiply Your pain in childbirth; In pain you will give birth to children; Yet your desire and longing will be for your husband, And he will rule [with authority] over you and be responsible for you." (Genesis 3:16 AMP)*

RP laid back in the chair all morning, and he didn't leave me at all. He dozed off and on while I was moaning, groaning, screaming and crying because of pain. He also helped me remember to breathe every time a contraction came. The pain was entirely unbearable.

"Nurse, can you please...see if you can get in touch with Dr. Brooks?" I asked her while breathing heavily. I couldn't take it anymore. I was ready to get up and leave. I couldn't believe that he had left me in pain for twenty- six hours.

When he finally arrived, I was angry, and he knew it. Suddenly, while he was examining my dilation, my water broke. I felt a hot gush pour out of me, but he said I still hadn't dilated enough: I only dilated five centimeters. I was closely built; therefore, they had to do a C-section.

Addressing me by my last name I shared with my husband, he said "Mrs. P, if you decide to have any more babies, this will be the case for you. Before we decide to do a C-section, we want to wait and try every possible option to not cut a patient.

"I understand," I responded.

"Are you ready?" he asked while smiling at me.

"I've been ready. Are you going to put me to sleep? You're lucky doctor. I was about to walk up out of here," I told him.

"Yes, you will be put to sleep. Oh, no, we can't have you getting up and leaving," he chuckled.

I was on my way to the operating room, and once we got there, they gave RP dressing to wear. He was ready for me to have this baby but not as ready as I was.

Afterwards, I woke up in my hospital room in pain from being cut. I gave birth to a baby girl, and I was glad that she was in the nursery. I know that you probably won't be able to wrap your mind around this, but I wasn't ready to see her. I had a lot of feelings and emotions that I couldn't explain, and I was sore and in excruciating pain. They had to drug me through the I.V. to give me a little relief from the pain.

"Thank you. She is beautiful." RP said when he came into the room and kissed me.

"Hey Trish, God is truly with you because she looked just like RP. Our genes run strong. He definitely can't deny her," his mom said entering the room with him.

I didn't respond to her comment.

"Nope. I definitely can't deny her. The judge would throw the good book at me if I did," RP said laughing.

In my mind, I thought, *"Yes, God is on my side."* I started laughing to myself and thanking God in my heart.

"You did good, Trish. She's a big baby: 7 lbs15oz. Shucks, that's almost eight pounds, she has a head full of curly hair," his mother said chuckling.

"Thank you," I said with a smile.

Then, RP took her home, and he went home to take a shower and change. I just rested.

"Would you like to see the baby and feed her?" the nurse asked.

"No. I am tired. I just want to rest," I said

They told me they would feed her in the nursery.

Thereafter, RP came back to the hospital and went to the nursery to hold and feed her he told me when he returned.

"She's beautiful," he said. Then, we started talking about her name.

"I like the name P, but you know my family had something to say about it," he said.

We named her after his favorite cartoon character. He always thought that the cartoon character, P was adorable, and I did too.

"This is *our* baby. We will name her what we want to name her. If she looks like a P, that will be her name."

"Yes, PPP," he said calling out her full name.

"Oh, you added a little bit of me into her name," I said surprisingly.

Her middle name was very similar to my first name. I smiled at her full name; I liked it.

The next day, the nurse woke me up and told me that I needed to feed her, so that I could bond with her. I couldn't breastfeed because I smoked, but she told me that the bonding begins when she could look into my eyes.

"How about later? Then I'll be ready," I told her.

I was undergoing so much pain, and I was blaming everybody even the baby. Also, the nurse had stated that they were going to start getting me up, so I could walk. The C-section had left me very sore.

Later, they brought her in and put her into my arms. I looked into those big, beautiful brown eyes and saw her chubby cheeks, and I started to cry. She was so beautiful that she turned my stony heart into flesh. My heart was overwhelmed with joy a day and a half later. She was born on September 15, 1994.

> *"A woman, when she is in labor, has pain because her time [to give birth] has come; but when she has given birth to the child, she no longer remembers the anguish because of her joy that a child has come into the world." (John 16:21 AMP)*

She was such a good baby. They allowed her to nap in the room with me, and I just kept smiling to myself at how precious she was. Now, I couldn't wait to get home; therefore, I was very cooperative with Dr. Brooks when he came to check on me from time to time. He told me I was coming along fine, and that I would be going home real soon.

After staying in the hospital for about a week, it was good to be home. I was still experiencing a little pain, but it wasn't as bad. I still didn't want RP near me nor did I want him touching me. I was angry as if it was his fault. I believe I was suffering slight postpartum depression. I would sleep at the other end of the bed to keep him from touching me. Also, the baby's crib was in our room, so I could keep an eye on her.

A couple of weeks had passed, and RP's family gave us a beautiful baby shower. She had so many gifts; PPP didn't want for anything. By the way, the family loved her name, and her grandmother laughed at the name; she thought it was cute. Well, if they hadn't liked it, I didn't care because she was our baby and the decision was ours. I didn't care too much about what people thought, especially if it's negative.

> *"But I, like a deaf man, do not hear; I am like a mute man who does not open his mouth." (Psalms 38:13 AMP)*

Now, that the baby was here, things became even more rocky. RP started acting crazy towards me in front of Naomi and her daughter as if I was his enemy. Once, he snatched the baby out of my arms as if I didn't know what I was doing. I was convinced that he was trying to drive me crazy. When I went to try to get my baby back, he pushed me. Although he may have gotten the best of me, we went to war (fighting). Naomi tried to stop it, but I called the police on him. He said he wasn't scared of the police and waited until they arrived. I told the police what happened, and they escorted him out while Naomi held PPP in another room. When RP went out the door, Naomi was ready to leave, and I was ready for her to leave. She wasn't fulfilling her obligations in what we agreed upon, and she was a liar as well. I truly believe that both of them were on something. She had called someone to come get her because my car wasn't going to move out the driveway.

Subsequently, one by one, his family called me. First, his mother called me and said,

"You called the police on my son talking about how he hit you? Don't you ever call the police on my son."

"Tell your son to keep his hands to himself, and then you will never have to worry about me calling the police on him. I am not going to sit up here and argue with you," I said before hanging up.

The next call came from his cousin B, and she seemed to be concerned.

"Trish, please tell me what happened," she said.

"Naomi is my witness." I said and when I told her what happen.

"Well, Naomi said he didn't slap you around he pushed you around," she said.

"And that's okay? He shouldn't have put his hands on me in the first place," I told her.

"If you call the police on him again, I am going to beat your a-- myself," she threatened and began to go off on me.

I was shocked. I thought she would be the who had some sense.

"Therefore, you just be ready for me to call the police on you to," I said before hanging up on her.

They didn't put any fear in my heart because right is right and wrong is wrong. They took up for him in his wrong, and that was sickening to my stomach. I guess blood is thicker than water whether they're right or wrong.

"Do not judge by appearance [superficially and arrogantly], but judge fairly and righteously." (John 7:24 AMP)

They tried to make me feel like I wasn't important, and that it was okay for him to put his hands on me. Yes, I thought they were out of their mind. They thought he was top tier, but no; they had it all wrong. I knew that I was someone's child, and I meant something to myself. I care about me even if no one else does; however, when things calmed down, he came back.

I had gone back to work, and so did Dale. It wasn't long after me that she had her baby. Since our husbands had been going out while we were pregnant, we made a deal with them: they needed to stay home take care of the babies, and allow us to go out. Since they agreed that weekend, Dale picked me up, and we went out to a club that she knew about. We drank and danced a bit; it was alright. We acted like we had a good time even if we really didn't. I don't know going out just wasn't the same after we had our baby. Nevertheless, we didn't want our husbands to know that we really didn't have a good time.

After Dale dropped me off, I knocked on the door because the screen door was locked. RP let me in, and the baby was asleep. We got in an argument because of sarcasm comments and responses, and RP started talking about putting me out of my own home.

"Oh no, you're not!" I told him.

He got up, he pushed, and pulled me out of the house. He even locked the door. I banged and hollered for him to let me in.

"I'm calling the police, RP," I said.

I went next door to my cousin's and called the police. Then, he opened the door, and the police talked to him about what he did.

"Oh, you called the police?" he said when I got back in.

"Just like you put me out? You won't do that no more," I said.

After that, I just wasn't feeling the same. Even when he wanted to have sex, I felt funny. I felt ashamed to have sex with him as if he wasn't my husband. One morning, he was talking in his sleep, and he called out another woman's name. I smacked the daylights out of him. I fought with him as I repeatedly asked him who she was. **Of course, he lied and said, "I don't know what you're talking about, Trish." Other times,** I felt like I was being chased by God because of the dreams that I would have. One particular dream, I was running towards the light

"There is no way in the world that I would be able to live a saved life while being married to RP. I know he's cheating on me. I would end up hurting him," I told God

This allowed me to think about God a lot more.

Therefore, RP and I decided to have PPP's christening at his mother's church, and we chose Pat and Mag as her Godparents. Also, I decided to get baptize as well. Everything turned out beautiful that night; it was a sacred moment. RP was really surprised when I decided to get baptize.

One day, I asked RP if he had ever thought about getting saved?

"No, I'm not ready yet," he said in an obnoxious tone,

When he responded, I was saddened in my heart. I truly knew that this marriage wasn't going to work if I got saved, and he wasn't.

I thought, *"Lord, you are going to have to do something."*

"I have [a] other sheep [beside these] that are not of this fold. I must bring those also, and they will listen to My voice and

pay attention to My call, and they will become [b] one flock with one Shepherd." (John 10:16 AMP)

The next day, while Dale and I were on our lunch break, this young lady named Espanola said to us that she could take our husbands. She knew our husbands because they would visit her house to play cards and to drink. So, Dale and I looked at each other and said,

"Oh, so that's where they go."

"I will put something on both yawls husbands, and you both would want to let them go," she said with a sly smirk.

"Don't even waste your time doing all of that. You could have mine; as a matter of fact, I will give him to you," she said seriously.

"I feel the same way. I could pack his bags if you want me too," I told her.

We voiced that at the same time.

"There will be no fussing or fighting. You can have them both, and maybe you can do better with them than we can."

Then we burst out laughing as she walked away.

"Trish, Espanola thought she was saying something. She didn't know it was nothing but a word." Dale said.

"I know right." I said with laughter as tears began running out of our eyes.

You just had to be there to see the look on her face. She was stunned at our response. We knew that she was a witch, but she didn't scare us; especially me.

"Thou shalt not suffer a witch to live." (Exodus 22:18 KJV)

> *"Regard not them that have familiar spirits, neither seek after wizards, to be defiled by them: I am the LORD your God." (Leviticus 19:31 KJV)*

Amid, when we are finished doing our job, we could go and help others at their station, so I went over to help Espanola at her workstation.

"Are you afraid of me?" she asked.

"No, because I know deep down inside you are a sweet person," I told her.

"What makes you know that?" she asked with a puzzled look.

"I don't know, I just know," I said shrugging with confidence.

She started talking about her children, and she named them. I knew her son because he hung out with my cousins. Remember, they would come over, play cards, and I would feed them. Yes, he was one them who came over and played spades while I was pregnant.

"Not my son. He doesn't eat other people's food," she said.

"He ate mine. Ask him. He did tell me that he usually doesn't, but he trusted me; he liked my food," I told her.

"He must have trusted you," she said.

"Yes, I wouldn't do anything to harm him," I told her.

I smiled at her as I left her machine. She had acted as if she didn't believe that her son ate at my house with her warped countenance.

The next encounter that Dale and I had with Espanola was when we had to ask her for a ride because Dale's car broke down. She was sweet about taking us home, and she was our only option. We didn't converse while we were in her car. We asked her how much we owed her, and she said that we didn't owe her anything. Dale and I was very grateful.

Well, as the months passed, RP began talking about moving to Virginia because there was no money in North Carolina, **and he was tired of traveling back and forth**. He would randomly bring it up, so that gave me time to think about it. He started talking about it even more as it got closer to our three-year anniversary.

At the same time, I was having problems with my hands. I couldn't hold anything, and pain was shooting from my wrist up to my arms. When I tried to cook or hold the baby, I would be in tears because of the pain; it was getting worse. When I went to the doctor, I was diagnosed with *Carpal Tunnel Syndrome* in one of my hands, I was put-on long-term leave, and I had to visit the Wranglers physician as well. RP didn't like the fact that I was released from work.

RP took PPP and I to Virginia for the weekend to visit his family. Once again, he brought up the idea of moving to Virginia. He had it all figured out: we could sell the house and move into an apartment in Virginia. When he told me his plan, I thought he was crazy. I was asking myself, *"Why would he think that I would say yes to moving out of our beautiful home and into an apartment? He just doesn't know that I always wanted a house, not an apartment."* Also, there was something telling me not to make that move; therefore, the answer was obvious.

"No, RP. I'm not leaving our home," I told him.

What he was talking about made no sense to me. Plus, I didn't trust him at this point.

When we arrived back to North Carolina, some things had come to my attention: he was messing up our money. He would say that he was paying this and paying that, but there were letters and the lack of receipts that stated otherwise; he wasn't paying anything. He was still lying through his teeth when I confronted him with it.

"You shall not steal, nor deal deceptively, nor lie to one another." (Leviticus 19:11)

"You must have forgotten where I'm from: New York City streets. You can't out-slick someone that use to be slicker. I have played dumb for too long. You're going to start seeing the true me. I will not be dumbing down for you any longer," I said angrily.

He sat there looking like a deer caught in headlights as he held the baby. I guess she was supposed to save him from my mouth. He took the money and gambled it up, did drugs, and there wasn't any telling of what else he done.

"This is not going to happen again. I'm on to your little games. You thought I was stupid, but I'm not. I lowered my intelligence because I knew I was way smarter than you," I said while shaking my head. I was just so disappointed.

He went to work all that week, and on that Friday, he came home and said,

"Patricia, I don't want to be married anymore. All you want is somebody to take care of you. One time it was your back: you had muscle spasms. Second, it was the pregnancy, and now your hands. Forget that. I'm not doing it no more," he said.

Oh, when I had muscle spasms, he wasn't compassionate at all. He just didn't know how much pain I was in.

431

"You took us to Virginia for our anniversary to celebrate. I mean, why in the world would you do all of that and you knew what you had planned in the first place?" I asked.

"I just want to wait to do it after our three- year anniversary." he said.

"What?" I shouted. I looked at him, picked up the iron, and I started to hit him with it. Then a voice said,

"Don't do it, he is not worth it. He is doing you a favor. Think about the hitting, the lying, and the cheating." I slowly put the iron down.

"You're not even worth it. That's okay. God is going to bless me with someone who is going to love me and your child," I told him with confidence.

"Who is going to be with someone who has a child?" he asked.

"Oh, there is somebody out there who is not going to mind. Negro, it's no low-self-esteem here. You can play and save those mind games for someone else because it doesn't work here," I told him confidently.

He stood there looking stupid. He didn't expect that to come out of my mouth. He expected me to be crying and begging him to stay, but that wasn't the case.

"I'll sleep right here on the couch until the morning. Then, I'll pack up my things," he said.

I went into the bedroom with P and I laid down, but I couldn't sleep as long as he was here. I said to myself, *"This negro is getting up out of here. It's over so let it be over."*

I walked into the living room and looked at him.

"If I was you, I would sleep with both eyes open," I told him seriously.

"That's just what came to my mind. I will be back tomorrow to get my things," he said.

He was smart.

"Oh, no. You're getting your stuff out of here tonight because it may end up outside," I told him angrily.

"Okay," he replied.

I stood there to ensure that he had every piece of clothing, so there would be no excuses to come back. Afterwards, he took his black tail right out the door. I felt so much better after he left, but at the same time, I was hurt. I thought maybe that this was a phase that he was going through.

Next morning, it hit me that he was truly gone. I started crying as I held baby P; I felt like I wanted to die. I thought to myself, *"What in the world am I going to do?"* I had so much pain going through my arms. *"How am I going to take care of P by myself? This wasn't supposed to have happened. What happened to my happily ever after? All of my dreams- shattered."* Then, the strangest thing happened while I was crying. Baby P placed her hands on my back, and she began to pat me on my back as if she were saying, "Mommy everything is going to be okay." It was like a ray of hope sparked in me out of nowhere.

"Yes, we are going to be okay," I said as I looked into her beautiful eyes.

I continued to look at her, I began to realize that I had plenty to live for.

> *"After you have suffered for a little while, the God of all grace [who imparts His blessing and favor], who called you to His own eternal glory in Christ, will Himself complete, confirm, strengthen, and establish you [making you what you ought to be]." (1 Peter 5:10 AMP)*

> *"For His anger is but for a moment,[a] His favor is for a lifetime. Weeping may endure for a night, But a shout of joy comes in the morning." (Psalms 30:5 AMP)*

In addition, I needed to call someone to take me to the doctor to get a hand brace, so it came to me to call Gail because she was there for me. I remembered that she told me to call her anytime I needed her. Even if she wasn't available, she'd find someone else to take me. When I went to the doctors, it was odd because they couldn't understand why my other hand was so swollen; they didn't see anything. The swellings caused my hands to feel like there were pins and needles in them. Therefore, I had to be very careful and mindful when holding the baby because she was heavy. My little skinny arms had to carry the weight of the baby carrier because I couldn't use my hands until I had my hand brace.

During the week, I received a call from RP's mom, during which, she said that we needed to try and work it out because their family reunion was that weekend. She wanted the baby, and I to come, but I told her that I wasn't going anywhere but the baby could. I would never keep the baby from him.

"I'm not a good pretender. I am not going to pretend or live a lie to satisfy everybody else," I told her truthfully.

"Well, please, just think about it," she said.

Meanwhile, I was so heartbroken. I smoked back to back. By this time, I was smoking two packs of cigarettes a day. All kinds of things were going through my mind, then. "*Did he leave me for someone else?*" I thought.

The next weekend, RP called because he wanted to spend time with the baby, so he asked me could he come and pick her up. I agreed, and he came to get her.

"I need to get away from Lewiston while she was away," I said speaking to Tanya on the phone. A few minutes later, she came and picked me up.

When we arrived at her home, all I did was drink and cry from the hurt that was embedded in my heart. I just couldn't wrap my mind around it. I wondered why did it had to hurt so bad. There was a big hole in my heart, and it was bleeding. I tried to ignored it, and even poor Tanya tried to make me laugh and cheer me up, but it was no use. I guess, I just needed the time to pass by. The end of the weekend came pretty fast, and I didn't want to go home and face him when he brought P home.

After a couple of weeks passed, RP wanted to talk to me about working it out. I was willing to work it out, so he came over since he still had a key anyway. We slept in the same bed that night, but we didn't do anything. Sleeping in the same bed together just didn't feel the same.

"Didn't you tell me that you and RP was going to work things out?" she ask when Charlotte called the next night.

"Yes," I responded.

"You're my friend, so I thought that you should know that his car is here in the trailer park at Cookie's house. You know her, don't you?" she asked.

"Yes, she is a light skinned girl who was fifteen years old when RP introduced me to her. As a matter of fact, she is related to RP's best friend. That sneaky dog. My instincts are never wrong when it comes to that n----. He's trying to play me. He didn't have any intentions on working it out," I ranted.

"Nope. I can try and see if I can get her number, so you can talk to her. I believe she would tell you," she said.

"Yeah do that, so I can trap his butt."

Charlotte did exactly that: she got me Cookies number. I called Cookie, and she got RP on a three-way call. It was on and popping. When he came on, he felt that something was up.

"Oh yawl, is trying to trick me!" he exclaimed.

"Oh n----, you're already caught! You're right: it is over. You're still cheating. I want a divorce. Cookie, he is truly a free man! You can have him," I said before hanging up the phone.

This is when I learned a powerful lesson that you cannot make someone love you nor stay with you if they don't want to. Love yourself enough to let them go.

> *"But if the unbelieving partner leaves, let him leave. In such cases the [remaining] brother or sister is not [spiritually or morally] bound. But God has called us to [a]peace."* (1 Corinthian 7:15 AMP)

> *"But whoever commits adultery with a woman lacks common sense and sound judgment and an understanding [of moral principles]; He who would destroy his soul does it."* (Proverbs 6:32 AMP)

See, his selfish problem was that he didn't want me, and he didn't want anyone else to have me. I figured it out:

he was running a game, but I wasn't the one. He left me. I didn't leave him, and I was willing to work it out. I guess I was too broke down for him. He wanted to cash me out for something new. He wanted to cease having the responsibility of taking care of me. I thought that's what a husband was supposed to do. Those were the wedding vows: through sickness and in health, for richer or for poorer, to death do us part.

> *"In the same way, you husbands, live with your wives in an understanding way [with great gentleness and tact, and with an intelligent regard for the marriage relationship], as with [a]someone physically weaker, since she is a woman. Show her honor and respect as a fellow heir of the grace of life, so that your prayers will not be hindered or ineffective."* (1 Peter 3:7 AMP)

> *"Husbands, love your wives [seek the highest good for her and surround her with a caring, unselfish love], just as Christ also loved the church and gave Himself up for her,"* (Ephesians 5:25 AMP)

> *"Let her be as a loving hind and graceful doe, Let her breasts refresh and satisfy you at all times; Always be [a]exhilarated and delight in her love."* (Proverbs 5:19 AMP)

Unfortunately, my long-term pay was taking a long time to kick in; therefore, I was looking for RP to continue to pay the bills. He took care of them, but he told me that next month I was on my own.

"Your daughter is here, and she needs food and pampers," I told him.

"I'll take care all of that," he told me. I said to myself, *"This negro is going to give me a hard time."* I felt like my back was up against the wall.

"And my God will liberally supply (fill until full) your every need according to His riches in glory in Christ Jesus." (Philippians 4:19 AMP)

At the same time, I am going through with RP, my cousin, Shug, called and asked me if I wanted to go to church with her on Sunday, and I told her yes. I was in pain all over my body: it was indescribable. I felt like an old lady: I needed a cane. I was walking bent over and not straight up. The pressure on me was so heavy like I was carrying a load. I was losing weight, and I was smoking terribly. Every time RP and I talked, he would pluck my nerve, and we'd end up arguing. I would completely cuss him out.

"The thief cometh not, but for to steal, and to kill, and to destroy: I am come that they might have life, and that they might have it more abundantly." (John 10:10 KJV)

Sunday came, and I went with Shug to church. Shug went to church every Sunday. She was always excited when talking about church. This was a day that I would never forget. I remember the Pastor of the church asked at the end of the service if anyone would like to come up for prayer. I walked up there bent over.

"Don't you want to get to know Jesus? Wait a minute you know Jesus don't you," she asked me in a bold tone.

"Yes, I do." I said with tears rolling down my face nodding my head.

"Now, are you ready?" she asked.

438

When she asked me that, I hesitated because **a small voice whispered in my left ear spoke and said,** *"No you are not ready there is still more out there."* All I could feel was pain while this was being said. Then, **the voice in my right ear said**, *"No there isn't anything else out there."* All I could see was the turmoil I was in, and I wanted it to stop.

The next thing I knew, I screamed out loud **Yes, I am Ready!**

Once I said I was ready, the Pastor said the sinner's prayer with me, and I repeated it after her. It felt like a load had been lifted off of me. I was repenting and asking God to forgive me for all of my sins, and for Jesus to come in to lead and guide my life. I walked into the church bent over, but I walked out tall and upright.

Ain't nobody mad but the devil. THE GENERATIONAL CURSES STOPS HERE! IN JESUS NAME.

> *"Come unto me, all ye that labour and are heavy laden, and I will give you rest. [29] Take my yoke upon you, and learn of me; for I am meek and lowly in heart: and ye shall find rest unto your souls. [30] For my yoke is easy, and my burden is light." (Matthew 11:28-30 KJV)*

> *"That if thou shalt confess with thy mouth the Lord Jesus, and shalt believe in thine heart that God hath raised him from the dead, thou shalt be saved." (Romans 10:9 KJV)*

When I gave my life over to Jesus Christ, my Lord and Savior, *the Chains of Generational Curses BROKE.*

COMING SOON!!

The Sequel of *MY STORY*...
NEW BEGINNINGS, MY REDEMPTION

Also, a special treat My dear husband Apostle Prophet Stacey Shannon's Book *'In Defense of the True Names of the Father and the Son'* Exposing the cover up

In Memory Of,

My Parents and Aunt the late: Biological father Charlie Slaughter, Mother Shirley Crawford, My Daddy Willie Mccoy Bazemore and My Aunt Lola.

I missed you all and Love you. As my parents and aunt, I thank God for you all because I wouldn't be the Woman that I am today.

May you all REST IN PEACE! You all will always be Remembered a Special place in my Heart.

"We are confident, I say, and willing rather to be absent from the body, and to be present with the Lord" (2 Corinthians 5:8 KJV)

Biological Father,
Charlie Slaughter

Mother, Shirley Crawford
and Stepfather,
Willie McCoy Bazemore

Aunt, Lola Williams

ACKNOWLEDGEMENTS

I like to take the time to acknowledge those who played an intricate part in my life and have made a difference in my life by being obedient in hearing the voice of God. Prophetically speaking, I believe that Jesus wanted me to know future events to come. Of course, throughout this book, I had visions and dreams, but it was if God turned up the volume as I grew in HIM. Somethings that were prophetically spoken to me, I felt that I wasn't ready for. For instance, I had the pleasure of meeting Margaret Sanford who stood in my kitchen while I was seven months pregnant. She prayed for me and then began to prophesy. The Lord spoke through her and voiced, "You have a double anointing an apostolic anointing. You are called to the Office of Apostle-Prophet". I took a look at myself and thought, "I do not see it." I was in my emotions. I just cried and ignored what was said.

However, God was working on me without me knowing it. The more I spoke in my heavenly language, the more I prophesied to others. I believe I was in training. Then, I met my friend, Stacey Shannon (who is now my husband) because he heard me pray for someone. He prophesied to me saying, "You have the Apostolic anointing". I thought, "Not another one" as I remembered to what was said to me eight years ago by Margaret.

444

My third encounter was when I was introduced, by my husband, to Apostle David B. Wanyonyi, who lives in Africa. As a matter fact, he prophesied to both of us. I was in amazement because he hadn't known anything about us. He told me things that only the Holy Spirit could have revealed to him including "You are Apostle Prophet". He started to laugh because he was fascinated by what God was revealing to him. He also said, "You are not Prophetess. You are Prophet," and that was extraordinary because the Holy Spirit had spoken to me three days beforehand and said, "You are Prophet." Apostle Wanyoni went on to say, "God has given me a Spirit of a man. You are very bold, and you have backbone." I began to cry because everything he was saying was confirmed. He also wanted to affirm my husband and I as Apostles Prophets, but it wasn't possible at that particular time.

God's plan is absolutely divine providence. He will provide a ram in the bush when he brings forth the person who is going to affirm you after much prayer. I told Jesus, "I have said yes to Your will, Your Way, and the Call finally. Now can you send some one to affirm my husband and I. I know You called us, but the papers are for man". Not long after, a dear friend of my husband showed up after many years. Chief Apostle Kevin Barber and his lovely wife Apostle Shelly Barber could see the call and the anointing on our lives. They asked if we had been affirmed. My husband looked at me in amazement because he knew what I had been praying for. The rest is History.

AUTHOR BIO

Apostle Prophet Patricia Veal-Shannon *is a Prayer Warrior who is on fire and on the battlefield for Jesus.*

She is a servant who loves the Lord and love serving God's people. She is a wife, mother, and grandmother who loves her family dearly. In her spare time, she is writing and creating God-given delicious Vegan recipes.

CPSIA information can be obtained
at www.ICGtesting.com
Printed in the USA
LVHW112001120521
687236LV00003B/24